WOMEN AND FOOD SECURITY

WOMEN AND FOOD SECURITY

The experience of the SADCC *countries*

Edited by MARILYN CARR

With an introduction by Anna Makinda

IT PUBLICATIONS 1991

Intermediate Technology Publications,
103/105 Southampton Row, London WC1B 4HH, UK.

© IT Publications 1991

ISBN Paperback 1 85339 109 3
ISBN Hardback 1 85339 118 2

A CIP catalogue record for this book is available from the British Library

Typeset by Inforum Typesetting, Portsmouth
Printed in Great Britain by SRP, Exeter

Contents

Introduction

Women in the SADCC Region play a major role in the production, processing, and marketing of food but, for the main part, they have been constrained from contributing fully to the development of this sector by the lack of availability of efficient technologies relating to their tasks, as well as lack of access to those technologies which do exist.

In recognition of this fact, and in light of the vitally important role which women have to play in the enhancement of food security in the Region, the Government of Tanzania hosted a Regional Conference in Arusha in May 1988 to identify food technology projects of benefit to women which could be channelled through the SADCC mechanism. The meeting was attended by Ministers responsible for women's affairs, Heads of Women's Machineries, technical experts from SADCC Sectoral Co-ordinating Units, and practitioners in appropriate technology and small industry development.

In order to have as much information as possible on women and food technologies, each of the nine member states was asked to prepare a background country paper on women's access to and use of improved food-related technologies. These technologies were to cover the full range of 'hardware' relevant to food security: simple tools and equipment for land preparation; seeding, weeding, harvesting, threshing, and winnowing; storage and drying devices; various types of crop-processing machines; small-scale irrigation devices; fish, fruit, and vegetable processing devices; low-cost transport devices; and energy conservation technologies; as well as 'software' techniques such as village woodlots and vegetable gardening.

The papers were to look in depth at the important facts which influence successful introduction and diffusion of these technologies to women, such as access to credit and training; involvement of women in technology design and adaptation; availability of raw materials, infrastructure, and markets; and the policy environment. Where possible, examples of successful projects were to be included which could serve as a basis for discussion of potential replication in other countries in the Region.

This was the first attempt to undertake a review of the situation concerning women and food technology in the SADCC Region as a whole, and the result is a collection of country papers which should be of great interest to all those concerned with improved food security in the Region.

Through publishing the papers for wider distribution, the Government of Tanzania hopes that more attention will be focused on women's need for improved food technologies and that the assistance they deserve can be acquired without further delay.

Hon. Ms Anna Makinda, Minister for
Community Development, Women and Children, Dar es Salaam

1
Malawi

1. Introduction

Improved appropriate technologies represent one among many areas to which the Malawi Government attaches great importance in its efforts to assist women to participate more fully in the national development process.

This paper attempts to share with other SADCC member states the Malawian experience in the area of improved appropriate technologies in assisting women to promote food security in an effort to improve their welfare and that of their families. More specifically, it sets out to provide an understanding of the existing technologies that are currently used by women in Malawi, and the constraints these technologies impose on the productive capacities of women and the overall welfare of their families. The paper also describes the programmes of action and types of technologies associated with women's activities that have been and are being tried in the country. Finally, it identifies potentially viable technologies and appropriate institutional support structures that could be introduced and/or strengthened in the country, to enable women to promote food security.

1.1 Socio-economic profile

Malawi's post-independence efforts to stimulate smallholder agriculture have been necessitated by the country's almost complete reliance on agriculture and associated industries.

Agriculture employs over 90 per cent of the population. The Government's objective is to develop the rural sector in an attempt to improve the standards of living of the ordinary people and to promote equitable distribution of social and economic benefits between the rural and urban areas. Since the attainment of independence in 1964, agriculture has remained the 'engine of growth' of the country's economy.

Of total national export earnings, 88 per cent originate from the agricultural sector. Although agriculture's contribution to Gross Domestic Product (GPD) has decreased from 55 per cent in 1964 through 46 per cent in 1976 to 38 per cent in 1986 due to the increasing importance of the other sectors in the economy, it has had a marked expansionary influence on the economy in general.

Malawi's agricultural development strategy is characterized by a two-pronged approach based on smallholder and estate agriculture. The former accounts for the bulk of the country's food supply as well as providing some export surplus; the latter has been the main source of the country's expanding exports.

1

This paper focuses on the smallholder sector, where the involvement of women is considerable. Subsistence farming in this sector is in women's hands and so is processing food for family consumption. In this sector the Government's approach stresses the need to meet the challenges of regionally balanced rural development activities. The emphasis is on increasing agricultural productivity and family income in those areas which are already developed as well as those that still lag behind. The intention is not only to reduce economic deprivation and the social maladies that accompany it, but also to try to stem the tide of migration to urban areas.

2. Women, food production, and indigenous technologies

It is estimated that 52 per cent of Malawi's population of 7 million are women, 93 per cent of whom live in rural areas. Of these, about 85 per cent are involved full time on their own holdings in subsistence agriculture and marginal cash cropping. More importantly, the Malawi National Sample Survey of Agriculture, undertaken in 1980–81, estimated that as many as 28.8 per cent of the rural households were headed by women who were divorced, separated, widowed, unmarried, married to polygamous husbands, or married to husbands who were away from home (within the country or abroad) in search of employment. Table 1 shows the incidence of female-headed households throughout Malawi by Agricultural Development Divisions (ADD).

Table 1 Percentage of female household heads by ADD

ADD	Female-headed households (Percentage of total number of households)
Karonga	15.8
Mzuzu	21.9
Kasungu	14.1
Salima	28.4
Lilongwe	27.4
Liwonde	36.5
Blantyre	34.3
Ngabu	24.8
ALL MALAWI	28.8

Source: Malawi Government, National Statistical Office, National Sample Survey of Agriculture, 1980–81 Zomba, 1984.

The high incidence of female-headed households in rural areas has far-reaching consequences for agricultural development efforts. In all these households, women undertake the central decisions regarding how to allocate land, labour, and other resources between competing needs in an

2

attempt to optimize family welfare. Moreover, in quite a number of male-headed households (especially in areas with marginal agricultural potential) the women again make most of the decisions connected with farming activities (be it cash or subsistence production). This is because the men are preoccupied with non-farm activities such as wage employment outside the farm (part time and full time), fishing, trading, self-employment in trades, and so on. This means that most of the time the women are left on their own to carry on with agricultural production. Hence, although men may from time to time assist in various farming operations, the majority of the tasks associated with food production are in women's hands.

In Malawi women can therefore be considered as the mainstay of agriculture. Clark (1975) found that approximately 50–70 per cent of all farming activities are accomplished by women. Kydd and Christiansen (1982) found that 69.3 per cent of those working full time on their own farm holdings were women, and that the amount of women's work was determined more by the type of crop than by whether marriage was monogamous or polygamous. Clark (1975) also discovered that the proportion of agricultural work carried out by women was twice that done by, men in villages cultivating maize — the major staple crop (54 per cent for women against 25 per cent for men) — and equal to that done by men or somewhat higher for cash crops. Women in Malawi therefore carry out most of the agricultural work for both subsistence and cash crops, even for those that are traditionally considered 'male' crops, such as cotton, tobacco, and tea.

A survey carried out in Karonga in the Northern Region of Malawi showed that women are involved in all aspects of farming activity (Spring, Smith and Kayuni, 1983). A more recent study carried out in three different areas in Malawi by Mkandawire, Asiedu, and Mtimuni (1988) supports the findings of Spring *et al.* For instance, in the cultivation of rice, primary land tillage or ploughing and levelling with oxen is considered men's work, but it is not uncommon to find women doing these operations. When levelling is done by hand, women often do it. Both men and women plant, apply fertilizer, and weed. Harvesting and threshing are mostly done by women, with occasional support from men.

Women are responsible for most of the food processing, whether it is winnowing, hulling, milling, pounding, grating, peeling, or drying, and for much of the food storage for family consumption and for sale.

Most of the farm activities and post-harvest operations are carried out using basic tools and equipment. Only in rare cases do we find women using improved tools and equipment for these tasks. Land cultivation is still mostly done by hand, predominantly with the traditional hoe or the tanged hoe. Since most of the crops are grown on ridges, the hoe is used primarily in digging and making the ridges. Although traditional

3

handwork still dominates, mechanization in the form of animal-drawn implements has been adopted to a limited extent, especially in the Northern Region of Malawi.

After the land has been tilled comes the sowing of the seeds and/or transplanting the seedlings. Usually the seeds or seedlings are planted or transplanted by hand, in rows to facilitate weeding. The crop harvesting equipment available to women has changed very little, if at all, over the years. Machetes and sickles continue to be the traditional tools used to harvest crops.

In food processing, too, the various operations are carried out by women using mostly indigenous techniques and equipment. In the case of rice, for example, bunches of panicles are threshed by beating them against the ground, a stone, a bamboo frame, or the edge of a wooden structure. For most staples the basic equipment used in processing food includes mortar, pestle, grinding stones, pots of various sizes and shapes, baskets, and mats.

Traditional drying of cereals, fish, flour, and vegetables is widespread. This usually means placing the produce on the ground in the open, in house compounds, and/or on roadsides for various lengths of time. This practice invites contamination and infestation by blowing fecal dust and parasite eggs, insects, chickens, and other domestic animals.

The importance of food storage in Malawian society stems from the role storage plays in food distribution, availability, prices, and production. While supplies can be abundant soon after harvest, shortages can be experienced within a month or two. Traditional ways of storing cereals, vegetables, and fruits include granaries ('Nkhokwe'), sacks, baskets, barns, clay pots, gourds, ordinary rooms, and roofs of dwellings, especially the part over the kitchens. Bags (sacks), granaries, and baskets are mainly used for the storage of maize, rice, and cassava. Clay pots and gourds are used to store cereal grains and pulses, especially those intended for seed in the next season. Some of the crops (maize, rice, sorghum) are stored in specifically designed structures, while others have no such structures. Cassava, a tuber crop, for example, may be stored (a) by delaying harvesting till required, (b) underground in pits, and (c) by simply drying and keeping them in any available receptacle, usually in bags or baskets. The sweet potato, another tuber crop, is stored mainly in pits.

Vegetables which lend themselves to drying are stored in that form in any suitable container, notably pots, gourds, baskets, and sacks. For example, fresh pumpkin leaves intended for storage are first boiled and then sun-dried. This method of preservation and storage is widespread in the country for most of the leafy vegetables.

Traditional methods have persisted partly because improved appropriate techniques are not readily available and partly because women generally lack the requisite knowledge to handle the few improved techniques that are available.

4

2.1 Time spent on working with traditional technologies

In the absence of improved appropriate technologies, women spend a considerable proportion of their time in food production. The Malawi experience demonstrates that women generally spend more hours than men in farming operations and food processing, besides their involvement in various domestic activities. (See Appendix for various crops and various farming operations for selected localities.)

The enormous workload women cope with in farming and food processing has serious unintended consequences on the welfare of the household. Very often family nutritional status suffers in a variety of ways. For example, it is common practice for women, in an attempt to save time, to reduce the frequency of cooked meals. Besides the children being adversely affected by longer gaps between meals, there is the risk of spoilage and food-borne infection if cooked food is kept for several hours before it is eaten. Another unintended consequence of women's workload is the tendency of some rural households to consume unboiled water. The effects of such practices are usually worst for pre-school children with immature immune systems.

It seems, therefore, that the introduction of improved appropriate technologies in the women's day-to-day tasks would not only reduce both the time and the drudgery associated with traditional technologies, but would also promote food production and allow additional time to be spent on income-generating and social activities.

2.2 Areas of concern in the food production chain

The solutions to many of the problems being faced by women in Malawi will rest largely on the development, availability, and dissemination of improved technologies which are appropriate to exsiting conditions. Some of the areas that need to be looked into are highlighted briefly in this section.

2.2.1 Hand tools

There are a number of hand tools for soil cultivation in Malawi and the energy requirements for some of these tools are relatively high. Very little improvement can be expected in the design, efficiency, and energy requirements of these simple tools. A study of the relationship between energy inputs and crops yields shows that higher energy inputs are required, if yields are to be increased (Giles, 1975). The challenges for the country in this repect lie in finding ways to increase energy input. Some possible areas that could be looked into are (a) the design and development of less energy-demanding hand tools based on local production and aimed at farmers cultivating land of less than 1 hectare; (b) increase in animal and mechanical power; (c) use of solar and wind energy.

2.2.2 Animal power

Medium-sized farms of 6–8 hectares could constitute a considerable part of

5

the arable land holdings in Malawi, if animal power technology could be extended or introduced over a wider area. Experience gained so far in North Africa and the Middle East indicates that with a pair of oxen and appropriate equipment arable land that can be managed by a smallholder can be extended from 2 to 7 hectares (Wieneke, 1977). Oxen and camels need no diesel fuel, or petrol, or spare parts. However, factors such as inadequate feed, lack of adequate veterinary stations and the problem of tsetse flies limit the wide application of animal power, especially in Malawi.

Any scheme for the improvement of the use of animal power in Malawi must therefore include the following components:

Consideration of the socio-economic and ecological character of the area concerned.
Training centres for 'man/woman and animal'.
Veterinary stations and technicians.

2.2.3 Irrigation

Irrigation is an important component in crop production for many reasons. Vegetables, considered a 'women's' crop, for instance, require a continuous supply of water for good growth and high yields, so that irrigation is needed in the dry seasons to ensure optimum moisture conditions throughout the growing season. Inadequate attention has hitherto been paid to small-scale irrigation systems. More emphasis on appropriate irrigation systems, using relatively low levels of power inputs, will be required if high levels of productivity are to be achieved.

2.2.4 Storage

The need for better and more secure storage of food is one which does not call for a 'revolutionary' solution in Malawi, since developed and more or less effective technologies related to food storage already exist. What is certainly needed is the constant encouragement of women to use simple improvements such as raising the traditional structures off the ground, adding rodent baffles to the legs, and coating the structures with mud. There are also a few traditional techniques for discouraging predatory insects. One common method is mixing ash with the grain; this technique has a sound scientific basis, since sharp particles of ash will damage the outer skin of an insect and lead to its death by dehydration. Other equally well-known methods involve mixing locally available insect-repellent plants with the grain, or mixing in an appropriate amount of dried sand, filling up the spaces between individual grains and thus creating a solid mass which insects cannot penetrate.

2.2.5 Food processing

It has generally been recognized that there is an urgent need for improved food processing technologies in Malawi. Despite being a largely agricultural country producing a diverse range of crops and foods, very little improved local processing of these crops is undertaken either for home consumption or for sale.

Malawi is an exporter of many agricultural products in raw form. At the same time, the country imports significant quantities of these products in processed form. Even when products are processed locally, they are far too expensive for the bulk of the population because of the high-level technologies used. For example, groundnuts are largely exported, with only a small proportion of the crop going to Lever Brothers' factory for processing into oil. This oil is too expensive for the majority of the people who, in the absence of cheaper alternatives, have to forgo oil in their diets possibly to the detriment of nutritional standards.

Similarly, there is virtually no local processing of fruit and vegetables in Malawi and much of this produce is either sold at give-away prices during the peak season or wasted. Production of cereal-based foods such as bread, using improved appropriate technologies, is also rare. Processing of staple crops such as maize, sorghum, and cassava mostly still involves such time-consuming and energy-demanding operations as pounding, peeling, and dehulling.

Traditional fish processing, too, is cumbersome and time-consuming, sometimes done under unhygienic conditions.

Smoking and sun-drying are the methods mostly used to process and preserve fish. Women play a central role in fish processing as well as marketing in Malawi. In fish-smoking, for example, they are responsible not only for the collection of firewood and grass for smoking, but also for attending to the actual smoking, and/or packing and transporting the fish to the house or the market. Smoking fish involves very simple steps. Once the fish has been gutted, it is placed on a raised wooden platform and a fire is lit in the open space beneath. The fish is continually turned over to ensure uniform smoking. Conrol of the fire is a problem in this method, and losses due to charring and burning can be considerable, while excessive heat in the initial stage of smoking tends to reduce the amount of protein content in fish.

Sun-drying in the open as an alternative simple way of preserving fish also has its problems. Often drying tends to be superficial, particularly in the rainy season. As a result most fish become susceptible to spoilage due to moulding, yeast, and bacterial action and from maggot attack.

2.2.6 Fuelwood

Fuelwood is the primary, and most probably the only, source of energy for most households in Malawi. Fuelwood shortages are noticeable and felt in many parts of the country. Women now find it difficult to get firewood and men, too, find it hard to find good building poles. In some parts of the country the environmental consequences of the fuelwood shortages are becoming dramatic. The effect of deforestation on erosion, climatic changes, and desertification are well known. Agricultural production is also affected by the demand for fuelwood substitutes. Some agricultural residues are used for burning at the expense of livestock feeding or soil fertility. Women and children have to walk very far to find fuelwood at the expense of their health and that of other household tasks.

The results of the Malawi Rural Energy Survey (1981) by the Energy Studies Unit found that 60 per cent of women felt that firewood collection is difficult and the results of Malawi Smallholder Tree Planting Survey (1982) indicate that 82 per cent of men feel that it is difficult to get building poles.

3. Improved appropriate technologies

In an attempt to improve living standards, particularly those of women in the rural areas, through the use of improved technologies, various items both indigenous and foreign have been and are being tried in the country. Also, a variety of programmes of action is being implemented by the Government with the ultimate objective of reducing or eliminating the monotony and drudgery associated with the daily tasks of women. Some of the technologies are outlined briefly in this section.

3.1 Fuel energy

One popular suggestion to eliminate the need for firewood for household activities was the use of solar cookers. However, these are virtually non-existent because of their disadvantages (socio-economic, design problems, cost). At present, one of the most practical ways of solving the problem of fetching firewood is by introducing and promoting stoves which use wood and/or charcoal in a more efficient way. The stoves in question are the adapted Jiko stoves, improved mud stoves, and 'Kynder Mbaulas.'

3.1.1 Fuelwood projects

The other approach which the Government of Malawi has taken to tackle the problem of energy is the creation of Fuelwood Projects. In all, wood fuel represents 35 per cent of the total primary energy consumed in the country, with agricultural residues 6 per cent, petroleum products 5 per cent, hydroelectric power 3 per cent, and coal 1 per cent. In 1983 wood consumption (effective demand) was 10.6 million m³ (roundwood). Woodfuel users consumed that total in the following quantities and proportions: rural households 5.1 Mm³ (60 per cent), urban households 0.9 Mm³ (11 per cent), tobacco industry 2.0 Mm³ (23 per cent), and other agro-based/allied rural industries 0.5 Mm³ (6 per cent). The strategies being adopted in the Government's policy involve the planting of trees and establishment of woodlots and plantations, the protection, control, and management of existing natural forests, and energy-saving systems (development and promotion of efficient utilization of wood and the investigation of wood-conserving technologies).

As many as 175 retail nurseries have been established throughout the country, from which the public, institutions, government and non-governmental organizations can purchase both exotic and indigenous tree seedlings. There exists a National Tree Planting Day which is aimed at educating, training, and promoting in students and the public awareness of the value of trees and also a knowledge of methods employed in establishing, tending, and protecting trees and woodlots. Smallholder Tree Planting shows that 39 per cent of the Malawi population have planted on average 40 trees per family during the past five years.

3.1.2 Charcoal project

The Malawi Charcoal project is being executed by the Forestry Department and is funded by the World Bank. The project is looking into the establishment and operation of semi-industrial charcoal production schemes from waste wood generated within Government forest plantations. The recommendations of the project (methods and technologies) have already been introduced on a pilot scale in the Viphya Forest, one of the largest forest plantations in Africa and the single most important wood resource in Malawi.

In addition to the above projects the Ministry of Forestry and Natural Resources has started the production of briquettes from sawdust for use as fuel. Three sawmills, one each in Blantyre, Zomba, and Dedza, are producing briquettes and selling them to the public.

The Government recognizes the fact that the strategies of reafforestation, forest conservation, and energy-saving systems will, however, have relatively little impact in meeting the sustainable needs of the people as well as of industries unless constraints such as land availability, land tenure, and competing uses, lack of a tradition of forestry, inadequate forestry extension systems, and the shortages of qualified manpower and finance are all under control.

3.2 Food processing

It is probably in food processing the simple and improved technologies can be of the greatest help to women because of the back-breaking and time-consuming nature of the work involved. The Malawi Government, having recognized the need for alleviating these problems, has been collaborating with other governments and non-governmental organizations to implement women-related projects. Some of these projects are briefly outlined below.

3.2.1 Maize

In Malawi, as in many parts of the SADCC region, maize is the staple food. To make the maize available for food preparation, the grain has first to be shelled, or stripped from the cob, a time-consuming and laborious task.

Several simple maize shellers are now available to Malawian women. Some of these are: (a) wooden hand-held sheller, (b) internally ribbed tube, (c) internally ribbed tube with rivets, (d) Chitedze sheller. The basic and common limitations of all these shellers are the cost of shelling output, and ergonomic aspects (Atiemo, 1983). Two prominent reasons for the limited use of these maize shellers by women are:
– the cost of the shellers;
– most women are not aware of their existence.

Efforts are also underway to reduce the energy and time involved in traditional methods of pounding maize. A project known as 'Grain Dehuller' has been established in the country to test dehullers for maize and sorghum, and so far three dehullers have been introduced. If proved suitable, as they have been in Botswana and Zimbabwe, and depending on local demand, a local company will be requested to start manufacturing the dehullers. The project is funded by the International Development Research Centre (IDRC), Canada.

Another project, implemented in May 1987 at Chikwina Rural Growth Centre in Nkhata Bay District, is intended to enhance the self-help capability of the women living there. An essential part of the project was the installation of a maize mill, which is now run by 17 women after having acquired the necessary technical and commercial knowledge in a form specially designed for them.

3.2.2 Groundnuts

A number of devices have been and are being tried for groundnut processing, such as shelling and oil extraction.

A wooden groundnut sheller, constructed at Chitedze Research Station, has been tested in the field. Improvements regarding level of nut breakages and suitability for the Mani Pintar variety (the main oil extraction variety) are being considered. Extraction of oil from groundnuts using simple, inexpensive equipment has presented a problem in the past, but recently a major breakthrough has taken place.

At Lobi Rural Growth Centre in Dedza district a spindle press and a roller mill have been installed for the extraction of oil from groundnuts. A group of women in the area have been trained to manage the project. At present the oil mill employs ten women, and can produce up to 15 litres of oil from 40kg of groundnuts a day. Recent feedback indicates that marketing of the oil and management of the mill constitute the main problems at present. Also at Lobi, a group of 10 women has just received training in fruit processing.

4. Proposed and potentially viable technologies

Basically there are two important ways in which improved technologies can help women to promote food security. These are:

10

(*a*) Labour-saving devices to reduce time and drudgery spent on tasks such as land preparation, weeding, fetching water and fuel, and processing grains.

(*b*) Equipment to assist women in processing staple crops and vegetables and fruits.

Women spend 9–10 hours every day in farming tasks such as hoeing, planting, weeding, harvesting, and processing. The outputs of their labour are low. Technologies which can help to reduce the time and drudgery involved in these operatirons and raise the productivity of women's labour would make a considerable contribution to food security.

Most women in Malawi still till their fields with short-handled hoes. If ergonomically improved hoes were made available (hoes with longer handles), this would eliminate much of the hard work which is associated with tilling since less bending is involved. Taking into consideration the present low technical knowledge and small-sized farms of women, the improvement and use of long-handled hoes and hoes with toothed blades for hard soils should be encouraged.

There are a number of simple yet improved methods of fish processing/preservation. For example in Ghana, as in most places along the coast of West Africa, fish processing/preservation (whether it be smoking, salting, or drying) is a part of a social system as well as a livelihood. The social organization, the division of labour, is already fixed. By and large, fishing is the domain of men, while processing and marketing belong to women. With the introduction and use of improved smoke ovens more women have become involved in fish processing and marketing. The improved smoke oven has had a very high acceptance rate among the processors because its design corresponds very closely to the traditional smoke oven, differing only in that trays can be stacked, allowing a greater number of fish to be smoked at one time. The improved smoke oven is designed so that the wooden frames of the trays will rest along mud ridges on the oven walls. The smoke oven has a capacity of up to 18kg of fish per tray, and as many as 15 trays can be used per oven. Because the smoke oven is a closed system, with the trays acting as a type of chimney, it uses less fuel and the heat is more evenly distributed. Losses due to charring are minimized because of better control over the fire.

It is recommended that such an improved smoke oven be introduced and tested in the lakeshore areas of Malawi. However, the adoption of such an improved processing technology will have one important consequence: since more fish can be smoked at one time, there would need to be an increase in fish caught. The introduction of the improved oven, which would allow women to smoke more fish, would be pointless without a corresponding rise in the fish supply. Such situations could discourage the women and can result in the rejection of a technology which appears to be useful.

Methods of processing, and the equipment used, affect food values and the deterioration and availability of food. Next to maize, cassava, rice, and sorghum are the most important food crops in Malawi. Increasing the yields of these crops has for many years been one of the Government's priorities. Rice forms an important part of the farming systems of the lowland areas in the country, more particularly along the lakeshore and on the plain around Lake Chilwa and in the Shire Valley. Women play a vital role in both the cultivation and the processing of the crop. The technologies used remain basically traditional.

Post-harvest processing of rice starts with threshing, when the grain is separated from the panicle. The equipment used is a stick or hinged flail with which the crop, spread on the floor, is beaten repeatedly. Such equipment is simple and cheap, but also slow and energy-demanding to operate. Output per person-hour varies considerably, but is on the whole between 25 and 50 person-hours per tonne. A study conducted by Mkandawire, Asiedu, and Mtimuni (1988) indicates that it takes about 4 hours for one woman to thresh 75kg of rice. After threshing and winnowing, rice is normally pounded in a mortar to remove the husks. Pounding or dehusking takes 6 hours for one woman to complete 75kg of rice. Paddy threshing and dehusking are the most arduous and time-consuming tasks that women have to face in the rice-growing areas of the country. Rice/maize mills are available, but their number seems to be so limited that in certain areas women have to walk up to 8 kilometres to have their rice dehusked. There is obviously a need for rice threshers and more rice mills.

For small-scale or village use, pedal-operated threshers having an output of about 150kg of grain per hour, and Engleberg hullers, should be considered. Engleberg hullers are commonly available in small hand-operated sizes or motorized versions of 3–10kW. Throughput varies from roughly 10kg/h for hand operation up to 300kg/h for the bigger models.

Cassava presents a staple crop for about 15 per cent of the population in Malawi. While the farming operations associated with cassava are not as cumbersome as those necessary for other crops, the processing of cassava into flour is long and taxing. Peeling and crushing/chipping are found to be the most time-consuming unit operations in the processing of cassava tubers into flour. The enormous workload women have to cope with in cassava processing limits the time they can allocate to other activities. Introduction of labour-saving technologies (peelers, chippers/crushers) would be an important consideration. Also worthy of consideration is the use of raised drying platforms for cassava instead of the usual drying on rocks or simply on mats on the ground.

5. Extension/technical advice on transfer of improved appropriate technologies

One of the problems of transferring technology to smallholder farmers in general is the shortage of both trained personnel and appropriate technological packages.

Providing small farmers, and women in particular, with information on existing technologies does not result in technology transfer if the technology is not appropriate to their needs or if they do not have the necessary skills to interpret it and put it to use. The introduction of improved appropriate technologies to women therefore involves the transfer not only of information, but also of skills in ways that encourage the development and utilization of indigenous resources.

Before implementation of the proposed technologies careful planning will be required. There will be need for the development of appropriate extension/technical advice to persuade both women *and* men that the proposed technologies will reduce their labour and promote food security and income for their families. Both formal and informal training will be essential in building up the women's skills if the proposed technologies are to be appropriate in meeting their needs.

So far Malawi's experience in extension has been largely in the area of agriculture. Some of the lessons gained in agricultural extension could provide a useful base for the development of extension training for improved appropriate technologies. Agricultural extension at the local level (Extension Planning Area) in Malawi operates through the Block system, a modification of the Training and Visit system (TV) successfully developed in South East Asia. The Block system involves a group of farmers from an extension worker's sub-section coming together at a given venue to be taught a given set of subject matter in farming and animal husbandry. The block itself is determined either by the geographical character of the area, or by accessibility of the venue to the farmers. Each block is supposed to have a demonstration garden where farmers are provided with extension advice in a practical way.

One of the advantages of this extension strategy is that a wider cross-section of farmers can be contacted at one place at once; and, given the formal setting of the block and the emphasis on demonstrations, farmers are able to learn from each other. With regard to women, the approach gives them the opportunity to receive first-hand extension messages; it has been found that where farmers are contacted as individuals, this sometimes results in male farmers being the exclusive clientele of extension workers.

The block system, in our view, provides a useful forum for the dissemination of improved technologies to women. However, if the block is to be effective, it will be necessary to utilize more female extension workers, who will be in a position not only to train women in the use of improved appropriate technologies at the block level, but also will be able to follow up individual women or groups in their homes.

It must be admitted that, in a situation where women have limited education, it may not be possible for them to enter into technical professions such

13

as extension. Malawi, however, has a large pool of sufficiently educated women who can be trained as trainers of women in the area of improved appropriate technologies. Indeed, at the grass roots level, it may not be necessary to have highly educated women as trainers/extension workers for women. A special programme can be launched to train female paraprofessionals to serve as extension workers for women. Such 'indigenous change agents' have the advantage of not simply belonging to the same subculture as the women: they also have the ability to empathize with their clientele. Such female change agents need to be trained not only in the art of communication, but also in various technical skills so that they are able to learn and understand the engineering and related technical aspects of the technologies. Rural Trade Schools that train in basic skills such as carpentry and metal working could be used to give technical training to women paraprofessionals.

Planners will, however, need to look critically at the adaptability of the proposed technologies to different groups of rural women. What must be realized is that rural women themselves are not a homogeneous group. The conditions under which they work, even in a given ecological area, vary. Different women have different amounts of land, different levels of income, different attitudes towards technological change and towards risk, and so on. Many of these differences will influence their decisions with respect to the adoption of the proposed technologies. While it is not practical for planners to take into account the special needs of each and every woman, it is possible to offer recommendations that will be approximately correct for given groups of women.

6. Institutional financial support for improved appropriate technologies

The proposed technologies will require financial support. There are a number of financial institutions which would need to be involved in the process of establishing improved appropriate technologies for women. The key ones include commercial banks, the Development of Malawian Traders Trust (DEMATT), and the Small Enterprise Development Organization of Malawi (SEDOM). While the country's main commercial banks, that is, the National Bank of Malawi and Commercial Bank, offer small- and large-scale loans to their customers, the bulk of these loans has in the past been given to estate agriculture. It is DEMATT and SEDOM that are at present actively involved in supporting small- and medium-scale entrepreneurs, particularly women.

DEMATT offers business training and back-up advice to its clients, who are mostly small- and medium-scale entrepreneurs, and the services provided cover the following areas: retail, wholesale, production, manufacture, and business management. Business advice is provided by business promotion consultants who visit each client twice a month at their business premises.

DEMATT does not provide loans, but it assists through its credit-worthiness programme in the procedure of obtaining loans from appropriate organizations, such as commercial banks and SEDOM. Both men and women have in the past participated in the organization's programmes. According to DEMATT, however, although direct applications by women come only to 9 per cent of all the clients, indirectly the organization deals more with women than men through its assistance in providing entrepreneurs with management, marketing, and accounting skills.

SEDOM works closely with DEMATT and leaves much of the busines training needs of its clients to DEMATT's extension staff. The main objective of SEDOM is to provide credit to small- and medium-scale entrepreneurs in a wide range of enterprises such as charcoal production, maize hullers and millers, bakeries, wine production, fish and food processing, etc. The organization offers both small- and large-scale loans of MK1000–MK3000 and MK3000–MK50,000 respectively.

The organization identifies existing and potential entrepreneurs through advertising, through organizing village-level workshops to explain its work, and through other agencies such as DEMATT. Several Government ministries are also involved in identifying groups and individuals who can become involved in productive enterprises. The Ministry of Community Services, for example, helps to organize workshops through its Home Economics Groups, and the Ministry of Agriculture, through its farmers' clubs, also helps to identify potential clients and organize workshops.

SEDOM has several women staff and has an active interest in promoting women's enterprises. It is currently estimated that 35 per cent of SEDOM's beneficiaries are women. Most of the women are involved in either textiles (49 per cent) or food processing (31 per cent).

Unlike other financial institutions such as commercial banks, SEDOM does not insist on land or buildings as collateral on a loan, so long as the proposed enterprise appears to be financially viable in terms of the project's capacity to generate adequate revenue or 'additional returns' which are important for repayment purposes. This is useful for women, who often have no collateral.

SEDOM's experience in funding small- and medium-scale entrepreneurs, particularly women, could provide a useful base for assisting women entrepreneurs who may wish to procure improved appropriate technologies.

In providing loans to women at the local level a number of organizational and administrative considerations have to be taken into account. There are already a number of women who receive credit from different organizations, either as individuals or in groups. The majority of the women, however, receive credit, particularly production credit, in groups. And, judging from Malawi's experience, such groups could provide useful lessons in the management and administration of credit for improved appropriate technologies for women.

Most rural women's groups in Malawi remain fairly informal, they are small in scale, single-function, homogeneous, and characterized by reciprocal relationships. Group members receive credits in kind from the Ministry of Agriculture: normally seeds, fertilizers, chemicals, or farm implements. Given that group members are linked through ties of affinity it is common practice for members to engage in reciprocal labour exchange during various farm operations. In cases where a group member is taken ill, other group members feel morally obliged to assist her in farming. This reciprocity is partly facilitated because the security for credit repayment is usually provided by the joint liability of group members. In case of default by any one member of the group, credit to the whole group is usually stopped until the default is corrected. Hence failure to repay by one single person may jeopardize all group members' access to credit the following season. Thus there is a high social pressure on individuals to make full and timely payments of their credit. The creation of women's credit groups is therefore a useful means to offset individual financial liabilities by offering lending institutions the lower risk of joint liability. The groups also involve lower transaction costs than for individual loans and more expeditious application–disbursement procedures.

Experience gained with women's agricultural credit groups in Malawi can be used for the administration of credit geared towards the procurement of improved appropriate technology for women. On the basis of the Malawian experience, the following guidelines should be considered in setting up women's groups for improved appropriate technologies:

(a) The group should start with one task, not several.
(b) The proposed task should be one for which there is a genuine desire on the part of the women involved.
(c) The group should be small in scale; members should preferably be drawn from the same village or lineage.
(d) The tasks to be carried out by the group should be relatively informal, unsophisticated, using familiar forms of organization.

The formation of women's credit groups should not preclude women from embarking on projects as individuals. Indeed, organizations such as SEDOM have in the past offered credit to individuals as well as groups of women. As long as there is a felt need by a given community for the establishment of certain improved appropriate technologies, and as long as the proposed project(s) have been assessed as economically viable, depending on the prevailing local circumstances, credit could be given either to individual women entrepreneurs or to groups.

7. Summary and recommendations

Women's contribution to agriculture, and therefore to the national economy, is enormous. They provide most of the labour for all activities except probably land clearing and ploughing. For land preparation and weeding the existing equipment needs to be tailored to reduce women's workload. Just as the improvement of pre-harvest technologies can increase the local availability of food, so can improved techniques be applied to reduce post-harvest losses and thereby improve food security at both household and national levels. This area of improvement is gaining more importance in Malawi. The other areas of concern for women in Malawi have been identified in this paper, and the Government fully appreciates both the magnitude and the seriousness of the problems that limit full participation by women in pursuit of national development. The Government's concern is expressed in the number of programmes of action that it has already started. It also recognizes that more has to be done, especially in the area of extension/technical advice and institutional support.

It is the Government's strong belief that the major technological thrust towards augmenting food production, securing food supplies, and improving living conditions is the introduction of improved technologies and labour-saving devices from which women can benefit. Regional co-operation through meetings of this nature go a long way towards providing a useful learning experience for us all. However, meetings at the regional or national level on their own will accomplish only limited results unless women are actually involved in planning and charting the way for interventions aimed at introducing improved appropriate technologies to enable them to promote food security.

The following three sets of recommendations are therefore offered, recognizing that the experiences described in this paper are not unique to Malawi but are common throughout the SADCC region.

7.1 Research
It is recommended that more baseline information to monitor the efficiency of technologies, once introduced, should consistently be gathered. This type of research will be technology-oriented, focusing on problems that women are encountering with the new technologies being introduced. This research should be built in to any technologies being introduced and should be action-oriented.

Weeding presents a major problem in the existing farming system. It is the most time-consuming and probably also the most energy-demanding activity in the entire farm operation-chain. Improved equipment that increases ground cover and reduces the need for several weedings is required.

It is recommended, therefore, that means should be explored now on how the hand cultivator can be introduced to women farmers in all the districts. Ways have to be explored to find out why only a few women use the existing improved technologies in cultivating their land.

It is clear that women farmers' *storage* practices have hardly been influenced by foreign storage methods and structures. There is a strong

17

likelihood that, even if these were introduced, they would not readily be acceptable to the women for several reasons. What is deemed necessary in such situations is to *encourage* as many women as possible to use improved storage structures (e.g. raised maize cribs with rodent baffles) as well as traditional insect repellents.

Constant promotion of the *improved stoves* (tested and recommended by Forestry and Natural Resources) is absolutely necessary. Women must be helped to realize the importance of cooking in enclosed areas to conserve firewood.

Improved *drying* methods (e.g. the use of elevated platforms as practised extensively in West Africa, and the use of simple solar driers for vegetable drying) should be introduced.

Improved *smoking* ovens for processing fish, as practised in coastal areas of West Africa, should be tested in the lakeshore areas of Malawi.

There is need for more work on processing *groundnuts* into oil using inexpensive oil expellers.

It is suggested that *post-harvest processing* equipment which has proved successful in other parts of Africa (rice threshers, Engleberg rice thresher-polishers, cassava crushers, peelers) be tried under Malawian conditions, and if found satisfactory should be introduced into the areas concerned.

7.2 Training and extension services
Special courses in the fields of processing, preservation, and storage of agricultural produce should be run in local institutions/colleges for the present extension workers.

Machinery extension should be incorporated into the existing extension programmes, or strengthened if it has already been incorporated.

Additionally, it is recommended that women paraprofessionals associated with the identified technologies should be trained in the various technical skills so that they are able to acquire, learn, and understand the engineering and related details embodied in the technologies.

7.3 Financial support institutions
It is recommended that appropriate institutional credit arrangements be introduced. However, such credit institutions should be tailored to fit into the already existing credit arrangements.

Appendix

Table 1 Maize: Labour inputs per crop activity (hours and % per hectare)*

Type of labour		Land preparation	Planting and harvesting	Weeding	Harvesting and marketing
Man head	Hours	35.8	13.8	63.2	24
	%	37.8	42.0	36.0	23.5
Female head/ wives	Hours	36.8	17.8	90.0	67.9
	%	38.9	54.3	51.3	65.4
Hired labour	Hours	22.0	1.2	22.2	10.3
	%	23.3	3.7	12.7	10.1
Total	Hours	94.6	32.8	175.4	102.2
	%	100.0	100.0	100.0	100.0

* Adapted from A.E.S. Report No. 33, Tables 18–20, pp. 20–21

Table 2 Pulses: Labour inputs by crop activity (hours and % per hectare)*

Type of labour		Land preparation	Planting and fertilizing	Weeding	Harvesting and marketing
Man head	Hours	151.4	93.6	38.5	88.4
	%	37.7	45.6	20.7	18.3
Female head/wives	Hours	157.1	95.1	142.3	395.9
	%	39.2	46.3	76.5	81.7
Hired labour	Hours	92.6	16.6	5.2	0
	%	23.1	8.1	2.8	0
Total	Hours	401.1	205.3	186.0	484.3
	%	100.0	100.0	100.0	100.0

* Adapted from A.E.S. Report No. 33.

Table 3 Cotton: Labour inputs per crop activity (hours and % per hectare)*

Type of labour		Land preparation	Uprooting and burning	Planting and fertilizing	Weeding and thinning	Spraying	Picking	Grading and marketing
Man head	Hours	73.4	30.1	24.5	170.9	39.5	161.3	161.5
	%	47.3	39.6	60.4	48.4	56.1	48.5	45.5
Female head/wives	Hours	53.1	26.9	15.1	109.2	22.5	100.8	121.3
	%	34.2	35.4	37.2	30.9	32.0	30.3	34.2
Hired labour	Hours	28.7	19.0	19.9	73.1	8.4	70.2	72.1
	%	18.5	25.0	2.4	20.7	11.9	21.1	20.3
Total	Hours	155.2	76.0	40.59	353.2	70.4	332.3	354.9
	%	100.0	100.0	100.0	100.0	100.0	99.9	100.0

* Adapted from A.E.S. Report No. 33, Tables 23–5, pp. 22–3.

Table 4 Sweet potatoes: Labour inputs by crop activity (hours and % per hectare)*

Type of labour		Land preparation	Planting and fertilizing	Weeding	Harvesting and marketing
Man head	Hours	204.5	54.1	31.4	8.2
	%	44.2	50.0	25.8	16.1
Female head/wives	Hours	203.5	50.4	90.4	42.7
	%	44.0	46.6	74.2	83.9
Hired labour	Hours	54.8	3.7	–	–
	%	11.8	3.4	–	–
Total	Hours	462.8	108.2	121.8	50.9
	%	100.0	100.0	100.0	100.0

* Adapted from A.E.S. Report No. 33.

2

Zambia

1. Introduction

Zambia's most recent statements of policies and strategies for development of the agricultural sector have the following main objectives:

1. to achieve a satisfactory level of self-sufficiency in the production of staple foods;
2. to expand the production of exports;
3. to increase the import substitution of agricultural products and inputs; and
4. to improve rural employment and incomes.

The existing data have shown that women play a very important role in achieving the above objectives. The strategies and policies outlined for achieving three of the above most relevant objectives (1,2 and 4) will be analysed in terms of their implications for women farmers.

1.1 Achievement of self-sufficiency in staple food production

The basic strategy for achieving this objective is that preferential treatment will be given to small-scale farmers in line with their greater number, their development potential, and their relatively efficient use of foreign exchange resources. Thus special attention is being given to government programmes designed to reduce the constraints on the productivity of small-scale farmers.

Data on the participation of women in Zambian agriculture show that most small-scale farming is done by women and that there are serious constraints on their productivity (Rothschild, 1985). One of the major constraints is the amount of labour time available, particularly in Female Headed Households (FHH).

One of the policies stated by the Government is to promote the regional specialization of agricultural production by means of economic and technological improvements, for example by growing sorghum in drought-prone areas of the country. In Zambia sorghum is a 'women's' crop, as are other important food crops like finger millet, cassava, beans, groundnuts, and green vegetables. Thus the success of this particular policy objective will depend on the orientation of agricultural services and resources to women farmers.

Another policy is to streamline the provision of credit resources to producers in order to improve their access to and command over necessary production inputs. In order to achieve this objective and contribute to the larger objective of self-sufficiency in the production of staple foods, the distribution of credit will take account of the characteristics of smallholders so that women farmers receive credit proportionate to their numbers or the area they farm.

Yet another policy emphasizes the development and dissemination of appropriate technological packages. This policy cannot be successfully achieved unless it is recognized that different categories of smallholders need different technological improvements. Women farmers, for example, need technology relevant to both their agricultural tasks (planting, weeding, food storage and processing), as well as their off-farm, domestic tasks.

Finally, there is a policy specifying the 'periodic adjustments of floor producer prices, based on the cost of production of efficient producers'. When making such adjustments, since they will affect men's and women's crop production differently, it is important to assess the impact of price changes on women farmers' productivity and incomes. For example, if maize or other cash crop prices are drastically increased, the demand for women's labour for the cultivation of these crops may become so great that their food crop production suffers. This would in turn have negative implications for the households' nutrition status and for women's incomes.

1.2 Expanded production of agricultural exports
One policy relating to this objective is to 'promote the expansion of market-oriented production, particularly through the support of emergent farmers'. Since women's labour is significant in this area, it is important to orient agricultural extension services to women farmers.

1.3 Improvement of rural employment and incomes
Though women are not specifically mentioned as a separate target group for achieving this objective, one of several policies regarding 'upgrading the living conditions of the rural population' aims to upgrade and promote the active participation of women in all aspects of rural development.

The analysis of the policies, strategies, and objectives mentioned above shows that women are an important target group and that some recommendations have already been formulated for the reorientation of agricultural services and resources towards women farmers. However, research has shown that the recommendations are not being implemented and that women are not benefiting from the agricultural resources and services of the nation.

2. Categories of farmers

To give a clear understanding of farming systems in Zambia, a brief on categories of farmers is provided here. Analysis of the needs of different categories of farmers is based on the various types of farming enterprises. Studies have shown that there are numerous systems of classification in use.

However, the categories used in the *Food Strategy Study* (1983) describe a number of the types of farming enterprises in the country as follows:

1. *Large-scale commercial farmers* have more than 40 hectares under cultivation.

2. *Medium-scale commercial farmers* have farms of 10–40 hectares.

3. *Small-scale commercial farmers* have farms of 1–10 hectares, use some purchased inputs, and market some of their produce.

4. *Traditional farmers* have farms of one hectare or less, do not use purchased inputs, and market only a little of their agricultural produce.

Based on 1980 estimates, the number and proportion in the respective categories were as follows:

Farm type	Number	Proportion (%)
Large-scale commercial	800	0.1
Medium-scale commercial	28,000	3.5
Small-scale commercial	161,600	20.2
Traditional	609,600	76.2

Other systems of classification use different criteria. For example, the Crop Forecasting System employed in Zambia defines peasants or traditional farmers as those who have farms of less than five hectares and/or realize a cash turnover of less than ZK1000 or US$125.

Given the classification generally accepted in Zambia and the important national agricultural objectives, to 'achieve a satisfactory level of self-sufficiency in the production of staple foods' and to 'expand the production of agricultural exports', there is one clear conclusion. The objectives can only be achieved if preferential treatment is given to the traditional and small-scale farmers who constitute more than 95 per cent of the nation's farmers.

Household food security for these two groups is essential to the nation's overall food security. Further, the nation's ability to achieve a sizeable production of agricultural surplus for the urban population in this most urbanized country of Africa, and for export, depends on increasing the productivity of small-scale commercial farmers. Thus any initiative designed to improve agricultural production should focus on the needs of these two farm household categories.

3. Women farmers

Although it is widely recognized that women do most of the agricultural work throughout Africa, including Zambia, it is important to document the extent to which they are independent farmers and to describe in some detail the character of the work that they perform. There is in rural Zambia a disproportionate number of adult women to men. The overall rural average is 85 men to every 100 women and some outlying areas have even greater imbalances. In addition to their numerical dominance in the rural labour force, individual rural women spend more time on average than individual men in both food crop and cash crop production in both traditional and small-scale commercial farms.

Regardless of their marital status, most rural women spend a significant amount of their time in agricultural work. Further, they make a disproportionate contribution to the nation's agricultural production. However, women farmers have *less* access to basic resources and agricultural services than men. In general this is the result of an interrelated set of factors including their relative poverty and educational level, together with other cultural practices and attitudes which result in a number of institutionalized constraints on rural women.

Farmers, including women farmers, need access to improved technology, to credit so as to employ the techniques available, and to training and other forms of education that will give them an understanding of the production and technological choices available. For the most part women farmers are significantly disadvantaged with respect to access to these services.

Part of the problem arises from the fact that rural women are not perceived as farmers by extension workers and other government officials. Despite the fact that women perform most of the agricultural work, extension workers are accustomed to dealing with a man, as head of a household, rather than with a woman, as the primary person involved in agricultural production. Thus, just as extension programmes are struggling to see small-scale and traditional farmers as legitimate clients, they must also struggle with acknowledging women farmers as a specific target group for their activities.

4. Female headed households (FHH)

In Zambian agriculture the gender factor has been widely cited as one of the most important variables influencing farming decisions and practices in the system. Adaptive Research Programme Teams' community surveys have shown that female farmers, especially as heads of households, were least advantaged in terms of access to production resources and had the greatest need for all kinds of assistance. Further, their problems and priorities are different from those of male farmers.

Female headed farm households are increasing in Zambia. A 1982–3 farm survey shows that on average 31.2 per cent of rural households were headed by women. An examination of the primary sources of income of rural female headed households indicates that for the most part, and with only a few exceptions, agricultural activities were significant in the family subsistence and income.

25

The character of agricultural activities undertaken by women – women's agriculture – was also revealing and suggested factors that should be taken into consideration when designing and implementing agricultural programmes and projects. Of the households in which livestock, including poultry, constitutes a significant part of the farming activities, there is a disproportionate representation of female headed households. In Luangwea district, Lusaka Province, over 66 per cent of the households raising livestock and poultry were female headed. Further, of those farming households that specialized in livestock and/or poultry and engaged in little or no other agricultural activity, a majority were female headed. Thus programmes aimed at animal agriculture, including poultry, must take cognizance of the importance of women decision-makers in those farming enterprises.

5. Sexual division of labour in agriculture

The sexual division of labour has important implications for agricultural development. Studies undertaken in several Zambian provinces show that tasks such as harvesting, weeding, shelling, winnowing, storage, and preparation are predominantly done by women. Also, depending on the method being used, women share the work of planting and transportation with men. In fact, when transportation of produce is to the local rather than national market, it is predominantly done by women. There is considerable variation in the division of labour according to the crop cultivated, the intensity of labour required, and whether it is considered as a 'female' crop or not.

Due and Mudenda (1984) have shown that on average, during the farming season, women contribute 53 per cent of total hours of labour in agriculture while men contribute 47 per cent. In another study conducted in 1981, in five areas of varying socio-economic characteristics, it was found that 26 per cent of the women but only 15.7 per cent of the men were working full time on the farm. Shula (1979) studied 69 subsistence households in the less accessible areas of Zambia's Central Province and showed that 55.6 per cent of the women and 34.1 per cent of men reported working full time. The latter data make the case that women bear the responsibility of subsistence cultivation. An Integrated Rural Development Programmes baseline survey (1984) reports that only in land preparation and the application of fertilizer do women do slightly less of the work than men (32 per cent of all women versus 36 per cent of all men).

As farms expand, weeding becomes the most serious constraining factor because there is a relatively short time in which it is valuable. Furthermore, if weeding is done at the best time it will clearly overlap with land cultivation. This in part explains why it is frequently done late. Using oxen could shorten the cultivation season and stop this overlapping of activities.

Weeding, however, is bound to overlap with planting of the main crops, because one occurs immediately after the other. Since both tasks are predominantly women's activities, it has been observed that this constraint will probably not be lifted without a change in technology that facilitates and lightens women's tasks.

Because men are inclined to take on jobs involving machinery and/or chemicals, a change in technology in that direction could bring men's labour into greater play. The same would also apply to harvesting and threshing. Men have no greater non-farm calls on their time than women, so there does seem to be a considerable amount of surplus male capacity which might be productively employed in agriculture. There is some question whether it is desirable to ease this labour constraint by reinforcing a sex-segregated labour pattern that leaves women outside the realm of agricultural modernization. Such a pattern might further weaken women's ability to control income and thus decrease their incentive to achieve higher agricultural productivity.

6. Institutional barriers to women's access to agricultural technology

New agricultural technology can provide rural women with the means to improve their traditional tasks. It can be used to encourage community self-help and to improve life-styles, as well as developing self-reliance. Though some technologies are developed, there are barriers to women's access to them. Others that should be developed are not in the scientific pipeline. This part of the paper will try to look at some of the barriers that either obstruct women's access to existing technologies or that prevent technologies important to them from being developed. In general we identify the following major institutional barriers:

1. access to credit (to use the technology);
2. access to existing knowledge:
    (a) attitude of agricultural extension workers who carry the new technology messages;
    (b) content of extension programmes for women;
3. new knowledge – the character of the research agenda.

6.1 Women's access to credit

While many poor households have difficulty in gaining access to agricultural credit, women face even greater constraints because of a number of attitudinal and structural barriers. While no comprehensive statistics are available, the limited existing data show women's very low access to credit. It has been reported that in 1984 only 5 per cent of agricultural loans were granted to women, and that the amounts lent were very low – in the order of ZK100–200. The Bank of Zambia also reported that during the 1982–3 season only 2 per cent of all applicants were women and the value of requested loans represented only about a half of one per cent (0.5%) of all loans.

Finally, data presented by the Standard Bank of Zambia show that in 1982–3, loans to women represented only 10 per cent of all individual agricultural sector lendings (Agricultural Lending Policies in Zambia with Special Reference to Women, 1983).

These data indicate that a very small number of women apply for and receive loans. The following reasons have been suggested:

(a) Many female farmers could not meet the lending criteria because they grow subsistence crops and their surplus could not be sold officially. However, new pricing policies since 1987 have taken the situation into consideration and all women's staples, such as sorghum, millet, and cassava are officially priced.

(b) Women farmers are not aware of lending policies, criteria, and requirements. Information and applications for loans are distributed by agricultural extension workers who seldom visit female farmers.

(c) Female headed households, which cannot rely on a husband's labour, depend mainly on hiring oxen or labour in order to increase agricultural productivity, often cannot assume the risk of a loan.

Gaobepe and Mwenda (1980) have shown that credit has very high transaction costs – the time and energy necessary to complete the application and other forms – that is especially costly for women heads of household with serious time constraints.

Recent experience with credit funds earmarked for women has shown that such initiatives help increase women's access to credit. In 1983–4, for example, the proportion of women receiving loans from the Zambia Cooperative Federation (ZCF) improved because it was requested that the ZK100,000 or US$12,500 earmarked for the People's Participation Programme (PPP) be biased towards women. Most of these funds (ZK89,00 or US$11,125) have already been allocated to women's agricultural groups. Similarly, the proportion of women LIMA loanees in Eastern and Northern Provinces went up to 36 per cent when credit funds became earmarked for women. Through these programmes women have increased and diversified their agricultural production. Technologies such as the use of oxen for ploughing and shellers for groundnuts and maize have been adopted.

It seems advisable, therefore, for agricultural loan programmes for smallholders to earmark funds for women farmers in order to safeguard their access to agricultural credit. This, however, should be considered as an interim strategy leading to women's equal participation with men in mainstream credit programmes. It is clear that small, isolated agricultural projects for women only have a very small probability of successfully utilizing credit and increasing agricultural productivity and incomes. The success of loan programmes for women and men smallholders depends on the extent to which integrated systems of credit, incentives, pricing policy, input supply, marketing, and extension services are provided in concert.

6.2 Women's access to extension programmes

Participation in Agricultural Programmes first of all means using new methods of production at all levels. Agricultural Extension Services are very important to every farmer. The Food Strategy Study (1983) reported a favourable ratio of extension staff to agricultural units of 1:300, but warned that there were fewer qualified staff members for non-commercial farmers.

The objectives of agricultural extension are to increase agricultural output and to reduce poverty. Up to now the focus has been primarily on the commercial farmer and, hence, on well-off farmers who can better afford modern agricultural inputs. The advice given has been concentrated on maize, cotton, sunflowers, and groundnuts together with a package of cultivation methods and inputs designed to encourage an intensive approach to production.

Women farmers have little access to agricultural extension staff for a number of reasons. One is that they have been viewed as subsistence farmers and not involved in mainstream agricultural production – the crops mentioned above – despite the fact that considerable numbers of women cultivate cash crops as well as food and most women sell some surplus food crops.

6.2.1 Attitudes of extension workers

There are very few female extension staff. It was shown in 1981 that there were 1449 agricultural extension staff members at the provincial and district level and that 9.6 per cent of them were women. About 65 per cent of all staff members were commodity demonstrators without any theoretical training, and 10 per cent of these were women. A 1984 survey of extension agents conducted by the Department of Agriculture showed that female extension workers (212 in all) represent only 8.6 per cent of the total number of all extension workers despite the involvement of women in agricultural production.

In addition to their relatively smaller numerical presence in extension, women's status and prospects are also more limited than men's. A larger percentage of all female extension workers (35.9 per cent) than of male workers (23.2 per cent) is at the bottom of the scale as commodity demonstrators. Very few female agents (12.3 per cent) continue with the two-year training to obtain a certificate and become agricultural assistants. On the other hand more than one-third of all male agents (37.2 per cent) do so. At the Senior Agricultural Assistant level about an equal percentage of male and female agents is represented. Finally, while more than a quarter (27.4

per cent) of female agents are agricultural supervisors with a diploma, and only 9.4 per cent of men fall in this category, more than half of these women are concentrated in the Lusaka, Central, and Copperbelt provinces in provincial offices rather than in the field.

A particularly disturbing trend is that there are very few female extension workers in the provinces with a high percentage of female headed households, while the concentration is high in provinces with big cities and very low agricultural production. This trend is shown below:

Northern Province	5.8%
Luapula Province	5.3%
Eastern Province	6.2%
Western Province	8.7%
North Western Province	6.6%
Lusaka Province	23.8%
Copperbelt Province	15.5%
Central Province	11.6%

While there is a clear need to step up the training of female extension workers in agriculture and to post them in the field, there are many prob-, lems associated with both measures that must be dealt with within the context of reorganization of the agricultural extension services. With that in mind, it is imperative that male extension workers be sensitized to reach female farmers including female heads of households.

In Zambia, provision of agricultural extension to women has been concentrated in the Home Economics section of the extension branch of the Department of Agriculture. In the past, staff in this section provided rural women with training in food handling and preparation, nutrition, child care, and hygiene – not in agricultural production information. Granted, these are essential subjects, but they have some limitations as far as participation in agricultural production is concerned. Women who attended courses at Farmers' Training Centres typically received training in domestic science, including sewing and knitting, with little emphasis on agricultural production, even though they were actively engaged in agriculture and animal husbandry.

More recently, the Home Economics section has expanded its activities to include teaching of production skills related to improved household food security. However, this section continues to be mistakenly perceived as having primarily a domestic science focus. Despite its increased attempts to reach its clients, the number of staff in this section is far too small to serve its target population. Further, because many of its staff have received specialized home economics training, some do not feel confident about their ability to impart production-oriented training on crop and animal husbandry to women farmers.

As stated above, cultivation skills are taught by government extension workers, most of whom are men. An observation was made which showed how easily, if not intentionally, women can be excluded:

A meeting was held in the yard of the branch chairman to demonstrate how to measure the size of a LIMA maize field. All farmers, regardless of sex, were present. The extension worker sat in the shade surrounded by men. The women sat ten metres behind them in the cooking area. After a short speech, which was impossible for the women to understand because of the distance, the men went to a nearby field, where they learned how to measure a LIMA while the women went home.

Women farmers should be assisted by general extension staff at camp level, as well as by specialists from the Home Economics section. The prevailing opinion is that male extension staff are inhibited from interaction with women farmers because of cultural constraints and attitudes.

In addition, the introduction and implementation of the World Bank Training and Visit system of agricultural extension in several provinces rarely benefits women. Women farmers are not generally selected by their communities as contact farmers. For example, only 5 per cent of contact farmers in 1985 in the Eastern Province were women. It should therefore be clear that existing general extension staff, predominantly male, will have to work with women farmers if the current change of emphasis away from large-scale commercial farmers and towards traditional and small-scale farmers is to become a reality. All woman, regardless of their marital status, need extension services. It will be necessary to adapt the Training and Visit system to local conditions and to reflect the fact that most rural women are contributing substantially to agricultural production. This adaptation requires that extension staff become aware of the contribution, needs, and constraints of women farmers.

The so-called cultural constraints and attitudes are not immutable, as is shown by the willingness and success of some general extension male staff in working with women farmers, both individually and in groups, in particular projects. For example, the 2000 women who take part in the Women's Participation in Rural Development Programme, co-ordinated by the Department of Agriculture in Central, Lusaka, and Southern provinces, have generally received adequate extension services; primarily because the district co-ordinators of the programme have mobilized individual camp staff.

Furthermore, in areas where there are women's agricultural groups, these groups could be used to demonstrate improved techniques, the dissemination of agricultural information, and the delivery of inputs. The use of such groups there would avoid the cultural constraints on male extension workers' contact with women farmers. Also, taking into account the labour constraints of female headed farm households, extension workers could test the Adaptive Research Planning Team's technical messages and packages,

31

alleviating acute labour shortages and thus allowing female farmers to participate in meetings and to have better access to agricultural information and technology.

6.2.2 Women's access to training and the content of training

Women farmers' access to training has been limited due to the fact that most of it is offered at the farming training centres. Studies of the Northern, Central, and Southern provinces have shown that in 1980 only 5 per cent of the women had attended farmer training courses. In the same year Eastern Province had the following sexual representation: 33.31 per cent men; 15.19 per cent women; 51.50 per cent schoolchildren and members of the Youth Farmers Clubs.

When this was realized an attempt was made to increase women's participation to 25 per cent, but that target was not reached even in areas where transportation was made available. This, of course, is not surprising since women farmers, especially heads of households, cannot take several weeks off to attend classes away from the village. The evaluation report of the Agricultural Sector Support Programme (1983) has underlined the importance of mobile farmers' training courses for small-scale farmers, especially women. Recent experience with mobile courses in Western Province has shown that the participation of women in mobile courses was 23 per cent (Niesten, 1984), which is much higher than that reported for Farmers' Training Centres. Within the context of this information, the recent decision by the Department of Agriculture to shift the emphasis from Farmers' Training Centres to mobile-type training is very encouraging.

Attention must, however, be paid to the contents of training offered both to extension workers and eventually to women farmers. The type of training offered to extension workers has its own limitations. Keller and Phiri (1986) have shown that one of the two agriculture colleges in the country has continued to give Home Economics or Home Science courses to their female students, whereas male students are trained in agricultural engineering. The Home Science syllabus does not currently include material on the inter-relationships between agricultural production and household nutritional status, nor does it make students aware of the production characteristics, needs, and constraints of women.

The animal and crop production courses are heavily biased towards commercial production by medium- and large-scale farmers. For example, a 'smallholder' of animals is one who has a herd of two to ten dairy cows and/or about six pigs or sows. Traditional animal husbandry, in which women are very much involved, and methods for improving existing practices are not taught. Similarly, the crop production courses include practical work in management of maize, cotton, groundnuts, soya beans, sunflowers, and various fruits and vegetables. Important staple foods such as cassava, sorghum, and millet are not much stressed. The Farm Management syllabus introduces students to budgeting, investment planning, financing, record keeping, etc., techniques which are more relevant to very commercially oriented farmers.

The Farm Engineering syllabus includes training in ox mechanization, appropriate technology, and numerous other subject areas, many of which are relevant to the needs of rural women. However, students are not taught to analyse the gender relevance of individual technologies such as the possibility, for example, that the use of oxen may benefit men more than the women in the same households who are still required to weed and harvest by hand.

Finally, the Extension Methods syllabus includes a rural sociology component and students do spend some time in villages. However, gender as an important factor in the division of labour in rural areas is not stressed to the degree that is warranted and as a result extension methods for reaching women farmers are not explicitly taught.

The above analysis of the type of training given to extension workers is in itself an illustration of the type of training women get, whether at the Farmers' Training Centres or through mobile units. Women are often offered courses in Home Economics, with only minor parts in production-oriented activities. If the agricultural productivity of small-scale farmers is to be enhanced and rural poverty alleviated, the focus of agricultural extension should be dictated by the type of farmers' agricultural activities and not by their gender.

6.3 The character of agricultural research

In earlier comments on agricultural research, there was a strong emphasis on the need for all agricultural research programmes to collect data on the differential resources, constraints, and needs of wives and of different types of female headed households. Depending on the results, appropriate technical messages and packages must be developed and tested by Adaptive Research Planning Teams in different provinces. This will show whether or not female headed farm households have different needs and constraints from male headed households; and what the needs, constraints, and potential are for different types of female headed households in developing and testing appropriate technical packages.

The lack of such research and information was identified as one of the barriers to women's access to agricultural technologies. The gaps identified are being commented on by ARPT's recent approaches to research. For the past three years several Adaptive Research Planning Teams have carried out considerable research on traditional crops such as cassava and sorghum. This trend should be strengthened and continued.

Discussions held in Zambia on the subject of agricultural research have revealed that most research has focused on improved methods of cash-crop oriented production such as hybrid maize, sunflower, cotton, soya beans, and very little has been done on staple foods such as cassava. Although

33

research efforts have been applied to sorghum varieties for the dry areas, results have not been disseminated to female farmers in those areas.

The Adaptive Research Planning Team in Luapula Province has been working on high-yielding cassava varieties. Some female contact farmers were selected for trials. The varieties that have been tried have not been successful with women. They say that although they produce more tubers, the tubers are very small in size, making the subsequent processing activities difficult. In addition, the leaves of these varieties are very small and sparse, making it difficult for households to use them as relish (a vegetable dish eaten with thick porridge or nshima). This is a very important observation for future research.

One technological package examined by ARPT is the use of draught animals for cultivation instead of hoes. In some areas where animals have not yet been used for draught purposes there are very few oxen being trained for such purposes and as a result demand for those animals is very high. Only those people who have special connections with the few owners of oxen, or those who have ox-drawn implements, have access to draught power. In other words, there are strong reciprocal economic linkages between the more affluent households in the community. Most of the resource-poor households who can afford neither oxen nor draught implements are excluded from these draught power-sharing relationships. Most women farmers belong to this category.

A Research Case Example

Efforts to take account of the differential impact of new agricultural technologies on various groups, in this case gender-specific groups, produce instructive case examples of the kind of considerations that must be taken. The negative impact on women of the introduction of draught oxen has prompted the ARPT to start looking at the possibility of introducing new tillage techniques such as replacing the conventional mouldboard plough with a tine plough in a reduced tillage technology. The reduced tillage technique with the tine plough could make it possible for larger areas of land to be cultivated in a shorter period of time and hence increase the availability of draught power to a larger population of farmers in the community.

However, in the area where this has been tried it has been observed that while the labour time required for ploughing is reduced with the tine plough, the time required for weeding is greatly increased. Since ploughing is a man's job and weeding a woman's job, this technology could very well shift the burden of labour in favour of men and at the expense of women. For the reduced tillage technology to be viable, it should come in a package that includes better weed control techniques.

Two alternatives to ease weeding problems are being considered: (*a*) the use of herbicides; and (*b*) a non-technical solution. The use of herbicides is being tested on farms rather than in scientific trials, because their effectiveness is already known; the tests are intended to evaluate farmers' responses to using herbicides. Techniques for using herbicides for women farmers should be simple, inexpensive, and save time, as well as being acceptable to farmers.

In a system where cash is a constraint, technologies that require higher cash investments than the traditional methods are less likely to be accepted. Given the inefficiency of the extension system mentioned earlier, the skills required to apply this unfamiliar technology will not be widespread among farmers. A further consideration is that the use of herbicides in maize fields will prevent families from using edible weeds, which normally grow randomly between the maize, as local vegetables.

Because of the possible drawbacks associated with herbicides, it was felt that a parallel non-technical solution should be developed at the same time. The non-technical solution inolves liaising with policy-making institutions and other relevant agricultural research teams such as agricultural engineering units, to identify suitable ox-drawn implements which would relieve the weeding burden, and to make these available to interested female farmers on a sale or credit basis.

Another interesting observation on the use of draught oxen is that farmers using ploughs, and thus cultivating bigger fields, are unable to plant desired hectarages within the current planting period. This means that maize varieties of differing maturing periods and whose planting dates can be spread over a long period of time (currently available through the co-operative unions or developed by the Zambian Research Branch) should be introduced to farmers. Investigations on the possibility of introducing suitable ox-drawn planters are also being undertaken.

The foregoing case discussion illustrates the importance of developing and introducing suitable agricultural technologies to reduce women's workloads. The research necessary to develop those technologies requires some considerations not normally taken into account in agricultural research. We are pleased that some such efforts are beginning to be made in Zambia.

7. Other technologies of interest to women

Thus far we have looked primarily at women's involvement in agricultural production in Zambia and their access to resources and technologies. In this part of the paper we try to look briefly at other activities in the food cycle that women are involved with and some of the technologies available in the country.

Some of the implements that have been developed in the food industry are maize and groundnut shellers, storage and solar driers, decorticators, fruit and vegetable processing techniques.

Groups of women, both urban and rural, have at one time and another been involved in the construction of the above devices. As a package

35

women have been taught food processing techniques to improve the quality of their dried products such as vegetables.

In Zambia most households use indigenous vegetables for relish, such as amaranthus, garden eggs, etc. These vegetables (which are very nutritious) are in abundance during the rainy season, but the supply tapers off after the rains. To enable households to utilize these vegetables all the year round, improved seeds have been developed and sold at a very cheap rate.

Improved fuel-efficient stoves programmes are being introduced. Such stoves include smokeless stoves made out of mud bricks, mbaulas (brassierrers), etc. These were being demonstrated at a Technology Centre in Central Province to groups of both farmers and farmer's wives. The smokeless cookers have become very popular in these areas.

Village-level grinding mills have been introduced to groups of women in all provinces of Zambia. These are being operated by women themselves once they have undergone intensive training in simple mechanics before project implementation.

Oil Seed Processing – A Case Example

An interesting case study to illustrate the place of women and technology in the food cycle is based on sunflower-seed oil-pressing units. Sunflower is one of the cash-crops and earns a lot of income for large- and medium-scale farmers. Oil processed from seeds is very important in the country's diet. The oil-pressing units were introduced to groups of women and installed in three areas of Zambia. This study is based on the oil press project in the Gweembe Valley Self Help Promotion (VSP), where the identified target groups were already in existence. Group membership was 30, including chairperson, treasurer, and secretary who were nominated by the group itself.

The women were involved in the installation of the processing unit. This unit was seen to be of potential benefit to both group members and non-members in the community. The women were trained to operate the machine by the Agricultural Extension Officer.

Before the introduction of the presser the women were engaged in cooking, sewing, and gardening. It proved helpful that the group was already organized and involved in other group activities.

Development

The installation of this unit has brought about some development in the area:

1. many people have been encouraged to grow sunflowers;
2. women have learnt to process cooking oil;
3. they have acquired simple techniques of operation and maintenance;
4. there is an availability of cooking oil, a rare commodity in rural areas;
5. oil cake is available for their animals.

Operation

Six women a day are required to operate the presser. Some know-how and a lot of interest are required for the smooth running of the process. There are a lot of people growing sunflowers in the area, and so far sunflower growing has not reduced the extent of growing staple food. Cooking oil is sought after, but the cake is in low demand although one farmer has indicated some interest in buying the cake for animal feed.

Prospects

The group intends to increase the output and satisfy the demand for oil. It hopes to process 10 bags of sunflower seed per week. The institutional and economic impacts of this project to both group members and nearby communities have not yet been assessed. It is, however, hoped that this will be done during the 1988–9 season.

8. Conclusions

Women as heads of households, as wives, as members of households, are central in the labour force of Zambian agriculture. As heads of households and as the cultivators of the major subsistence crops they are significant decision-makers. Women are central to agricultural development and to the food security of rural people in Zambia, and until now their concerns have been too little recognized.

Zambian female farmers need help. Unfortunately, many of the existing initiatives to assist farmers are directed at men rather than at farmers in general and as such will have only limited impact. Only as Government officials, most of whom are male, become aware of the gender distortion in policies and programmes of research, extension, credit, land, and labour access, and a host of other issues of agricultural development, will they be able to bring about the agricultural transformation they desire.

3

Botswana

1. Background

Over the years several countries including international co-operating partners (Donors) have devised policies and programmes that are intended, among other things, to improve both the living standards of women, in general, and their food security, in particular. This positive attitudinal and behavioural development follows decades of concern over the poor socio-economic conditions and glaring inequalities faced by women and children especially in the rural areas of Third World small countries. Botswana has over the years designed programmes and projects in several sectors of the economy including agriculture, which is the backbone of rural development, to improve the quality of life for women. However, a lot still needs to be done to promote equality for women as well as other disadvantaged groups.

Botswana's population was estimated at 1,231,972 in 1988, of which about 52 per cent were females. Over 70 per cent of the country's population lives in the rural areas and derives its livelihood from agriculture and off-farm activities (basketry, clothing, beer brewing, woodwork, etc.). The majority of the rural population are women and children; most able-bodied men emigrate to towns in search of job opportunities. Most of the agricultural activities, including decision-making, are therefore undertaken by women. For instance, of the estimated 84,000 farming families in Botswana, about 35 per cent are female headed households. However, when decision-making on the day-to-day management of the farming enterprise is considered, since most men are away in towns, mines, etc., the percentage of women engaged in key production, management, and other related agricultural activities is overwhelmingly higher. Except for ploughing, practically all the cropping activities are undertaken by women in Botswana.

Despite this significant representation of women in rural and agricultural activities, their living standards and food security in most cases leave much to be desired. If by food security, in this context, we refer to 'access to calorie-adequate diet for all people all the time to live a healthy and normal life', it is clear that in a socio-economic environment where agriculture is largely constrained by erratic and unfavourable weather conditions, access to productive inputs such as technology, implements, credit, and draught power is poor, and alternative employment and income-generating activities are painfully limited, nutritional stress including chronic hunger among both women and children is likely to be serious. In fact, most

38

farming families in Botswana hardly produce sufficient food for themselves. Fortunately, since the onset of drought about six years ago, Botswana has launched country-wide relief programmes including supplementary feeding and cash-for-work (labour-based) which have covered both women and children. Obviously this humanitarian assistance could be attributed to the relatively healthy financial position of the country coupled with generous donor contributions. However, it is also important to note that the political commitment to allocate resources to such programmes, followed by timely monitoring and supervision, has also led to the success of the country's relief programme. Unfortunately, such short-term relief programmes cannot be relied upon in the long term because the financial and human resources that they require cannot be sustained by economically vulnerable countries. Botswana's major sources of income are diamonds and beef, which in turn are dependent on politically and economically volatile world markets.

To help in the improvement of the food security position of the majority of the people, including women and children, the Government has initiated deliberate policies and programmes which will, among other things, promote the socio-economic conditions of these chronically disadvantaged people typically found in several developing countries including the SADCC region. Not only should prices of commodities produced and sold by women be attractive in real terms; policy-supportive systems on taxation, interest rates, credit, and technology (both access and utilization) require periodic review and monitoring to ascertain whether or not they have a positive impact on the population in general and women in particular. Botswana strongly believes in a *multifaceted strategy* that improves overall opportunities in income and employment generation in agriculture, industry, agro-processing, etc. through credit, pricing, and marketing policies, training, technology, and research. Africa and SADCC have had several lessons and experiences of how piecemeal approaches have brought more harm than good to their people. At least in Botswana through the National Food Strategy, where efforts are being intensified to increase both household and national food security (i.e. through domestic production on income and employment creation), an integrated approach is pursued. Physical and social infrastructure together with economic incentives are being provided and developed. For instance, farmers in Botswana are free to sell their produce to anyone at a price determined by market forces, not by government as is the case in most countries. The negative effects of producer price control are well known, including the adverse effects on nutrition, food security, etc. for women and children in particular. Similarly, the supply of inputs such as field implements, seeds, etc. is not accomplished by any one agency.

This paper summarizes the various Government and non-government intervention programmes and projects that are intended to improve access to and utilization of food cycle technologies in Botswana in order to enhance the food security situation of women in the long term. Besides improving women's food security situation, these food cycle technologies are also intended to remove bottle-necks such as shortage of labour and capital among households in order to raise their productivity. Lack of appropriate technology has been one of the major constraints responsible for low incomes, hence poverty and malnutrition, among the disadvantaged groups. Further, four case studies are provided to enable us to learn from the implementation of some of these programmes and suggest improvements to achieve the intended socio-economic objectives, such as social justice and non-discrimination on the basis of sex. Finally, the paper identifies constraints that could hamper efforts to promote access to and use of food cycle technologies, in particular, and the food security situation in general. However, as experience elsewhere has amply shown, efforts to resolve these constraints without strong political commitment backed by decisive action to improve implementation capacity, efficiency, and accountability may not yield the desired results.

2. Research and technology development

2.1 Ministry of Agriculture

The Agricultural Research Station deals with research subjects such as sorghum/millet improvement and production, oil seed and legume research, weed control, crop rotation, plant protection, horticulture, plant nutrition, machinery development, and tillage systems.

In Botswana, technology design and improvement is based on the problems of production which generally reflect women's problems, since all operations in arable agriculture except ploughing are predominantly done by women. Improved technology covers a wide spectrum such as land preparation, crop management, crop improvement, and storage techniques, to mention a few.

2.1.1 Land preparation

Under traditional systems of raising crops, land utilization involved the use of hand hoes and ploughs which needed a lot of labour and draught power respectively. The current recommendation is the use of tractor-drawn implements such as mouldboard ploughs with planter attachments, plough planters, and harrows. Ox-drawn implements are made lighter to reduce draught power requirements, both to facilitate easy handling by women and also to use labour effectively so that operations are performed faster. Although the technologies for land preparation concentrate on techniques which are traditionally men's domain (animal power), women benefit in that part of their workload is shifted to the men, e.g. by the use of plough planters. The hiring or purchase of these implements is available through different farmers' assistance schemes, most of which have a clause that favours women, e.g. the Arable Land Development Policy (ALDEP).

2.1.2 Planting
Traditionally broadcasting was done by women, but with row planting the introduction of plough planters has shifted this responsibility to men and therefore gives women time for other chores. Row planting makes weeding and harvesting easier (especially in mixed cropping systems). It also facilitates the use of inter-row cultivators which reduce the hand weeding load. Use of jabb planters provides an improvement of the back-breaking operation of hand hoe planting.

2.1.3 Seed dressing
The problem of poor stand and low plant populations has been addressed partly through the use of seed dressing (fungicides and insecticides). This gives better emergence by protecting the seed against soil micro-organisms and insects. The recommended seed dressings are captan and malchion, which are fairly cheap and easily available. Women's labour, saved on gap filling, is available for other duties.

2.1.4 Certified seed
The Seed Multiplication Unit (SMU) of the Department of Agricultural Research (DAR) makes certified seed available to the farmer through extension personnel. This provides better quality, clean, and treated seed of high germination percentage at subsidized prices. Seed is produced for recommended varieties of sorghum, millet, maize, cowpeas, and groundnuts. Farmers who keep their own seed are recommended to send it to the research station for germination and purity tests.

2.1.5 Improved varieties
Crop production in Botswana is characterized by low and inconsistent yields which are affected by factors such as pests and diseases, poor economic practices, lack of suitable varieties, and the large variations in amount and distribution of rainfall. The recommended varieties are basically those which are drought tolerant, high yielding, early maturing (for drought avoidance). For legumes the recommendation is for varieties that mature synchronously, facilitating easy harvesting and reduced labour requirement. The high labour input demanded by legume crops such as cowpeas mostly goes into harvesting and is generally provided by women and girls.

2.1.6 Weeding
Mechanical weeding through use of ox-drawn or tractor-drawn cultivators

reduces the necessity for hand weeding labour provided by women. Use of herbicides for problem weeds is directly beneficial to women.

2.1.7 Storage
Better management and improvement of the existing traditional storage structures are promoted. These stress good sanitation and chemical treatment to reduce storage losses.

2.1.8 Soil and water conservation techniques
Harvesting water by building contour ridges gives it enough time for infiltration. Although a lot of labour is involved in the construction of ridges, moisture made available by this system facilitates longer planting times, lengthens the season, and creates the potential for double cropping and therefore high yields. This system favours weed growth, but with improved weeding technology, this can be handled. Contour ridge building fits well into the soil conservation programme, labour intensive projects (drought relief), and ALDEP packages so that labour or draught for building ridges can be obtained through one of the farmer assistance schemes.

Technology adaptation is primarily hampered by lack of knowledge about the technology itself or the different farmer assistance schemes which are available.

The Animal Production Research Unit conducts research on livestock and range research; this includes trials relating to livestock productivity, mortality, stocking rates, grazing systems, fodder species, dairy production, and small stock.

The Unit provides trainees with high breed cattle and assistance in animal husbandry in the hope of doubling the production of milk. In conjunction with the Botswana Food Laboratory (BFL), it runs biological and chemical analysis on milk to improve and standardize 'madila' production. 'Madila' is a traditional milk product made by women and if milk surpluses do become available the findings of the pilot project can be replicated and the information can be disseminated. There are two women participants in this project.

2.2 Rural Industrial Innovation Centre (RIIC)
This non-profit association has the following objectives:
1. To promote the creation of rural employment, including self-employment, by providing training programmes and other activities.
2. To endeavour to make Botswana more economically self-sufficient by producing goods and services that would otherwise be imported.
3. To promote and support the development of job-creating industries by:
   – identifying, adapting, and developing labour-intensive technologies and processes geared to local resources.
   – designing, testing, producing, and distributing implements and

equipment for small-scale industries and for the development of agriculture.

– providing technical training to rural Botswana to enable farmers to be more productive and self-sufficient.

– developing technologies suitable for local conditions which are based on renewable energy rather than imported non-renewable energy resources.

– RIIC's projects that are relevant to this paper are:

(*a*) the sorghum dehuller.

(*b*) the Village Artisan Programme – particularly the bakery programme.

(*c*) water lifting devices – handpumps, animal-drawn pumps, monopumps.

(*d*) solar batch water heater (not directly related to food security, but a time- and energy-saving device for heating water at home – facilitates more time for income-generating activities).

(*e*) salt production.

(*f*) sorghum thresher.

(*g*) animal-drawn implements.

2.3 Botswana Technology Centre (BTC) – Botswana Food Laboratory (BFL)

A summary of the aims and objectives of the Botswana Food Laboratory is:

– job creation, both rural and urban.

– building food security at a local, national, and regional level.

– raising the nutritional status of the population, a long-term aim.

– improving the quality of processed foods, both microbiologically and otherwise.

– export quality assurance.

– import substitution.

The BFL also focuses on advising local entrepreneurs on how to produce economically viable food products based on local agriculture or wild foodstuffs.

2.4 Southern African Agricultural Research Centre for Cooperation (SACCAR)

SACCAR's programmes and projects aim at generating technology for use by farmers, both men and women. On-farm testing deals with farmers to ensure that they get maximum benefit from these technologies. Co-operative agricultural research in SADCC started off as a political directive in Lusaka, April 1980, when the leaders of the nine independent states of Southern Africa set up SADCC and committed themselves to 'policies aimed at the economic liberation and integrated development' of their national economies. Agriculture and animal husbandry were identified as priority areas for Southern African co-operation.

A number of programmes and projects are already in operation:

2.4.1 Sorghum and Millet Improvement Programme (SMIP)

This programme was set up as a result of the Lusaka Declaration and ICRISAT was identified as the external agency particularly equipped to provide assistance in a regional programme aimed at improving sorghum and millet. The institution of this programme was mainly stimulated by the drought conditions which were widespread in the SADCC region at that time.

The programme is based at Matopos in Bulawayo, Zimbabwe, and run by ICRISAT on behalf of SACCAR. The main objective of the programme is to create the basis for improving sorghum and millet varieties available to farmers throughout the region and in general to raise the level of technology available for the production of sorghum and millet; also to assist national programmes to design and improve technology relevant to their cropping systems.

The project has a strong programme of on-the-job training, both informal and formal. On the informal side, the project staff visit research institutions within the region on a regular basis to discuss issues of mutual interest and offer advice and assistance where appropriate.

2.4.2 Land and Water Management Research Programme (LWMRP)

This programme is based on Botswana and it is funded by the Overseas Development Administration (ODA). The project was started in 1987 and its main objective is to carry out research on watershed management and rainwater harvesting, and to develop techniques generally concerned with maximizing the availability of rainfall and moisture for crop production.

SACCAR's potential role in promoting food security in the Southern African region includes:

Grain Legume Improvement Programme (GLIP).

Agricultural Research Resources Assessment (ARRA).

Small Research Grants Programme.

Travel Grants Programme

SACCAR Newsletter.

3. Financial assistance and credit

Botswana has several sources of financial support for women in food production, including Government financial schemes, parastatal agencies, commercial banks, and foreign development agencies.

In this paper only a few of the important financial assistance and credit schemes are outlined.

Government Assistance includes:

3.1 Small Village Projects (LG 17)

Although most of the funding so far has been allocated to construction projects, many other initiatives could be funded under LG 17. Examples of food production projects might include fencing vegetable gardens and water points, starting a vegetable garden, or constructing and operating a village market.

It should be noted that more of the projects funded under LG 17 could be of a directly commercial or money-making nature. Projects which support or assist commercial activities are very acceptable.

3.2 Agricultural Extension – Small Projects Programme (AE 10)

This programme is aimed at overcoming some of the problems attached to increasing agricultural production at village level. This will be done by providing funds to assist with the setting up of agricultural support facilities in villages and agricultural areas, as well as assisting the setting up of agriculture-related production projects.

Projects under this programme should be small and community-based. They should aim at creating agricultural infrastructure or at directly increasing agricultural production. Examples of projects which should be included are:

– village horticultural projects.
– bookkeeping.
– storage facilities for crops and/or seeds.
– market places.
– drift fencing.
– soil conservation.
– water development for agricultural purposes.

This project specifically excludes cattle-oriented projects. Projects under the AE 10 programme should be small, low cost, labour intensive, and answering an immediate problem or need felt by the community.

3.3 Service to Livestock Owners in Communal Areas (SLOCA) (AG 15)

SLOCA attempts to address the needs of communal livestock owners. The formation of groups of farmers has been encouraged by the Ministry of Agriculture and it is to these groups that funds are provided under SLOCA. The second phase of SLOCA will continue to build upon developments already achieved, with the aim of encouraging the use of improved animal husbandry techniques and increased offtake, improving the provision of livestock inputs and marketing services, increasing technical assistance, information and training for livestock owners in communal areas. SLOCA has 40% participation from women for small stock projects, for example the erection of dipping facilities.

3.4 Financial Assistance Policy (FAP)

FAP has made a special 10% inducement provision for women.

Table 1 No. of women grantees out of total FAP small-scale agricultural grants 1982–6

Type of project	Rural areas			Urban areas		
	Total grt	Female £	Female %	Total grt	Female £	Female %
Horticulture	79	19	19.39	0	0	0
Fishing	278	0	0	0	0	0
Poultry	72	16	18.18	11	5	31.25
Small stock	7	2	22.22	0	0	0
Dairy	3	0	0	0	0	
Piggery	7	3	30	2	0	0
	446	40		13	5	

Source: Calculated from FAP Small Scale Agricultural Projects Status report.

Though the returns from labour and financial inputs are not immediately realizable (particularly in horticulture), agricultural income-generating activities have the most potential viability over the long term. The number of women involved in small-scale agricultural projects, however, accounts for less than 10% of the grantees. This is lower than female participation rates in industrial projects.

3.5 National Development Bank (NDB)

NDB finances the following sectors related to food security: horticultural projects, dairy projects, poultry, piggery, field crops (for seeds, fuel, fertilizer), tractors and all agricultural implements, livestock ranching, purchases of breeding stock, commercial crop farming, food processing, and the fencing of fields.

The Bank must finance viable well-secured projects (33 per cent security margin minimum). Project promoters should participate by providing a 15 per cent or 25 per cent contribution, depending on the total cost of the project. Loans of P20,000 need a 25 per cent contribution of the total cost of the project. Management of the project should be sound to ensure sustainability.

NDB does not have special arrangements for funding women as such, although they are considered as eligible for loans as any other sector of society. This is with particular reference to the Small Borrower Fund (SBF) for borrowing up to P10,000 (recently extended to P20,000) at a low interest of 10 per cent for viable projects. Security or collateral in such small loans is not a major bottleneck, since the loans are guaranteed in conjunction with Government. Sound management skills are a prerequisite, with a minimum of 15 per cent of the total cost of the project having to be provided by the applicant. For loans exceeding the total project cost of P20,000, the equity contribution in participation has to be at least 25 per cent.

The collateral requirements for loans include assets not otherwise acceptable to many commercial banks in Botswana, for example livestock and equipment.

Generally, women apply for loans for food production projects as groups – syndicates, management associations, co-operatives, and companies. Loans are then granted to them in this capacity.

3.5.1 Agricultural Credit Guarantee Scheme (ACGS)
The constraints regarding loans to women are:
(a) Some farmers, including women, can not afford 15% of the contribution.
(b) Some farmers, including women, may not have sufficient skills for project management.
(c) Some farmers, including women, may not have enough assets to secure loans.
(d) The need to present a viable project proposition for long-term survival and sustenance.
(e) As men are traditionally the heads of households, women do not have the collateral to apply for loans. Women, however, are heavily involved in the management of the projects on a day-to-day basis, particularly in projects like cereal production, poultry, and horticulture. Approximately 40 per cent of the credit extended to men has substantial female participation in the project, particularly in agriculture and food processing projects.

Women are treated equally at NDB as far as loan applications are concerned. They are very eligible for credit facilities as they have tended to be better managers of projects and are more likely to be assisted under the SBF, for small amounts which are more suitable for most female headed households.

4. Manpower development

4.1 Ministry of Agriculture
The Ministry has a number of training institutions and programmes for men and women to increase and improve food production. Several non-government organizations offer training facilities and programmes; only the major ones are listed here.

The Ministry of Agriculture is itself the largest institution in terms of providing services to farmers. The Department of Agricultural Field Services (DAFS) incorporates both crop production and animal rearing divisions, and is responsible for extension services to farmers. The country is divided into six agricultural regions, each region is divided into districts (22 in all), and the districts are divided into extension areas. Regional Agricultural Officers (RAOs) are responsible for co-ordination of the extension programme at the regional level. There is one District Agricultural Officer (DAO) in each district and one Agricultural Demonstrator (AD) in each extension area. There are 225 extension areas, which gives a ratio of approximately 364 farming households to one AD. This compares quite favourably with other developing countries.

Table 2 Staffing of the Department of Agriculture Field Services

Position	Male	Female	% female
Field services:			
Regional Agricultural Officer	4	2	33
District Agricultural Officer	22	0	100
Agricultural Supervisor	21	1	5
Crop Production Officer	8	2	20
Agricultural Demonstrator	200	50	20
ALDEP	2	2	50
Horticulture	1	1	50
Agricultural research:			
Arable crops:			
Technical Officers & Assistants	34	15	31
Agricultural Research Officer	14	5	26
Animal production:			
Technical Officers & Assistants	9	2	18
Agricultural Research Officer	8	3	27
Soil & Plant Analysis	5	6	55
	306	111	27

The field service District Agricultural Officers are all male, which is rather disappointing. Although staffing for ALDEP and horticulture is 50% female, the numbers should still increase since women are very active in these two sectors. The number of females employed as Technical Officers and Assistants is very low and should be increased. All sections of the DAFS should increase the number of women employed, particularly since most small-scale farmers are female. The services of female extension officers could make the extension services more accessible to women farmers, since communication and the dissemination of information would be easier.

4.1.1 Botswana Agricultural College
This is the main instrument for agricultural training in Botswana. Courses offered include certificates and diplomas in agriculture and animal health.

Some courses are pre-service courses such as the certificate courses. The graduates go out and work, and return later to do upgrading courses such as the diploma courses. They then function as Agricultural Demonstrators, Crop Production Officers, and Technical Officers.

Table 3 Enrolment at Botswana Agricultural College

Course	1985	1986	1987	1988	Total
Certificate in Agriculture					
Male	17	37	26	39	119
Female	9	11	10	15	45
Certificate in Animal Health					
Male	20	19	19	25	83
Female	8	10	5	8	31
Diploma in Agriculture					
Male	7	17	14	21	59
Female	3	5	8	3	19
Diploma in Animal Health					
Male	13	9	17	11	50
Female	1	3	0	2	6
Total male enrolment					311
Total female enrolment					101
% of female enrolment					24.51

The main reason for the low female enrolment over the past four years is the lack of accommodation at the College. The Government should seriously consider providing facilities for women students since the potential for increased enrolment exists.

4.1.2 Rural Training Centres

The Ministry of Agriculture's Rural Training Centres (RTCs) train men and women in a range of agricultural skills that are aimed at improving subsistence farming and farm-based income-generating activities.

There are five Rural Training Centres, serving the Southern, Gaborone, Central, Maun, and Francistown Agricultural Regions. The Western agricultural region has temporary facilities. These RTCs have dormitory facilities for trainees. Agricultural demonstrators suggest through the District Agricultural Officer the types of courses needed by the farmers, and the RTC staff plan and execute them. These courses cover all areas of agricultural production.

Two of the RTCs, Gaborone and Mahalapye, have Rural Home Instruction (RHI) programmes designed specifically for female farmers and consisting of home economics subjects (home management, nutrition, sewing, knitting, food processing and preservation). Other RTCs use the services of home economists from other organizations as temporary resource persons.

Several specialized programmes at the Ministry of Agriculture have strong training and technical assistance components. These include horticulture, small stock, fisheries, poultry, dairy, and bookkeeping. Table 4 shows a high (47.6 per cent) female attendance in RTC-run agricultural courses for 1984–5.

Table 4 Male/female attendance in RTC-run agricultural courses 1984–5

District	Male	Female	Total	% female
Chobe	196	164	360	45.5
Ngamiland East	160	68	228	29.8
Ngamiland West	188	20	208	9.6
Gantsi	187	130	317	41.0
Tati	119	300	419	71.6
Tutume	176	133	309	43.0
Mahalapye East	84	130	214	60.7
Mahalapye West	144	256	400	64.0
Bobonong	53	67	120	55.9
Palapye	177	223	400	55.8
Serowe	117	98	215	45.6
Bamalete/Tlokweng	249	314	563	55.8
Kgatleng	188	107	295	36.3
Kweneng South	384	347	731	47.5
Barolong	59	37	96	38.5
Ngwaketse South	220	131	351	37.3
Ngwaketse North	179	127	306	41.5
Ngwaketse Central	49	31	80	38.8
Kgalagadi South	43	33	76	43.4
Kgalagadi North	62	40	102	39.2
Total all districts	3034	2756	5790	47.6

Training under these programmes is usually provided directly through specialized extension personnel or at RTCs. At some centres, like the Mahalapye RTC, women form the majority of participants in courses such as small stock management, dry land farming, vegetable production, and poultry. Even in courses like livestock management and soil conservation, women are in the majority as trainees over a number of years. Table 5 presents data on male/female participation in selected courses during the last three years.

The only course for which no female participants are recorded is the tractor maintenance course. Similar trends of female participants are noticeable at the Francistown and Sebele RTCs. At the Maun RTC, women

Table 5 Male/female participation in selected courses at Mahalapye Rural Training Centre

Subject	1983–4			1984–5			1985–6		
	Male	Female	% female	Male	Female	% female	Male	Female	% female
Small stock mgt	64	102	61.45	4	20	83.33	48	89	64.9
Dryland farming	38	37	49.33	24	31	56.36	16	30	65.2
Livestock mgt	16	14	46.67	28	32	53.33	45	38	45.7
Disease ctrl									
Soil conservation									
Range mgt	14	31	68.89	2	9	81.82	60	17	22.0
Vegetable product	31	77	71.30	70	72	50.70	26	33	55.9
Poultry mgt	16	18	52.94	20	13	39.39	24	33	57.8
	179	279		148	177		219	240	

do take part in the specialized agricultural courses, but their participation rate is relatively much lower.

For example, during 1985–6, there was 1 woman out of a total of 24 in the fishing course. For vegetable production, 2 out of 10 participants were women. Only the poultry-keeping course attracted more women: 9 as compared to 8 men. The agricultural staff, interviewed by the consultant Laketch Dirasse, suggest that the low female participation rate in the Northwest District could be as a result of cultural values. In other parts of the country men are said to delegate women to attend courses like livestock management (a strictly male domain), but in the Northwest husbands are said to prefer their wives to stay at home and attend to their tasks.

The female enrolment for farmers' courses at Denman Rural Training Centre shows a marked improvement. In a six-year period the percentage had increased from 39.7 per cent to 52.3 per cent. This trend in the

Table 6 Enrolment at Denman Rural Training Centre: Farmer Course

Year	Male	Female	Total	% female
1983/4	1150	757	1907	39.70
1985/6	750	614	1364	45
1986/7	1296	678	1974	52.30
	3197	2049		5245

improvement of female participation is constantly increasing. This is a big step forward, since the overall food security of Botswana could be enhanced if women are helped by training to improve on their unskilled, subsistence tradition.

It should be noted that the trend in the courses over the years is the same.

Table 7 Enrolment by course at Denman Rural Training Centre 1985–6

Course	Male	Female	Total	% female
Parasite Control	77	47	124	37.90
Livestock Mgt	54	47	101	46.53
Horticulture	106	163	269	60.59
Poultry	32	41	73	56.16
Contouring	24	7	31	22.58
Ranch Mgt	13	9	22	40.91
ALDEP	20	9	29	31.03
Small Stock	46	32	78	41.03
Fencing	63	10	73	13.70
Soil Conservation	17	37	54	68.52
Dry Land Farming	50	60	110	54.55
Farmers Committee	24	34	58	58.62
Tractor Maintenance	11	0	11	0
Group Formation Mgt	93	76	169	44.97
Firebreak Construction	18	5	23	21.74
Bee-keeping	16	12	28	42.86
Pig-husbandry	20	1	21	4.76
Rabbit-keeping	4	15	19	78.95
Fodder Preservation	8	4	12	33.33
Tractor Owners	55	7	62	11.29
	751	616	1367	45.06

The enrolment by women at Denman Rural Training Centre for 1985–6 in the horticulture course was 60 per cent (163 female and 106 male), much higher than the male enrolment. Female enrolment for dryland farming, farmers' committee, and rabbit-keeping courses also exceeded male enrolment. These are all very encouraging developments.

However, enrolment for tractor maintenance was zero as compared to 11 male enrolments. This trend should be overcome, since the exclusion of women from highly technical subjects is a continuing issue for concern. In the subsistence and unskilled agricultural sector women predominate, and if their skills are to be increased and modern technology introduced, women should be encouraged to enrol for courses such as tractor maintenance. Their chances of acquiring these skills outside training centres are practically nil.

4.2 Parastatal and Non-Governmental Organizations
The programmes listed here represent only a few of those actually available in Botswana.

4.2.1 Partnership for Productivity (PFP)

PFP is a non-profit subsidiary of Botwana Development Corporation (BDC). PFP provides training, extension services, and micro credit to small-scale producers. Part of PFP's activities is aimed at small rural producers, especially women, in Southern District's Communal First Development Area (CFDA).

4.2.2 Rural Industries Promotions (RIP), Rural Industries Innovation Centre (RIIC)

While RIIC is engaged in research and development of appropriate technologies, it also provides a series of training programmes, known as the Village Artisan Training Programme. The course offered that is relevant to this paper is the bakery course.

Trainees learn to construct a rim oven, the theory and practice of making bread, buns, small cakes, scones, tarts and doughnuts, and an introduction to haybox cooking (*maikapei*). A short course in bookkeeping as well as advice on the finances needed to start a bakery business are included.

4.2.3 Foundation for Education with Production (FEP)

Ths is an international organization with its headquarters in Gaborone, registered in Botswana as a Development Trust. The FEP guiding principle is the promotion of social, cultural, education, and economic progress of people in various countries in a spirit of international co-operation and solidarity.

The training undertaken by FEP embodies the principles of education with production, the linking of manual and mental work to bridge the gap between education and real-life situations.

4.2.4 Botswana Mill Owners Association (BMOA)

The BMOA provides training for owners of sorghum mills, including technical, record-keeping, and marketing training. A number of women in Botswana have gained from this.

4.2.5 Botswana Food Laboratory (BFL)

BFL provides training for women in making achaar, curd, pickled beetroot, and biltong. It also helps women's co-operatives in the use of yeast in their bakery project. This is specific assistance in streamlining produce.

The laboratory is also experimenting on processing watermelon to make jam, squash, and beer. It is conducting experiments on drying marotse (a drought-resistant melon) to preserve it for use in the off-season.

In conjunction with the Animal Production Research Unit (APRU) at the research station in Sebele, BFL is conducting research to develop a technique for increasing the shelf life of madila.

5. Case studies

Four case studies are dealt with here. The first three are examples of technologies which have been successfully introduced to women. These successful programmes need to be constantly reviewed and improved. Not all technologies developed in Botswana have been successful in design and acceptance, for example, the sheet metal stove mentioned under Constraints and Potentials, Section 6. The last case study is a pilot project.

5.1 Arable Land Development Programme (ALDEP): benefits to women

Up to 1983 Arable Land Development Programme packages were given to small farmers on loan. In 1983 the Government modified this scheme to benefit more farmers, eliminated the loan component, and offered packages to farmers with a subsidy of 85 per cent because the poorer farmers were unable to produce the security for obtaining loans or take a second package without repaying the loan.

The ALDEP strategy is to make the small farmer owner of her/his inputs and free her/him from dependence upon larger farmers – a dependence which can make small farming unviable. ALDEP is intended to reach 11,000 farmers, 17 per cent of the total farming households in Botswana, over a five-year period. Farmers who own fewer than 40 cattle and plough less than 10 hectares are eligible to apply for ALDEP packages. Targets for the disbursement of packages in the first phase are: draught power 6000, implements 6980, water tanks 3470, fencing 2000, a total of 18,450 packages.

All ALDEP packages consist of: animal-drawn ploughs, planters for row sowing, and cultivators for removing weeds; fencing; water tanks; draught power (donkeys, oxen, mules). For these four packages the farmer pays only 15 per cent of the actual cost except for oxen, where the downpayment is 40 per cent.

Free fencing up to P1000 is provided for the poorest farmers with no cattle and an annual income of less than P500, who cannot afford the 15 per cent downpayment. Other provisions to help farmers include:
- Women farmers without family labour can hire labour for fence erection for P150 within the package.
- Small farmers, farming as little as one hectare, can receive packages.
- Farmers unable to destump, but who are still cultivating their land, can obtain packages excluding planters, cultivators, and harrows.
- The farmers' contribution of 15 per cent is reduced by P50 for the fencing package if she digs the holes etc.
- Tools for fence erection can be loaned to farmers by Agricultural Demonstrators.

5.1.1 Household and farm characteristics of aided farmers
Sex

Women's participation in ALDEP continues to grow, as is evident from Table 8.

Table 8 Sex composition of ALDEP participants (percentages)

Region	1982–3		1983–4		1984–5		1985–6	
	Male	Female	Male	Female	Male	Female	Male	Female
Southern	91	9	89	11	77	23	71	29
Gaborone	90	10	88	12	71	29	71	29
Central	84	16	71	29	67	33	61	39
Francistown	78	22	71	29	71	29	60	40
Maun	92	8	96	4	93	7	80	20
Total	85	15	84	16	74	26	67	33

Overall, participation of female farmers has gone up from 15 per cent in 1982–3 to 33 per cent in 1985–6 – good progress, considering that about 36 per cent of the farming households in the country are female-headed (1985 Agricultural Statistics) and do not have cattle. This is an encouraging feature of ALDEP implementation, demonstrating that the assistance is increasingly being channelled to the poorest and most vulnerable sections of the farming community which constitute the focus of the programme. In Model I category, the poorest of the target group, women farmers are in the majority (54 per cent). Increased women's participation is positive evidence of the strengthening extension outreach.

The regional picture reflects the same trend, except in the Gabarone region. But here too, women's participation has increased in all the districts except Bamalete/Tlokweng where it is still very low (10–15 per cent). This is to be explained largely by the acute shortage of draught power in the district, which has kept down the participation of the poorest group of farmers (Model I) in which female farmers predominate. This problem could be tackled by transporting draught animals from outside the district, but there is currently a government ban to prevent overgrazing.

Table 9 brings out the preferences of female participant farmers from different models for various types of packages:

There is a broad similarity in the preferences of both male and female farmers of different categories (Models I, II, III) for various types of packages. Fencing packages seem to be most popular with female farmers, as with males. Ploughs, being a basic package, seem to be in great demand with resource-poor women farmers. Thus, 78 per cent of the packages taken by female farmers consist of fencing and ploughs. The poorest among them (Model I) could not afford oxen and planters/cultivators. The slightly

55

Table 9 Female farmers' response pattern for farm packages
(% of total number of packages taken by female farmers)

	Donkeys	Oxen	Ploughs	Planters/ cultivators	Fencing	Tank	Total
Model I	1.4	–	11.3	–	7.7		20.4
Model II	3.5	7.0	20.4	6.3	31.0	1.4	69.6
Model III	–	0.8	2.8	0.8	4.9	0.7	10.0
Total	4.9	7.8	34.5	7.1	43.5	2.1	100.0

better-off among women farmers (Models II and III) have taken more oxen than donkeys. The relatively low uptake (12.7 per cent) of the draught power packages should not be taken to reflect low preference but unfulfilled demand due to the prevailing shortage of draught animals in the country.

Age

Table 10 summarizes the age distribution of ALDEP participants.

The 1985–5 Assessment Report referred to a shift towards lower age groups among the farmers joining the programme. This trend is observed during 1985–6 also: 30–31 per cent of the participants in 1984–5 and 1985–6 were in the younger age bracket of 44 years and under as compared to 18 per cent in 1983–4, 17.6 per cent in 1982–3 and 12.5 per cent in 1981–2. The proportion of farmers in the higher age bracket of 45–64 years declined. However, in the highest age group of 65 years and above the proportion of participants, declining up to 1984–5, showed a slight increase in 1985–6.

Age/sex distribution of ALDEP participants is shown in Table 11.

(i) 43.9% of female participants and 23.9% of male participants are seen to be in the younger age bracket of 44 years and under during 1985–6.

(ii) Among both male and female participants, the proportion in this younger age group was increasing every year, except for some de-cline noticed in male farmers in 1985–6. It is to be noted that the

Table 10 Age range of ALDEP participants

Age range of holder	1981–2	1982–3	1983–4	1984–5	1985–6
34 and under	12.5	4.4	4.2	13.3	9.5
35–44		13.2	14.0	17.9	20.4
45–54	29.2	32.1	29.9	30.9	28.3
55–64	37.3	31.1	36.0	23.0	24.2
65 and over	21.0	19.2	15.9	14.9	17.6
Total	100.0	100.0	100.0	100.0	100.0

Table 11 Age range of ALDEP participants by sex (percentages)

	1981–2			1982–3			1983–4			1984–5			1985–6		
	M	F	Total	M	F	Total	M	F	Total	M	F	Total	M	F	Total
34 and under	13.3	4.2	12.5	3.9	7.9	4.4	3.2	4.8	3.4	8.6	11.8	13.3	6.7	16.0	9.5
35–44				12.8	15.8	13.2	13.1	23.8	14.8	18.4	19.6	17.9	17.2	27.9	20.4
45–54	27.1	50.0	29.2	30.7	39.5	31.9	28.8	35.7	29.9	34.2	26.4	30.9	30.3	23.6	28.3
55–64	37.7	33.3	37.3	33.1	18.4	31.2	37.4	28.6	36.0	25.4	19.7	23.0	27.0	17.4	24.2
65 and above	21.9	12.5	21.0	19.5	18.4	19.3	17.5	7.1	15.9	13.4	22.5	14.9	18.8	15.1	17.6
Total	100.0	100.0	100.0	100.0	100.0	100.0	100.0	100.0	100.0	100.0	100.0	100.0	100.0	100.0	100.0

proportion of female participants in this younger age group of 44 years and under was higher every year than that of male participants.

(iii) As compared to 1984–5, in the highest age bracket of 65 years and above, while the proportion of female farmers declined that of male farmers increased.

One plausible explanation for the growing proportion of female participants in the younger age groups may be the recent trend of female dependants of a large number of farming households joining the programme to benefit from ALDEP packages, mainly ploughs. A recent study of ploughs distributed under ALDEP in Tutume district of Francistown region revealed that as many as 80 per cent of the beneficiaries were females.

It can be concluded that more and more female farmers (who preponderate in the poorest segment of the ALDEP target group) are coming into the fold of the programme, and a large proportion of them belong to the younger age group.

5.2 Impact of sorghum dehulling on women and food security in Botswana: RIIC dehuller

5.2.1 Brief history

African peoples produce and consume the following basic cereals: sorghum, millet, maize, wheat, rice, barley, and a variety of oilseeds. In the semi-arid tropics of sub-Saharan Africa sorghum and millets are grown primarily by smallholder subsistence farmers and are mostly consumed by the producers and their families. Studies by the RIIC extension team during the 1977 Needs Assessment Study made apparent that the most significant constraint to the subsistence farmer in adopting improved food production processes lay in the post-production systems. During the identification survey of 1977, it was noted that the responsibility for food processing rested on the women and children in the household, and that a significant amount of time was spent on pounding the cereal.

RIIC translated this expressed field need into a research and development programme to develop a village-level sorghum dehuller. The overall programme objectives could be summarized as:

1. To encourage increased consumption of domestic sorghum and millets, thereby stimulating the market for these grains. This would have three desired effects:

   (*a*) to increase food security.

   (*b*) to reduce dependence on imports, thus saving foreign exchange.

   (*c*) to release women's and children's time for more economically and socially rewarding activities.

2. Based on these objectives a strategy was developed aimed at:

   (*a*) Developing a suitable village-level milling system for processing

58

sorghum to produce flour of comparable quality and price to imported maize flour.

(b) Testing the performance and economic feasibility of small village sorghum systems.

(c) Determining the acceptance of these mills by rural households and the influence on sorghum demand and utilization.

Following which the RIIC established the programmes:

– a 'post-harvest technology' extension programme to provide advice to mill owners;

– training mill operators in storage, production, record-keeping, supply; organizing an end-user fraternity.

The programme achieved all the above objectives.

5.2.2 Acceptance and impact

The extension-cycle

RIIC adopts the approach in developing any new technology that technological research *must* be 'problem-led' to have any useful bearing on the intended beneficiaries. Any solution, to be useful to the intended beneficiary, has to be technically sound, economically viable, and socially acceptable. Thus the problem addressed by the introduction of a technology has to be defined in all three dimensions and continually rechecked with subsequent field testing against the initial objectives before proceeding to wider dissemination.

Many improved technology intervention programmes have failed in Africa because they have failed to adhere strictly to the extension-cycle.

Distribution and capacity

At present, there are a total of 31 sorghum mill operators established in Botswana, using over 50 dehullers. The mills have been established on the eastern flank of the country, primarily along the railway line servicing 85 per cent of the population. However, the sorghum milling industry has remained decentralized and rural-based. Within this belt the mills are located in both small rural villages and the peri-urban area around the capital. Mills initiated to operate mainly as service mills are located in the small villages and 'land-areas'.

A total milling capacity of 52,000 tonnes has been created by the development and acceptance of this technology. This capacity of food processing at village level, as against multinational/urban food processors, is an important step towards food security. The RIIC dehuller has been exported from Botswana to ten countries, including SADCC member states. RIIC has also played an important role in transferring the technology and experience gained in Botswana to other SADCC member countries.

Social and economic impact

A survey was carried out in 1981 by Parker-Nayaran to assess the impact of the mills in four rural communities, looking in particular at the issue of time

Table 12 Distribution, capacity, and employment

Location	Mills	Capacity (tonnes)	Employment Female	Male
Servie mills:				
Rural/village	25	34,500	61	33
Peri-urban	2	5000	19	10
Commercial mills	4	12,000	43	20

Table 13 Time saved and redistribution

Family member	Food prep. time (hrs)	Time saved	Saved time redistributed Household	Production	Other
Women	4–6	2.5 hrs	57%	41%	2%
Children	2–3	2 hrs	31%	50%	19%

saved. The research indicated that the intervention of the RIIC dehuller in the post-production food-cycle has eased the burdensome task of soaking, pounding, and winnowing staple grain-foods. Table 13 shows 'time saved' and the use of this time in other activities.

Of the time saved by women, 57 per cent was spent on household activities (washing clothes, cleaning yard, collecting firewood) and 41 per cent was spent on production activities such as pottery, agricultural work, beer brewing, and others. Children stated that they helped with household activities, and spent 50 per cent of their time reading and 19 per cent playing.

J. Hardie in his 'Development Impact Case Study' (1982) comments:

> The important fixed point is that large numbers of people have preferred to pay the going price for service milling than to persist with hand processing. One way of estimating the benefits from the service mill would be to put values on the different activities that are undertaken with the new-found time. Empirical evidence to measure this would be extremely difficult to obtain, and according to one approach is neither necessary nor desirable. There is an appealing economic principle, that the consumer is the best judge of the value of goods or a service, and that this value can be measured by the consumer's willingness to pay (wtp). In terms of the service mill consumers have been willing to pay for the service in three broad categories.

The report concludes as follows:

> This analysis supports the general conclusions that the sorghum milling Research and Development effort in Botswana, with which IDRC has

been associated, has had and is having a positive development effect on society. The principal beneficiaries are the women and children who would otherwise have to process the daily family food by hand, and the Botswana consumer who is able to exercise his or her preference for local produce over imported flour.

Agricultural impact
Parker-Narayan's report draws attention to the relationship between the choice of grain sown, crop production, and the presence of grain processing technology. The report concludes that the food cycle is strengthened by the presence of local processing. The Ministry of Agriculture has played a major role in supplying funds and extension efforts to encourage subsistence farmers to grow drought-resistant crops. National production trends are indicated in Table 14; however, it must be remembered that these figures are depressed on account of the drought.

Table 14 National production trends

Harvest year	1979	1980	1981	1982	1983	1984
Production (000 t)						
Sorghum	4.3	29.1	28.3	3.8	5.2	5.7
Maize	2.3	11.6	21.4	12.4	8.5	0.5
Millet	0.9	2.9	1.8	0.5	0.4	0.7
Bean/pulses	1.0	1.8	2.7	0.5	0.3	0.4

Study of these figures, together with the statistics on grain imports, clearly shows that the consumption of sorghum over other cereals is steadily rising. This is not all attributable to the dehulling industry, of course; however, the peri-urban and commercial mills are significant markets for grain sorghum.

5.2.3 Concluding notes
In summary, the RIIC dehuller was a useful response to the following problems:
- where the homemaker customarily spends time in manually decorticating or pounding the grain;
- introducing a decentralized food processing industry at a village level;
- encouraging the consumption and production of traditional grain;
- studying alternative uses of traditional grain at the household level.

5.2.4 Personal case study: Mrs Molomo
This section attempts to outline a personal case study of all the factors and institutions that come into play when an entrepreneur wishes to purchase an RIIC dehuller. It must be noted that Mrs Molomo had to have a certain

amount of capital at her disposal to have made such a success of her business undertakings; but a high level of motivation and hard work was also needed. The case study does not suggest that success is guaranteed, especially for disadvantaged, illiterate rural women.

Initial approach

Mrs Molomo, from a small village in the Kweneng District, wrote to RIIC asking to purchase a sorghum milling package. She was interviewed by RIIC staff to assess the feasibility of a mill in Kopong, her management skills, the market size, crop production in the area, and the potential for commercial milling. This was followed by RIIC issuing a detailed pro forma invoice, which the entrepreneur could either forward to a finance agency, or submit for part grant (FAP, AE 10, etc.) and part loan. The finance agency obliges.

Credits and cash flows

The financing agency contacts RIIC for a description of the technology, economic feasibility, competitors, etc. This information is provided, including details on training accompanying the technology. The finance agency continues independent assessment. If all is well the agency informs Mrs Molomo and issues purchase orders in favour of RIIC.

Training

RIIC arranged for the client to be trained at RIIC on milling equipment, maintenance schedule, production processes, costing of final product, quality control, basic record keeping, packaging methods, marketing.

The training is usually done at RIIC; however, if the entrepreneur strongly prefers, training is decentralized and arranged at a mill convenient to the buyer. In this particular case Mrs Molomo and her chosen staff were trained at RIIC. RIIC encouraged Mrs Molomo to join the Botswana Mill Owners Association (BMOA) to ensure that she remains informed of the developments in the industry. She did so, and was later elected national treasurer of the executive committee.

Commissioning

The milling package was installed and commissioned, by the RIIC technical crew assisted by Mrs Molomo and her staff, to ensure that all the technical aspects of the installation are understood.

Follow-up

A visit is undertaken three months after installation as part of the sales agreement. Mrs Molomo decided to sign an annual service contract with RIIC, and her mill is visited regularly by the directors of the BMOA.

Finally, Mrs Molomo recently purchased other improved technologies from RIIC, a chaff cutter for better utilization of her crop, stoves, and a fence-making machine to produce her own fencing and that of neighbouring farmers. She has recently undergone the bakery training programme, purchased a rim-oven, and is producing bread for her family and village.

5.3 RIIC oven – impact of RIIC bakery programme on women and food security in Botswana

5.3.1 Brief history

The Village Artisan Training Programme (VAT) was first introduced in 1980 with the creation of the Village Tannery at RIIC in Kanye. This was followed within two years by the addition of training programmes in the areas of blacksmithing, carpentry, and baking. The RIIC's VAT programme is geared to increasing productivity in the informal sector. Maximization of local materials is encouraged and trainees are taught how to make their own production equipment. Courses are flexible in timing, location, and content.

The RIIC oven design emanated from a request from village women attempting to improve on the traditional methods of home baking. The traditional method included using ant-hills as baking ovens, using earth as an insulator, and building mud-ovens. RIIC's initial design (and the cheapest) comprised an old oil tin around which a mixture of clay, bricks, and soil is built. The tin, being of thin metal, burnt out relatively quickly, leading to the design engineers replacing it with two truck wheel rims, thereby increasing the durability and baking space (and cost!)

5.3.2 Acceptance and impact

Training attendance

RIIC has to date trained approximately 160 women from the informal sector in the techniques of setting up a village level bakery. The course outlined includes:
- Construction of the rim-oven.
- Theory and practice of bread and bun making.
- Introduction to the haybox.
- Making cakes, scones, tarts, doughnuts.
- Basic bookkeeping (including methods of financing).

The bakery programme is the most popular one and attendance is primarily made up of women.

Distribution

There are approximately 55 small rural bakeries in Botswana, many of which are thriving businesses. The bakeries close to major settlements have made major inroads in competing with industrial bakeries that normally deliver 'day-olds' to these points. The university and defence force canteens are all supplied by small-scale bakers.

Socio-economic impact

David Cownie in his report 'An evaluation of the Village Artisan Training Programme: Developing its full Potential' concludes:
- That a large percentage of trainees were found to be in production (45 out of 79 that were visited).

- Most producers have been in production for less than two years.
- Bakers were most successful at obtaining funds.
- Most women interviewed in this survey indicated that as a result of the training at RIIC they have increased production due to using improved technologies and/or greater efficiency in production.

V.A.T. Programme

Bakery

Year	Novice numbers	Upgrading numbers	Decentralized[1]	Total numbers
1985	31	16		47
1986	9	23	5	37
1987	33	11	55	99
1988 (to 16.5.88)	27[2]	4	18	49
Sub-total for year	100	54	78	232

[1] *Decentralized courses held in:*

1986	Pitsane	5
1987	Mochudi	10
1987	Good Hope	22
1987	Hukuntsi	5
1987	Mmadinare	10
1987	Takatokwane	8

[2] 20 females, 7 males

5.4 Concrete bench horticultural production skills (a pilot project)

5.4.1 Background

The Women's Affairs Unit (WAU) of the Ministry of Home Affairs provides links between various ministries and departments which are concerned with policies and programmes affecting the position of women. It also provides the link between non-government agencies and international organizations. The WAU prepares memorandums for Government, draws up papers for conferences and acts as a consulting body, disseminates information, and acts as a focal point on women's issues.

The WAU is strengthened and supported in its work by WODPLAC (Womens' Development Planning and Advisory Committee). There are representatives from various ministries, who have a wide range of skills, expertise and experience. It is made up of a diverse group of people, and is in a good position to offer advice on how women could benefit from Government programmes and how these services could be improved and extended to all women, in both urban and rural communities.

WAU has a pilot training programme in which disadvantaged urban women are trained in concrete bench horticultural production skills, combined with motivation for group work and production, simple business management and operation, entrepreneurship development, management of multiple roles, literacy and numeracy, available finance assistance and how to apply for it.

5.4.2 Project objectives
The project is aimed at enhancing women's productive roles and economic position in Botswana through the provision of holistic training in innovative horticultural production and management techniques. Over the long term, it is hoped to institutionalize the training programme at Denman Rural Training Centre, and replicate similar efforts in rural areas in order to stimulate viable horticultural income-generating activities.

5.4.3 Selection criteria
Potential trainees should be:
- female household heads
- unemployed
- landless
- over 25 years old
- maximum standard IV education
- interested in self-employment
- willing to undergo a three-month training.

Trainees are to be recruited only from the Broadhurst area because it has a high incidence of low-income settlements and because it is in close proximity to the Segoditshane site (the location for post-training production).

5.4.4 Production method
The method selected for horticultural production utilizes concrete benches filled with river sand to grow vegetables. This method was developed and refined by Dr Gus Nilsson of SANITAS (Pty) Ltd over a period of twenty years.

Compared to conventional methods of growing in soil, the concrete bench method affords many advantages:
- there is no need for ploughing and disking, therefore the need for fuel-consuming machines like rotovators is eliminated.
- any location can be used. There is no need for soil surveys and soil analysis. The availability of water and a market are the only criteria of a suitable place.
- the system requires only 30–50 per cent of the water needed for growing in soil because the concrete wall and floor confine water to the root growing area and reduce loss of water due to evaporation.

Therefore, over-watering is eliminated because excess water can be seen draining through the hole in the bench.
- there is practically no need for weeding because sand has no weed. Those that grow can easily be uprooted to avoid regrowth.
- plants grow faster in sand than in soil due to more aeration. (SANI-TAS has recorded a 20 per cent gain on time to maturity for vegetables.)
- harvesting and replanting can be done the same day.
- borehole water, collected surface water, or a combination can be used. Water with quite high salination can also be used because the salt will not build up in the sand as it will in soil. Excessive salts can be drained out of the drainage holes at the side of the benches with a single heavy watering.
- root diseases do not develop due to good aeration. All roots remain healthy and active.
- the productivity of the benches per square metre is much higher than that of soil. See the table below on comparative yield figures:

Table 15 Comparative average yield for selected vegetables (tonnes/hectare)

Vegetables	Sebele Research Station (open land)	SANITAS Farm (concrete benches)
Beetroot	40 (with leaves)	70 (with leaves)
Cabbage	40+	120
Carrots	35 (with leaves)	100 (with leaves)
Onions	60	150
Potatoes	25	60
Tomatoes	27+	100

5.4.5 Drawbacks: high initial capital cost

The system also has some drawbacks as far as its accessibility to small-scale local producers is concerned. These are mostly as a result of the high initial capital cost required to set up the system. The costly items are:

Cement for building the concrete benches. SANITAS uses a mixture of cement and river sand in a 1:4 ratio. The Botswana Technology Centre (Mr Enyantseng) recommends a mixture of cement, sand, and gravel in 1:3:6 ratio as a cost-cutting measure. But the cost of gravel is very high (about P31.00/m³ delivered). Furthermore, special care will be needed to get a dry mix to produce waterproof concrete.

A further cost-cutting measure that has been considered is using slaked lime mixed with cement to get a good concrete.

Irrigation system SANITAS currently uses two complementary irrigation systems. The first is drip irrigation (ultraviolet–resistant drip pipes in the benches under the river sand). The second is a modified system of sprinkler irrigation – a 'hose and nozzle' system. SANITAS mostly uses the latter for cooling purposes. However, an application of the concrete bench system at SOS Children's Village in Tlokweng utilizes only hose and nozzle for irrigation, with good results. A third alternative is the capillary irrigation system (buried clay tube blocks joined with plastic connectors).

Of course, hand watering is the way to avoid the high cost of installing irrigation systems. SANITAS used hand watering during the early years of its operation. But this also wastes water, all crops can never be watered evenly, and thus yields are reduced. The advantage of the three irrigation systems is that they save water and fertilizer (mixed in the water), and increase yields.

Shade netting is important for protecting plants from excessive summer heat and also from hail. This allows year-round production of vegetables.

While these are the major costly items, it should be noted that the system's high productivity make it cost-recovering after a few seasons of production. Furthermore, Government's financial assistance programmes (such as AE 10 and FAP) can be easily used to make the system affordable and accessible to small-scale local producers.

5.4.6 Marketing

The South East Growers Association (SEGA) is ready to purchase and market all vegetable crops produced by the trained producers. SEGA has also agreed to take responsibility for the supply of inputs such as seeds and fertilizers.

Trainees will be encouraged to join SEGA. This will enable the new producers to benefit from SEGA's cropping plans aimed at promoting a steady supply of vegetables while avoiding glut during some seasons.

The project vehicle will be used to transport produce to SEGA. It is recommended that this service be free to the trained producers during their first year of production. In subsequent years the groups should be in a position to pay nominal transport fees which can subsidize the operating costs of the vehicle after the pilot project phase terminates.

After one or two years in production, the groups should also be encouraged to set up stalls for direct selling to consumers. The location of the Segoditshane site in the rapidly growing Gaborone North area would make direct retailing of at least part of the groups' produce highly profitable.

Currently there is high demand for vegetables in Gaborone. Over 80 per cent of the demand is still being met by imports from South Africa. A study on 'Consumer Demand and Producer Relationships for Vegetables in Botswana' (1984) found that while the greatest impediment to a per capita increase in demand for fresh produce in villages and rural areas is the high price of vegetables or lack of money, in urban areas lack of availability was the greatest impediment. Furthermore, the same study found most vegetables to be inelastic (change in price will result in limited variation in demand). As such, with population increase, even if prices of vegetables increase, a proportional increase in demand can be expected.

Given the fact that the population of the Gaborone region is growing at an estimated 5-7 per cent per annum, and assuming there will be a relatively modest growth in employment and that Government's Selective Vegetable Imports Restriction Policy will continue and be implemented without loopholes, rapid expansion in local horticultural production is justified.

5.4.7 Location
The training will be based at Denman RTC in Sebele. This centre was chosen because of its mandate in providing training in all spheres of agricultural production, and readily available room and board facilities for trainees. Long-term institutionalization of the pilot training is assured because of the interest in and commitment to the project by Denman RTC and the Ministry of Agriculture.

Post-training production by the pilot group will take place at a site bordering the Segoditshane river.

5.4.8 Project implementation update
The first group of 19 women started their training on 15 January 1988. By the time they graduated on 22 April they had formed a group and officially registered. A revolving credit fund specifically designed to assist the trained producers was allocated to the group. They were also provided with a plot where they have now started production.

6. Constraints and potentials

6.1 Training
Despite the number of training institutions existing in Botswana, this submission has indicated that access to training for women remains inadequate. Enrolment figures at the Agricultural College indicate a 24 per cent female attendance. Considering that Agricultural Demonstrators are the initiators of most agricultural activity in the communities it is not surprising that there are fewer successful female farmers than there are males. The impediments to increasing the female intake must be overcome (hostel space, teacher/staff ratios).

Training programmes, especially the ones run by government structures, are well organized; however, many of them are stereotyped into male roles, making them difficult for women to relate to. Flexibility in venue, contents, teaching aids, and curriculum must be developed to heighten the pedagogical impact of all training. The NGOs listed are innovative in their approach and exercise much greater flexibility, but are restricted by the small numbers that can be trained at any one time. They are further constrained by the mono-disciplinary mode of teaching, expecting the Government network to fill in the gaps. For example, at RIIC women are trained in the operation of a bakery, but the problems of finance seeking, grant application forms, etc. are left to Government agencies. If synchronization between the different agencies is lacking, many a trained person fails to start the project.

There is a need to integrate the different agencies, attempting organizing-training programmes for the trainers of women to adopt a multi-disciplinary approach.

6.2 Finance

Financial institutions in Botswana, despite their healthy liquidity, are conservative in their approach to finance management. This conservative outlook has a direct bearing on the granting of loans, especially to the socially disadvantaged. 'The more you need the loan the less your chance of obtaining it.' The fact that only 9.8 per cent of all FAP grants were granted to female applicants in the small sector category indicates the problem women have in grant application. The success rate is better for the medium-scale sector in volume terms; however, these figures are distorted since medium-scale sector grants are almost always joint ventures with outside parties.

Loan application for women is directly related to their social status in Botswana. Acceptance of collateral, securities, inheritance, and land holding rights are guided by the law, making it extremely difficult for women to perform in the 'open economy'.

6.3 Technology

Unless technology is a tool of liberation, and is designed to qualitatively improve the life of the majority, it is of little use in developing Botswana. Choice of technology, design parameters, and end-user patterns must all be established with the potential *group* before dissemination. There are numerous examples in Africa of an 'appropriate technology' being designed independent of end-user participation: a very expensive programme in Botswana, managed by a group of expatriates, designed and produced a small tinmetal stove, allegedly to solve the problem of disappearing firewood. After many thousands of dollars and many hours of working people's time, hundreds of these stoves were manufactured that burnt your fingers, that needed to be fed with finger-long twigs, that denied the family a social place each evening, and that nobody bought. The project managers also departed.

Technology is only a means to an end . . . it is the people that matter. Technology transfer is only possible between equals, demanding that technology dissemination is possible through national institutions.

The Potential for Legume Crops in Botswana offers another area in the development of technology for food production. The growing of legumes is primarily undertaken by women as a mixed crop with cereal. The 1985–6 crop statistics indicated that about 18,000ha were planted with pulses, of which 4000ha were harvested and gave an average yield of 100kg/ha. The area planted is 14 per cent compared to that of sorghum, Botswana's national crop, underscoring the importance and popularity of legumes.

Agronomic conditions plague the success of the crop (cowpeas, groundnut, mungbean, bamboo), with production being characterized by low and inconsistent yields, greatly affected by factors such as pests, diseases, and poor agronomic practices. Variety choice is limited by paucity of research and erratic rainfall. However, the most serious constraint to wider use of this food crop is the intensive labour it demands: the lack of appropriate technology for weeding, picking, threshing, and processing diminishes the farmer's enthusiasm for this traditional crop.

This problem sums up the situation of women farmers in Botswana, and research is called for to study this particular food cycle and develop the necessary inputs to this sector.

6.4 Policy

Women's access to technology to improve national food security is a complex issue necessitating support from many quarters to be effective. In this restructuring, society's view of the role of women must be drastically redressed. In post-colonial Africa the social role of women has been intertwined with a modern economy. The economy slowly erodes social values, judging a woman's role only in labour value and collateral. In Botswana there is a need to re-schedule interest in favour of poor and subsistence farmers as an incentive to invest in their smallholdings. Credit lines must reflect Government's rural development programme by decreasing interest rates for subsistence women farmers.

The value of women's labour has been depressed financially, with terms of employment that denigrate their social role. However, great attention has been paid to labour laws related to women workers. Maternity leave pay has been increased to 50 per cent of the gross salary for 12 weeks around birth and there are proposals before Parliament to extend this paid leave further.

4
Zimbabwe

1. Introduction

Nearly 70 per cent of Zimbabwe's 7.5 million people live in communal areas. Of these 55 per cent are women (CSO, 1982 census). Subsistence agriculture is the main source of foodstuffs in the rural areas. Women constitute 80 per cent of subsistence farmers and are involved in all aspects of food production and post-harvest technology (GOZ, CSO, 1986).

These demographic and economic realities place women at the forefront of issues relating to food security at the household, community, and national levels. By food security is meant 'access by all people at all times to enough food for an active and healthy life' (World Bank, 1986). Women are the chief actors in the two main aspects of food security: (1) food availability through domestic production, storage, and/or trade and, (2) access to food through home production, and the market of food transfers.

Most of the activities undertaken by women to enhance food security, including production, storage, and processing, are arduous, time-consuming, and inefficient. Development and introduction of new technological change, particularly in women-controlled processes in the food cycle, would go a long way towards enhancing food self-sufficiency through increases in productivity and output as well as enabling women to allocate more time to other tasks.

Government policy is highly supportive of integrating women more fully into the development process. The First Five Year National Development Plan reiterates the government's commitment to women 'in promoting and facilitating community development in which women's participation is an essential precondition for success' (GOZ, 1986). Similarly, the government recognizes the need for investing in appropriate technology in order to facilitate suitable economic growth and employment for the masses of the people. There is growing realization, particularly in the Ministry of Community and Cooperative Development and Women's Affairs, that women's participation in rural development and their recognized role in the food security system cannot be meaningful without the necessary means and access to productive resources, including access to and training in appropriate technologies, specialized marketing and processing techniques, and practices ensuring optimum utilization of resources.

This paper is an attempt to look at the appropriate technology development and delivery system in Zimbabwe, the technologies that have been developed by that system, their stage in the delivery cycle, which begins at R & D and ends at widespread utilization, and the interplay of the system's components with women performing their roles in the food security system. A deliberate attempt has been made to provide an inventory of all the technologies available or potentially available to Zimbabwe's women. Specific technologies have been described either as case studies or in so far as they help to explain some factor(s) related to or impinging on women's access to technology.

The paper is divided into four main sections, dealing with:
- technologies that have been successfully introduced to women;
- technologies which are available in Zimbabwe but are not being used by women;
- technologies that are recently being disseminated to women; and
- technologies that are not available in Zimbabwe, but are known to exist in other countries.

The issue of appropriate technology is relatively new to both men and women in communal areas owing to the emphasis by colonial governments on high-tech hardware designed for large-scale commercial modes of production.

The overall picture that currently emerges in post-independence Zimbabwe is one of technologies that have been developed but are either museum pieces in the display cabinets of research institutions, or have been disseminated resulting mainly in gender shifts in employment patterns, with men partially or wholly taking over activities previously performed by women.

2. Technology delivery system

Various public sector organizations, NGOs, and private sector enterprises in Zimbabwe are involved in research and development, manufacturing, and dissemination of development technology.

2.1 Developers

Five government ministries stand out as the most active in the development and dissemination of technologies among rural people in Zimbabwe: the ministries of Lands, Agriculture and Rural Resettlement; Health, Energy and Water Resources; Local Government; Rural and Urban Development; and Community and Cooperative Development and Women's Affairs (MCCDWA).

The Ministry of Lands, Agriculture and Rural Resettlement (MLARR) through its Technical Department, the Institute of Agricultural Engineering (IAE), and the Ministry of Health through its research department, the Blair Research Laboratory, have developed a variety of technologies aimed at assisting rural people in Zimbabwe.

The IAE is the research branch of the Agricultural Technical and Extension Services (Agritex). Its role is to conduct agricultural research, design and test improved farming technologies, and provide extension services to meet the needs of agricultural sectors in Zimbabwe.

The work of the Institute is directed to all farming sectors, but the order of priority is: firstly, that which is relevant to communal farmers; secondly, resettlement farmers; thirdly, small-scale commercial farmers; and fourthly, large-scale commercial farmers (KIRTH, 1987).

The specific problems identified by the Institute in its research, and those that appear to have shaped the Institute's technology development techniques, have been mainly those stemming from the lack of draught power and the problem of soil erosion.

As an integrated technology development approach, some of the research areas being pursued are:

1. Reduced tillage and improved animal-drawn implements trials in communal areas.
2. Testing and development of hand tools and animal-drawn implements.
3. On-farm crop storage.
4. Crop processing equipment.
5. Renewable energy-powered water pumps.
6. Training and extension.

The technologies developed are field tested with the help of Agritex extension officers who work with communal farmers, the majority of whom are women.

The Blair Research Laboratory has been charged with the responsibility of developing water and sanitation technologies. The Laboratory began in 1975 with a principal focus on research on specific diseases prevalent in the communal areas of Zimbabwe. Over the years the Laboratory began to investigate ways of disease prevention in communal areas and this led to the development of improved and low-cost sanitation and water supply systems suitable for use in the communal and peri-urban areas.

Specific technologies such as protection of wells from contamination, hand pumps designed to draw water from different well depths, and toilet structures have since been developed in compliance with government policy to provide adequate health facilities for the majority in communal areas.

The Ministry of Energy and Water Resources and some non-governmental organizations have done a great deal of research in biogas digesters and solar cookers. The principal aim of those efforts is to try to optimize the utilization of natural resources.

The Scientific Council of Zimbabwe co-ordinates research activities carried out by research councils and institutions within various ministries. The Council also initiates and promotes scientific and technical research in the country.

Other institutions that are to a lesser extent involved in development technology R&D include the private sector and NGOs. The private sector was traditionally geared towards the development of capital intensive and complex agricultural technologies for commercial farms. Since independence, a few private sector companies have established development technology departments which could benefit rural women. Private sector developers have hitherto tended to be strongest in water delivery, and preparation and crop processing technology systems.

Only a few NGOs, such as ENDA and Silveira House, are involved in R&D of development technologies. Most participate in the pilot testing and dissemination phases of the delivery system.

2.2 Manufacturers

The responsibility for producing prototypes and manufacturing the technologies developed by the public research centres rests mainly with the private sector. Zimbabwe has a well developed private sector that has had several years of engineering and fabrication experience and expertise.

Despite this, the private sector abounds in conservative business practices. The sector has often been reluctant to produce technologies developed by, for example, the IAE, because business with communal peasants is considered both risky and unprofitable. The importance of this weak link in the technology delivery system, to women and communal people in general, is discussed later in this paper.

The informal sector also manufactures simple, low-cost technologies and implements, for use in both urban and rural areas. Some of these technologies manufactured include traditional hoes, ploughs, Scotch carts, household appliances, fences and other construction materials. These are often copied from prototypes of products already being manufactured by the formal sector and are made from new and scrap materials. Although these technologies tend to be of inferior quality, they are more accessible to women because of the price.

2.3 The disseminators

The dissemination system consists of numerous components including marketing, the provision of credit, extension, maintenance and repairs of the technologies and monitoring the performance of technologies, and impact on beneficiaries.

Public institutions, the private sector and NGOs all play a role in the dissemination of low-cost technologies. Since the activities and techniques of these institutions are governed by different policies, the impact these institutions have on rural people varies.

Technologies developed by IAE are disseminated through the MLARR's extension department, Agritex. Agritex extension officers attend regular training courses at the IAE both for the purpose of facilitating information exchange and for the identification of specific problems encountered by communal farmers. Although these officers are based throughout

74

Zimbabwe, lack of manpower and financial resources result in poor communications between the communal peasant and the IAE, leading to poor dissemination strategies.

Technologies developed by the Blair Research Laboratory are disseminated by Ministry of Health (MOM) assistants who work in conjunction with MCCDWA officers. It is the MOH policy target to provide one protected water supply and handpump for every ten families, and sanitation technology for every family in rural areas. MOH and MCCDWA officers mobilize villagers for community participation in the water programme, involving installation, well protection and maintenance. For household sanitation, such as the construction of Blair toilets, the beneficiaries provide all the material and manpower inputs except for two bags of cement which are donated by government.

The Ministry of Energy and Water Resources has a Rural Water Supply Division whose scope has been expanded from providing water and sanitation technology to rural schools, hospital and growth points to the dissemination of deep wells and boreholes in semi-arid communal areas. The department relies heavily on experts e.g. geophysicists and engineers for the siting, installation and maintenance of the technologies; community participation is generally ignored.

Another department in the Ministry of Energy and Water Resources is responsible for disseminating improved energy-saving cooking technologies.

The Ministry of Local Government, Rural and Urban Development (MLGRUD), through the District Development Fund (DDF), disseminates and maintains water technologies such as boreholes, deep wells and bush pumps in the marginal rainfall areas. The DDF has a team of engineers based in each of the country's 55 districts.

Private sector companies utilize their own existing marketing channels consisting of wholesale and retail outlets to sell technologies to end users in urban and rural areas. The activities of private companies tend to be centralized in urban areas; marketing in the rural areas is normally done through field officers and agents.

In Zimbabwe, NGOs play a significant role in the dissemination of development technology. Except for two NGOs identified in an ENDA survey as being involved in disseminating agricultural and processing technologies, most NGOs in Zimbabwe are involved in the dissemination of water and energy technologies.

Because of their flexibility, scope of activities, limited geographical coverage and grass-roots orientation, NGOs are in a better position to research the social, cultural, and socio-economic factors relating to technological interventions prior to their introduction in specific areas than are public or private institutions. They are also in a better position to evaluate the impact of the technology long after its introduction. For this reason,

NGO efforts could easily complement and supplement the government's development efforts. As a result, some government ministries are now considering the possibility of engaging selected NGOs to implement technology dissemination programmes on their behalf.

To summarize: one can conclude from the above structure of the appropriate technology dissemination system that the government, through its parastatals and departments, is the most prominent developer of technologies that could be made accessible to women in the communal areas. However, the manufacturing role is relegated to the private sector which in essence operates on the profit motive and has no developmental agenda. Both the developers and disseminators of appropriate technologies rest at the mercy of the private sector. In addition, there is no direct operational linkage between the departments in the same ministries that have been charged with developing and disseminating technologies respectively. For example, the operational linkage between IAE and Agritex is ineffective in providing free flow of information between women end-users of technologies and the scientists at the research centre.

It is therefore highly important for the government to integrate in the same institution all the necessary aspects of the technology transfer including R&D, development of prototypes, manufacturing and mass production, and dissemination of the technologies.

3. Technologies available in the country but not being used by women

In communal areas, food production activities including ploughing, planting, and application of fertilizer are normally done by women. A few technologies have been developed by the IAE to assist in performing these tasks, yet these technologies have not been successfully disseminated to rural women.

3.1 IAE technologies
1. Silver Medal Plough – this is an ox-drawn plough which weighs 3–5kg more than the national plough.
2. The Reversible Plough – with two opposite and symmetrical plough bodies one of which is in the working position for ploughing in one direction and the other for the opposite direction, so that the soil is thrown in the same direction.
3. Single-row ox-drawn planter can plant about 9 crops, including maize, groundnuts, sorghum, soya beans, wheat, sunflower, cotton, beans.
4. Two-row ox-drawn planter – plants two rows of crops: rice, sunflower, wheat, soya, beans.
   Both the single-row and two-row ox-planter incorporate fertilizer at the same time.

76

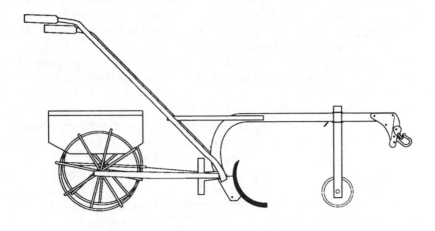

Fig 4.1   *Planter/fertilizer machine behind the tine*

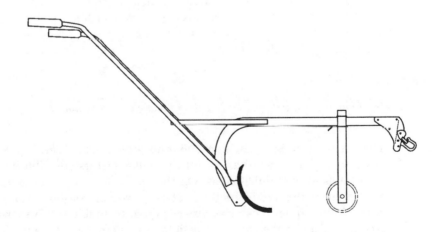

Fig 4.2   *Planting tine on plough beam*

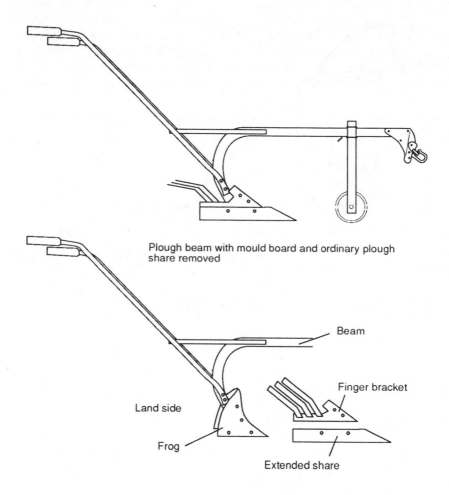

Plough beam with mould board and ordinary plough share removed

Beam

Finger bracket

Land side

Frog

Extended share

Fig 4.3   *Plough beam with mould board and plough share removed*

5. The planter/fertilizer machine and tine attachment. Timeliness of planting has been noted as one of the major factors contributing to crop yields in communal areas. On the basis of some research work carried out at the IAE on methods of early crop establishment, it was decided that an ox-drawn tine was required, to enable the farmers to establish crops in the shortest possible time after the first rains. The tine would be used for opening the ground at required inter-row spacings. Seed and fertilizer would then be applied by hand. The planter/fertilizer machine can therefore be used in two ways: on its own and behind the tine.

6. Groundnut lifter. Two simple attachments can be fitted to any single furrow mouldboard plough beam to convert it into an effective and inexpensive groundnut lifter. In the IAE groundnut lifter, the mouldboard and standard shear are removed from the plough. The shear is replaced by a similar but extended shear 445m long, and the mouldboard is replaced by a simple mounting to which the three lifting

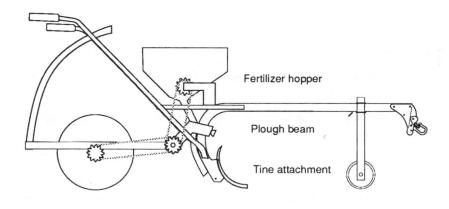

Fertilizer hopper

Plough beam

Tine attachment

Fig 4.4   *Fertilizer attachment on plough beam*

Fig 4.5   *Planter/fertilizer machine on its own*

79

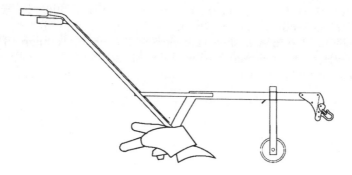

Fig 4.6   *Ridgerbody attachment and tie*

fingers are welded. The lifter can be pulled by two animals, minimizes crop losses and has low labour requirements.

7. Ridgerbody attachment and tie. 'Tie ridging' is a recommended tillage practice in low-rainfall areas and on soils where water infiltration rates are very slow. The usual method of tie construction is tedious and labour intensive: as a result it is not widely practised. The automatic tie-ridger is very simple in construction and is used in the ridging operation, attached behind the ridgerbody.

The machine consists of three blades set at 120mm from each other fixed to a central tube. The tip of each blade is bent backwards to an angle of 35–40 degrees. The blades rotate about an axle through the centre tube when pulled behind the ridgerbody. The leading blade gathers the soil and on rotating leaves a mound 70–100mm in height at intervals of approximately 700mm between the ridges, depending on the size of the machine.

The advantages of the machine are:
- the operation can be fully mechanized;
- when re-ridging and tieing, a single healthy ox can provide suffi-cient draft power;
- it is easily combined with a re-ridging operation;
- the ties are small and therefore present less of an erosion hazard when heavy rains fall, causing water to flow down between the ridges;
- small ties are also easier to traverse by a tractor than larger ones and cause less damage to machinery;
- no extra labour and operation when using the tie ridger.

The main disadvantage of the machine is that it cannot be easily made by communal farmers. It is hoped that because the machine is less labour intensive, and easy to operate, it will be more readily adopted. The implement can be easily adapted to both communal and commercial farms.

8. Home-made donkey harnesses. A well-designed and well-fitting harness is a basic essential if any draft animal is to work at maximum efficiency.

   Horses, mules, and donkeys are built differently from cattle and therefore require specially designed harnesses. Cattle have strong necks and withers, but weak chests and so the neck or head yoke suits them for heavy draft work. However, donkeys, horses and mules produce their main draft power when harnessed from the breast: their withers are weak and may be severely damaged by the use of an ox yoke.

   A simple machine to make a breast-bank donkey harness constructed from conveyor belting has been developed at the IAE.

   Although the above technologies have been developed and are available in Zimbabwe, they are not commonly accessible to communal farmers, and where they are being utilized it is the men, not women, who are using them to perform tasks that are traditionally performed by women. The next section discusses why this has been the case in Zimbabwe.

3.2 Technology and gender

The interplay of several factors explains why there has not been widespread adaption of technology by communal women. It is now generally recognized that technology, however appropriate, is neither value free, value neutral, nor gender blind. Contemporary literature suggests that the importance of gender and its linkages with technology transfer involves several related issues or critical aspects that dominate technological change including the issues of choice, cost, control, capacity and suitability.

On the issue of choice and appropriateness, the literature covers such crucial factors as the patterns of information dissemination, project planning, and the impact of cultural factors such as sex and status stratification. In cost factors, it addresses gender issues of labour displacement, cost benefit analyses from a female perspective and exacerbation of gender-related divisions of labour/work loads. In terms of suitability, it looks at priority needs and gender accommodations concerning time, location and cultural norms. Regarding the issue of acceptability, it considers such preparations as skills training and access to needed resources to master fully the transfer of technology.

The issue of technology choice and appropriateness is of particular importance in the Zimbabwean context. Some of the technologies developed at public research centres have been designed by scientists who have little or no understanding of the communal woman who should benefit from introduction of the technology. There is a general failure to address

81

women's real priorities, failure to include input from women in the planning or design of new technology, failure to provide women with a choice of alternatives, and failure to establish any viable communication networks at the local level to assess community-level impact.

The development and dissemination of different types and models of ploughs in Zimbabwe is a case in point. None of the women in a technology survey conducted by ENDA owned any of these ploughs. The women who were surveyed felt that the Silver Medal Plough (for example), currently being promoted by the IAE, does not address itself to the problems that the old National Plough also failed to address. The National Plough is heavy and makes ploughing a slow and difficult task for women. The Silver Medal Plough, supposedly an improvement, weighs 3–5 kg more than the National Plough. Had rural women been consulted and their needs and concerns considered at the design stage, more emphasis might have been placed on the weight of the plough. Instead, the IAE engineers considered retention of soil moisture content and the minimization of erosion as the most important factors in the plough design. While these environmental concerns are important, their overall emphasis precludes successful adoption of the technology.

Another example of the non-incorporation of the end-users preferences involves the development of solar cookers. Much work and resources have been invested on the design and development of solar cookers which could have had a significant impact in fuel-scarce areas. However, the women interviewed for the survey were not aware of this new technology and studies from around Africa (Ahmed, 1985) have revealed that the solar cooker is not popular with rural women because it deviates from the cultural and cooking practices of rural women in almost all parts of Africa. Had the end-users been consulted before solar cookers were developed, perhaps energy and money might have been saved.

The Blair Research Laboratory approach to development does not emphasize the social or cultural needs and perceptions of the rural people. Instead it emphasizes the health-related factors and technical functioning of the various technologies. Consequently, a series of handpumps, all of which are supposedly improvements on previous designs of the same technology, have been developed. The standard bush pump, developed in 1933 to lift water from deep wells, was of a design simple enough for maintenance to be possible. Subsequent bush pump models have become more and more complex, eliminating the possibility of village-level repairs and maintenance. Although efforts to simplify the technology are under way, no effort is being made to consult the women users of the technology.

3.3 Gender-based labour displacement
There are some cases in Zimbabwe where gender-based labour displacement as a result of technological change has been observed. This refers to situ-

ations where machinery was introduced in activities traditionally done by women with the result that men either completely replaced women or the activity became fragmented in such a way that men took over the tasks that used technology and required greater skill, while women were relegated to less skilled, menial tasks. In some cases these shifts are accompanied by loss of income-earning opportunities or marginalization of women.

The introduction of weeding technology in Zimbabwe is a case in point. Women are traditionally responsible for weeding the fields. An appropriate technology, the cultivator, which could only weed along and not across the field was introduced to assist women in performing this task. Men now use the cultivator for weeding along the field while women have been pushed to manually weeding across the field. The introduction of the cultivator has thus not eased women's work load but has in effect made it more difficult.

Another example of gender-based labour displacement relates to water and fuel procurement. In the absence of Scotch carts, women are primarily responsible for fetching both water and fuelwood. When a Scotch cart is available, it is the men who perform both of these tasks.

3.4 Costs and gender

Another issue that affects the access of women to technology is the relative costs associated with adopting the technology. Household incomes in communal areas are generally controlled by men. In such a situation buying a technology for women's work might not receive priority when the availability of funds is limited.

It was revealed in an ENDA survey that women were unable to purchase the technologies which they felt could help to solve some of their health problems. Most women expressed interest in constructing Blair toilets but could not afford to purchase them. It is not that the technologies are expensive but simply that the household money is controlled by the man, even when he is absent. In most cases, the women do not have a separate source of income and thus cannot undertake any discretionary expenditure.

In addition, women usually suffer from inadequate access to co-operative or credit facilities. Conservative lending practices in Zimbabwe including requirements for down payment, collateral, track record, and husbands approval all militate against a woman's ability to gain access to credit. It is therefore necessary to determine whether women can bear a part of the whole cost of a technology before its introduction or if a financing mechanism must be developed.

3.5 Women miss out

Several other complex needs arise out of technological change. These needs, including knowledge of new technology, extension services, and participation in rural organizations, determine the accessibility of the technology to rural women. Factor market imperfections in a Third World country such as Zimbabwe restrict availability of information and access to factors of production to privileged classes or groups. Women in communal areas generally belong in the lowest group of disadvantaged citizens. In some cases, cultural restraints often prevent women from dealing with male extension workers. The net result has been that the majority of rural women are completely unaware of the existence of the improved technologies.

Training and extension programmes should be an integral part of the application and dissemination stage of any appropriate technology. Chances of women being involved in training are very slim partly because most extension workers are male. As a result, women are given no training in the operation and maintenance of equipment intended for their use.

The Ministry of Health (MOH) and MLARD rely on MOH health assistants for the repair of waterpumps. Women, the end-users of the pumps, are not trained in maintenance. Because of the Ministry's lack of manpower in the rural area, women often have to hire someone to repair these pumps.

When information does filter down to the village level, it is usually the men who receive it mainly because men have the time to sit around at organized meetings. Unfortunately these same communication channels are rarely used simultaneously to inform the men about the importance of assisting their wives through the acquisition of improved technologies.

4. Current technology projects: case studies

4.1 Crop-processing equipment
Appropriate equipment has been developed in Zimbabwe to assist small-scale farmers in undertaking the processing activity.

4.1.1 Hand-operated alternating groundnut decorticators
The construction of these decorticators, which are used to remove the shells of groundnuts, comprises a pivot rasp bar fixed at a critical distance above a concave sieve. The pendular motion of the rasp bar cracks the shells of the groundnut pods and the broken shell and whole nuts fall through the sieve. Most of these models have interchangeable sieves ranging between 8mm and 16mm. Another operation is required to separate the cracked shells from the nuts. These decorticators can shell about 100kg pods/hr.

4.1.2 Maize shellers
These are available in two modes, and both modes are hand operated. There are single-cob and twin-cob shellers. The single-cob sheller can be attached either to a container or frame allowing the kernels to drop into the

container, and passing the shelled cobs out to the side. Tension is adjustable according to the diameter of the maize cobs.

The twin-cob machine operates on the same principle. These machines are designed to operate at village level. Hand-operated maize shellers are widely used in Zimbabwe.

4.2 The Small Grains Milling Project

A four-year Small Grains Milling Project is currently being implemented by ENDA on behalf of the Zimbabwe Government's MLARR. This CIDA-funded project seeks to raise the production and consumption of indigenous grains through the introduction and dissemination of sorghum dehullers attached to grinding mills. Mechanical dehulling replaces the arduous pounding normally undertaken by women in areas where small grains are much grown.

The project benefits to women are perceived as labour- and time-saving, and a desire to encourage women as consumers to revert to sorghum and millets as being more nutritious and agro-ecologically more appropriate crops for communal areas in marginal parts of the country. The overall goal is the enhancement of food security in marginal areas.

Although no women were involved in the design and planning of the technology itself, a socio-economic survey administered during the pilot phase solicited input from rural women, the intended beneficiaries of the project. Also, an affirmative quota of 25 per cent of the owners of the technology has been earmarked for women entreprencurs and groups.

The mini dehuller programme in Zimbabwe began in May 1985 when ENDA-Zimbabwe, a local development and research non-governmental organization, began an investigation into the application of grain-dehulling technology in the communal farming areas. A pilot hammer-mill site was launched in November 1985.

The pilot project enabled ENDA-Zimbabwe to:
- install five mini dehullers at rural hammer-mill sites and acquire operating experiences through a 12-month monitoring of the dehullers;
- verify that the dehuller is an appropriate response to the rural problem of hand pounding of sorghum and millets;
- determine the manufacturing capability of the informal sector;
- train a core national staff in technology transfer;
- prepare an action programme of nationwide dehuller dissemination.

ENDA has, beginning in 1988, embarked on a four-year dissemination programme.

The key components of the Small Grains Milling Project are:
- the manufacture of 40 grain dehullers by Zimbabwean engineering firms. The quality of manufactured dehullers will be controlled and tested against engineering specifications registered with the Central African Standards Association (CASA);

- the external procurement of capital equipment and materials for the manufacture of the dehulling units, i.e. carborundum stones and bearings, and the procurement of project support equipment, i.e. vehicles, office equipment and supplies;
- the selection of mill sites in the small grains producing areas of the country. Sites will be basically restricted to communities located in dryland farming areas. However, it is also planned that one or two of the mini-dehullers will be located in the peri-urban areas of Harare and Bulawayo to supply urban consumers with processed and packaged sorghum and millet flours.
- the sale and installation of dehulling units as part of an integrated small grains milling system. The complete system being offered for sale in part or in whole consists of the following components:
  ○ A grain dehuller
  ○ A hammer-mill
  ○ A power source (either diesel or electric)
  ○ An appropriate building to house the system.
- the selection of owners of milling systems. The primary criteria for ownership will be her/his ability to pay and effectively utilize the technology. While existing hammer-mill owners or other entrepreneurs in rural areas may be in a better position to raise the required capital to purchase the system, co-operatives and women's groups, already identified in many communities as potential owner/operators, may experience difficulty in raising the necessary funds. In such cases the project will assist these groups through the Project Credit Scheme;
- the management and administration of a 'lender-of-last-resort' credit scheme for prospective mill owners. This service will be aimed primarily at assisting co-operatives and women's groups to purchase and operate milling systems. In cases where credit is given, up to 25 per cent down payment will be required. Normal commercial interest rates in force in Zimbabwe at the time of sale will be applied. The Credit Scheme will become an integral part of the process of disseminating milling technology to rural areas;
- the operation of maintenance and repair programmes to assure owner/operators of a continuous supply of spare parts and technical service;
- the organization of training programmes for owner/operators and technology awareness seminars for government and non-government personnel in Zimbabwe;
- the carrying out of market surveys to determine the long term marketability of the technology in Zimbabwe and to explore opportunities for the commercial utilization of sorghum and millet flours in Zimbabwe's food industry;
- the preparation of a comprehensive Pathfinder Prospectus aimed at generating interest and promoting investment among individual

86

entrepreneurs, industry and financial institutions in Small Grains Milling Technology;
- the provision of management and administrative services and consultancies necessary to the effective implementation of the project.

Spence (1987) summarized her assessment of the Small Grains Milling Project with the following statements:

This form of technology and its impact upon women in crop processing in Zimbabwe has enormous potential. Simply as a technology to save women from the unproductive manual pounding and processing the sorghum dehuller/hammer mill is impressive: it does not appear to displace existing patterns of employment, it acts to encourage future production of more appropriate crops and allows women more free time for agricultural products or club work. But the real potential seems to exist in the opportunity it offers for women to be integrated into ownership and operation of mill sites. This project allows women the rare opportunity for access to credit and relevant skills training in both technology and management. It provides women with the chance of being absorbed into a viable and profitable mainstream income-generating project which enhances their stature in the community and recognizes their economic roles. It indicates the project's commitment to minimize the habitual 'gender shift in production roles' with the introduction of new technology.

4.3 Harvesting, drying and threshing

Research is being carried out by ENDA-Zimbabwe in conjunction with the Crop Science Department of the University of Zimbabwe on the above three activities in their grain storage programme in communal areas with farmers. The objective of this undertaking is to determine harvesting, drying and threshing methods and the quantitative losses in traditional on-farm storage structures.

Some representative case studies will be conducted. The major emphasis will be on techniques used, volumes of produce involved, estimated amounts lost, time taken and shortfalls observed.

5. Technologies which are not currently available in Zimbabwe but are known to exist in other countries

The bulk of the technologies known to exist outside Zimbabwe which could have relevance to Zimbabwe women are associated with processing of oilseeds and horticultural produce. Two examples of these are discussed in this section.

The Eastern districts of Zimbabwe, namely Nyanga, Mutoko, Mutare, Chimanaimani and Chipinge, are well endowed with a perennial production of tropical and sub-tropical fruits including mangoes, avocadoes, citrus fruits, bananas, papayas and pineapples. These fruits either grow wild or are planted, harvested and utilized by communal women in these districts. The surplus fruit that cannot be consumed locally is often wasted. There is the need therefore to introduce appropriate technologies for processing these horticultural products thereby adding value to the raw material at the local level and generating income and employment for the women.

One such technology is the banana chip technology. Banana chips are manufactured by a process in which bananas are made into deep fried chips, sealed hygenically in plastic bags and sold as snacks. Any type of banana can be used. The bananas are harvested when they are still green, peeled, sliced, salted, and cleaned, sun dried and finally deep fried. The chips are then salted and packed in polythene bags and sealed with a hacksaw blade and candle flame.

The banana chip project was initiated in Papua, New Guinea, in 1981. The technology uses surplus locally available raw materials, provides an income-generating activity requiring few or no skills, and is inexpensive to set up. There is a market for snacks in Zimbabwe and the banana skins can be fed to livestock.

Another technology that could have widespread application and impact in Zimbabwe is the oil mill or expeller which extracts cooking oil from oilseeds such as groundnuts and sunflowers. Both of these crops are grown as cash crops by communal farmers in semi-arid regions III, IV and V of Zimbabwe.

Two types of oil expellers, the Tinytech oil mill developed in India and the Komet Oil Expeller developed in Germany are suitable candidates for Zimbabwe.

The latter machine is more suited to operation by women and is simpler and cheaper than the former. The end products of these mills are cooking oil for household use and cake which can be used for livestock feed and the manufacture of soap.

The above two examples refer to imported technologies from different cultural, and socio-economic environments. Ahmed (1985) noted: 'More often than not, the problem of technical change lies not with technology innovation since what is not inappropriate is not its technical characteristics but the socio-political context within which it is introduced'.

Before these imported technologies can be put into widespread dissemination they should be pilot tested and monitored for technical viability, social and cultural acceptability and economic viability. The key questions that have a particular importance to women and appropriate technology issues should be answered prior to their dissemination. They fall into the following broad categories:

choice – who has it?

cost – who really pays?

control – is it transferable?

capacity – who masters it?

suitability – whose need is met?

Another framework or taxonomy that might be employed to evaluate the proposed investment in the appropriate technology involved analysis of the availability, practicability and profitability of the proposed technology:

Availability: Can the technology be made accessible to the target group?

Can she afford to buy it either directly or through some credit scheme?

Can it be purchased by collective effort?

Can she afford to pay for maintenance and repairs?

Can some of the component parts be manufactured locally?

Practicability: Is the technology viable given the local context?

Does the technology disrupt the prevailing social, cultural and economic life or blend with it?

Can it be operated by the woman herself?

Is it convenient for the woman to use?

Can it be maintained and repaired?

What skills and training are required?

Profitability: Will the woman gain or lose from using the technology?

What are the gains to her in terms of time, labour and money?

Does the technology provide more income?

What are the costs?

Are there any marketing or transportation problems?

Feasibility studies and socio-economic surveys should be conducted to answer these and many other questions relating to the new technology. In-house pilot tests should subsequently be carried out with a representative sample of intended end-users and beneficiaries prior to widespread dissemination.

5. Recommendations

So as to improve the situation regarding dissemination and access of new technologies in rural areas a different approach has to be followed:

i) Research organizations should not work in isolation from the reality of the rural people's world. Rural women should participate more in the identification of their needs and priorities. Organizations involved in the design, production and manufacturing production of appropriate technologies should concentrate on those needs and problems which rural women highlight. This would help alleviate the reflection of inappropriate technology. Conducting rural surveys, discussions with women's groups, and observations of rural women's activities would help achieve this.

ii) Community participation in the testing, adaption and modification of technologies must be encouraged. This could be done with representative women's groups in the rural areas.

iii) Training women in the operation and maintenance of communal technologies such as water pumps and any equipment, such as grinding mills, that they own co-operatively. Training should be organized at various levels for trainers, extension workers and supervisors, and of course the end-users themselves in courses long enough to impart knowledge and skills; follow up with proper monitoring and on-site supervision.

iv) Giving women equal access to co-operative and credit facilities. This would enable women to purchase equipment that they see as beneficial and would allow them to make use of improved technologies when it is convenient to do so rather than only when it suits their husbands' purposes.

v) More attention should be paid to introducing money-earning projects for women alongside the introduction of labour-saving devices. Having their own source of income would reduce the women's dependence on men in cases where crop processing is commercially available.

vi) Feasibility studies should be carried out to assess the capability of the informal sector to manufacture development activities at lower cost than the private sector.

vii) To help disseminate development activities – more rural fairs, agricultural shows, field days and demonstrations could be held. Local demonstrations could be held at growth points.

viii) Research projects, field testing and dissemination of technologies should be done jointly by IAE, Blair Research and NGOs so that duplication of efforts is minimized. Co-operation between these and other organizations would enable the formation of joint demonstration centres and a long-term work programme.

A national workshop of all parties involved in technology development and dissemination (including end-users) should be held after the technology trade fair in Zimbabwe in order to share experiences.

5

Tanzania

1. Introduction

Food security refers to the access of all people at all times to enough food for an active and healthy life (FAO, 1986). Existing technologies in Tanzania do not guarantee availability of food supply as such. This situation is more pronounced in rural Tanzania, where women play a greater role in ensuring that the family is fed. By and large much of agricultural production is small-scale and women are more involved in agricultural activities than men, as seen in Table 1.

Table 1 Length of time spent by women, men, and children performing different tasks in Tanzania (hours per annum)

	Adult females	Adult males	Children
Water collection	587	32	68
Firewood collection	324	20	44
Crop establishment	251	194	63
Crop weeding	99	76	25
Crop harvesting	91	64	23
Internal marketing	9	4	1
Health	73	25	0
Grinding mill	169	21	13
Trips to market	227	51	0
External marketing	12	5	2
Total	1842	492	239
	(71.6%)	(19.1%)	(9.3%)

Source: Marilyn Carr and Ruby Sandhu, Women, Technology and Rural Productivity, UNIFEM Occasional Paper No 6, New York 1988 p31.

Hand tools are used for 82 per cent of cultivation and the rest is done with tractors and animal-drawn ploughs.

In some regions of the country, building houses and herding livestock is also the responsibility of women. The extent to which women participate in livestock production (especially cattle) is directly related to the distance between their dwellings and the place where the animals are raised. In zero grazing areas and the nearer the animals are to the house, the greater the women's participation in animal keeping.

Traditionally livestock keeping has remained a rural occupation, but recently a tendency has developed within some urban households to keep a small number of cattle, chicken, ducks, and other small animals for consumption and to subsidize incomes. In most cases it is the women who care for these animals.

In addition to the above-mentioned tasks, women continue to be responsible for the collection of firewood and water and in some cases for constructing cooking stoves. Fuelwood collecting is not only time-consuming and a burden to women and children but also results into serious environmental degradation.

All the above tasks are in addition to bearing children and other household chores like cooking, sweeping, washing, nursing the young, handicrafts, etc.

The traditional methods used in performing the above tasks are labour-intensive, physically strenuous, inefficient, and time-consuming. To enable women, who are the main producers, to promote food security – that is, to produce enough to sustain our national needs and ensure that it reaches the consumers – application of appropriate technologies is vital. Among the criteria identified for choice of appropriate technology are:

- Low in capital investment.
- Uses locally available materials.
- Emphasizes job creation, using local skills and labour.
- Is affordable by the intended users.
- Can be understood, controlled, and maintained by the intended users.
- Is organizationally simple and adaptable to local circumstances.
- Will satisfy local wishes and needs.
- Can be locally produced, preferably at village level.

This paper discusses different technologies which can reduce the workload of women in the promotion of food security. Some of the technologies identified have successfully been introduced, others have been developed but not yet reached the women in the community. Section One deals with technologies in agriculture and livestock production. Section Two is on technologies for food processing and preservation. Section Three concentrates on household energy, and Section Four on domestic water supply technologies. The remaining sections deal with rural transportation, various factors that influence the introduction and diffusion of appropriate technologies, and finally general recommendations.

1. Agriculture and livestock production technologies

1.1 Agriculture
Generally, women more than men are involved in agricultural production. The traditional methods used are mainly labour-intensive. These include hand hoes and other hand tools which are used to cultivate 82 per cent of the total land area.

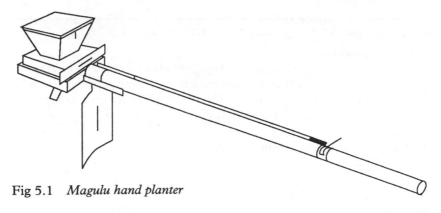

Fig 5.1 *Magulu hand planter*

Improved technologies which are being promoted to boost agricultural production include animal-drawn farm implements and innovatory hand planters. Oxen training centres are being strengthened.

Tractors are currently used on only 5 per cent of the total cultivated land. Steps are being taken to establish tractor service centres which will facilitate effective utilization of tractors in agricultural production. Those technologies are indicated in Table 2. Along with the appropriate technologies mentioned above, other inputs such as chemical fertilizers, insecticides, organic manures, etc. are being promoted.

1.2 Livestock
In livestock production existing technologies which could be considered as appropriate are as follows:

1.2.1 Incubators and hatchers
These will help the women to raise chicks easily and they can also sell chicks to others. However, imported incubators and hatchers are very expensive and out of reach for many women. There are a few individuals in the country who make kerosene operated incubators (in Kilimanjaro and Lindi) which are cheaper, but very few women know about them.

1.2.2 Animal food making machines
Grinders are locally made by Mang'ula Mechanical and Machine Tool Company and Dharam Singh but they are expensive, so not easily affordable by women.
Mixers are manufactured locally by the Institution of Production Innovation (IPI).

1.2.3 Drinkers and feeders
These are locally made by D'Salaam Small Scale Industries Company (DASICO) and Endelea Sheet Metal of Dar es Salaam Local Craftsmen. These are not expensive and women can easily afford them.

Table 2 Demand, distribution, and manufacturers of ATs in Tanzania

Technology/equipment/ tools/inputs	Accessibility			Remarks
	National demand	Manu- facturers (1984)†	Distri- bution (1983)	
Handtools		SIDO,	2,600,750	Readily
Hand hoes	3,700,000	Ufi		available to
Matchetes	1,200,000	Media, SIDO		women but are labour intensive and
Axes	264,000		70,375	inefficient
Sickles	300,000		128,221	
Planters	300	CARMATEC	unknown	Not readily available. Efficient
Animal-drawn				Limited use
Ploughs	100,000	Ufi, SIDO	32,337	by women
Harrows	680*	none	152	because of
Planters	300*	Themi, Ufi	unknown	high costs and lack of training
Engine-powered				Not
Harrows	680*	none	152	affordable by
Planters	300*	none		women
Ridgers	680*	none	1226	
Weeders	300	none	nil	
Chemical fertilizers, herbicides, and pesticides				Expensive, not easily available. Efficient
Animal manure				Limited to animal rearing areas
Sunnhemp (Marejea) Weedkiller Animal feed Soil conditioner Pesticide				Newly introduced. Limited to few areas

* The national demand does not specify whether hand, animal, or engine powered.
† Other manufacturers, including those in the informal sector, are not shown.

1.2.4 Introduction of improved breeds

Improved breeds of goats are available in the market, but they are expensive. So far, improved breeds of poultry are not easily accessible by women.

1.2.5 Other inputs

Drugs and minerals are scarce and expensive, as are tools for management practices, such as burdizzo and debeaking tools.

1.3 Irrigation

The country has 4 million hectares which can be cultivated by using irrigation technologies. Women are mainly found in the traditional small-holder irrigation system. The total area under this type of irrigation is estimated to be 120,000 hectares. The main source of water is rivers and streams, from which water is diverted to the farms and the hand hoe is used to excavate the channels.

Both large- and small-scale irrigation mostly involves diverting water from rivers/springs by using specially constructed weirs. Large-scale irrigation schemes are implemented, at low level especially, by both the private and public sectors where women are involved as wage labourers.

1.4 Soil conservation

Soil fertility loss is usually caused by several factors including overgrazing and improper farming systems. The lack of suitable soil conservation measures on cultivated land leads to severe loss of soil fertility due to water and wind erosion. Crop rotation, manuring, contour farming, formation of tie-ridges, and tree planting are being used by women in different areas. Of special interest is Kilimo cha Ngoro in Ruvuma Region, where tie ridges are constructed on the Matengo hills by both women and men.

Zero tillage, which involves minimum disturbance of the soil, is only restricted by small-scale farmers, of whom women are the majority, because it involves the use of chemicals which are too expensive. Besides, overuse of chemicals can pollute water-sources and even harm the health of local people.

2. Food processing, preservation and marketing

In these important post-harvest activities the involvement of women is substantial. At present, post-harvest losses are estimated at 30 per cent (FAO, 1986).

2.1 Food processing and preservation

In Tanzania, technologies involved in handling these activities are largely traditional. Existing improved technologies are described below along with traditional technologies, equipment, and tools.

These are discussed on the basis of the type of food processed and/or preserved. Details of manufacturers, prices, capacity, and distribution are shown in Annex 1.

2.1.1 Grains

Types of grain commonly grown are maize, sorghum, rice, and wheat. All these require similar processing techniques.

(a) *Threshing/Shelling*

This involves separating the kernel from the stalk/cob. Traditionally this is achieved by using sticks to beat the harvested crop, either spread on the floor or packed into sacks. CAMARTEC, SIDO, Sokoine University of Agriculture and TEMDO have developed threshers for rice and sorghum and shellers for maize.

These machines can shell/thresh in a shorter time and effectively. Hand-driven threshers have an average capacity of 3000kg per day. Manual maize shellers have a capacity of 500kg/hr, while the powered ones have a capacity of 750kg/hr (Fig. 5.2). Smaller hand-shellers are being developed and used although they are not as efficient.

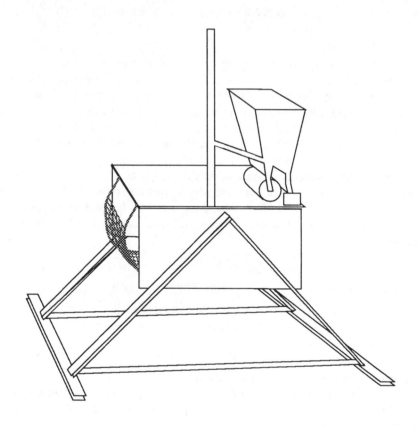

Fig 5.2   *Sheller*

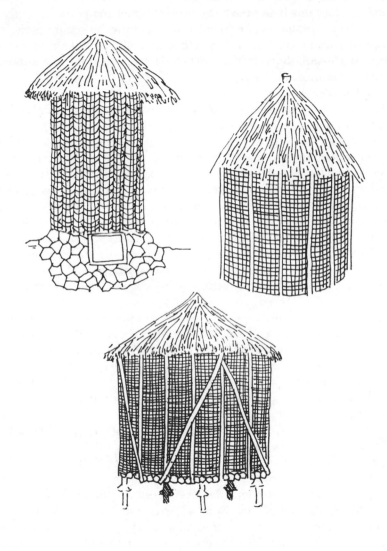

Fig 5.3 *Traditional means of preserving and storing grain*

(b) *Winnowing*

The process of separating the good grain from empty grains, stalk remnants, husks, and other impurities is called winnowing. Traditionally it is done by placing some of the grain on a flat or curved split bamboo tray and then, holding this high above the head, tossing the grain up in the wind. The process may have to be repeated several times before the grain is clean. Improved winnowers which are both electrically and diesel operated have been developed locally. In these winnowers a fan has been incorporated to guarantee enough blowing.

(c) *Storage*

There are many traditional means of preserving and storing grains (Fig. 5.3).

Despite the many names used in the country, storage structures can broadly be divided into two types: open types (cribs), largely found in the more humid climates, and the closed types (silos) found in hot, dry areas. Small quantities of grain, mainly seeds for the next season, are stored in clay pots, gourds, openwork baskets and used tins, and kept in the house. Many of these traditional stores need minor improvements such as raising them off the ground and fitting rat guards or baffles as well as use of pesticides.

The village godowns being constructed are to be used by co-operatives. CARMARTEC has also developed an airtight improved storage tank, but women's accessibility to the technologies is poor owing to high prices.

(d) *Dehulling/Dehusking*

This is the process of removing the husk or outer coat of the grain. Traditionally it is done by pestle and mortar. SIDO, CAMARTEC, and Hanspal and Sons manufacture electrically and diesel-operated dehuskers for rice and dehullers for maize and sorghum. The first sorghum dehuller was installed in Kilosa (Morogoro Region) in 1982 by SIDO and funded by IDRC. A sorghum dehuller consists of a dehuller and a hammer mill for grinding the grains into flour (Fig. 5.4).

The dehullers are owned by the villagers and are purchased through loans from SIDO or CRDB.

(e) *Grain milling*

Pounding grain into flour is traditionally done by women using pestle and mortar. The process also includes sieving out the flour and repounding the grits. Mang'ula Hanspal and Sons of Arusha and a few individuals manufacture electric and diesel-powered milling machines. Milling machines are still very thinly spread and are largely owned by individuals. Long queues are therefore still typical, even in urban areas. SIDO has developed a hand-operated grinding mill, but despite being cheap it has not attracted many women because it is laborious.

2.1.2 Fruits and vegetables

Tanzania has an abundant supply of fruits and vegetables suitable both for

98

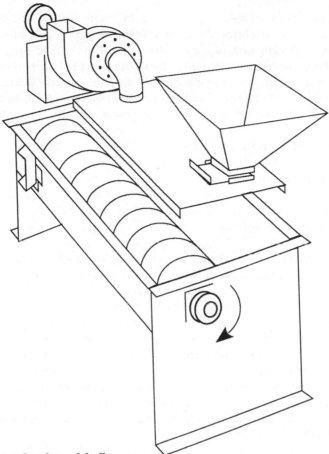

Fig 5.4 *Sorghum dehuller*

home consumption and export. The vegetables include spinach (*Amaranthus* sp.), cabbage, cassava leaves, sweet potato leaves, cowpea leaves, okra, pumpkin leaves, and many wild varieties. The fruits include mangoes, oranges, pineapples, pears, plums, tomatoes, pawpaws and bananas.

2.1.3 Root crops

Root crops (cassava, sweet potatoes, yams, etc.) are important staple foods in some parts of the country. These crops are drought resistant, and with the adverse weather conditions being experienced in many countries of the region, these crops hold a lot of hope in terms of food security.

Technologies

Traditionally the problem of storing cassava has been overcome by leaving the roots in the ground until needed. This practice has a disadvantage in that it occupies the land; also the roots become more fibrous and woody, and nutrient content declines. Another traditional method of processing cassava involves peeling, slicing, and sometimes soaking it in water overnight before it is sundried and stored. For short periods of time (3–4 days) cassava can be preserved by burying it in the ground. In the case of sweet potatoes the tubers are peeled, sliced, and boiled before they are sundried. In some parts of the country sweet potatoes are stored in pits with alternate layers of wood ash.

In general, there are no improved processing and preservation techniques for root crops. Elsewhere, however, e.g. Nigeria, cassava is grated by either a hand- or pedal-operated machine.

Since there are no adequate techniques for preservation at source, the need to transport fruits and vegetables to places where they can be processed and preserved is enormous.

(a) *Vegetables*

Traditional methods of processing and preserving vegetables include:

1. Direct sundrying, e.g. sweet potato leaves, spinach, and mushrooms.
2. Sundrying after boiling, e.g. cowpea leaves.
3. Sundrying after pounding, e.g. pumpkin leaves.
4. Sundrying after pounding and boiling, e.g. cassava leaves.

Some of the vegetables preserved traditionally lose their nutritional quality, flavour, and taste. This can be changed if the drying procedures result in a product which has not undergone drastic changes. To achieve this, improvements are needed to the boiling and sundrying techniques. Research has been undertaken at Sokoine University of Agriculture on solar driers for vegetables and grains, but adoption of this technology has lagged behind due to lack of funds.

(b) *Fruits*

By and large, fruits are consumed while they are still fresh, although to a limited extent some types are traditionally preserved by sundrying (e.g. mangoes and bananas), and pickling (e.g. mangoes).

Improved techniques for processing and preservation of fruits include dehydration, fermentation, juice extraction, jam-making, and confectionary. SIDO has a training centre for fruit canning at Lanzoni in Tanga region, where all these technologies are taught. Women represent 30 per cent of the participants for every intake.

2.1.4 Fish

Traditionally, fish processing, i.e. cleaning, gutting, and drying, is done manually. Preservation of fish is usually done by salting and sundrying, smoking, and frying. These methods, however, have disadvantages: they are not very hygienic; they consume a lot of fuelwood; and they require constant attention to safeguard against animals and birds. The improved techniques are:

(a) *Improved sundrying*
This can be achieved by using racks or concrete floors instead of spreading the fish on the ground.

(b) *Improved smoking methods*
A smoker which uses an enclosed fire box (Fig. 5.5) is better than an open fire.

The smoker is cheap in that it can be made using locally available materials and it is efficient in terms of fuel consumption.

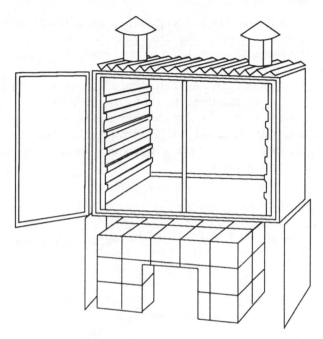

Fig. 5.5   *Enclosed fire box*

2.1.5 *Oil seeds*

Oil seeds grown are cotton, sunflower, simsim, soyabeans, groundnut, coconut, and palm kernel. These seeds have a high oil content and local women have been making oil from these seeds using pestle and mortar, stones, and graters. These processes are slow and inefficient, and the oil obtained is of poor quality. Faster and more efficient machines for oil extraction, oil expellers and oil pressers, are being locally manufactured. However, expellers are extremely expensive and pressers, although relatively cheap, are difficult for the women to operate owing to their mechanical construction (see case study, Annex 2).

2.2 Marketing

An important factor in marketing, and one which merits attention, relates to packaging and quality control of products. Traditional packaging tech-

101

nologies include gourds, gunny bags, and baskets. However, these have proved inadequate. Improved technologies which are currently being promoted involve packaging such as canning, bottling, tetrapaks, refrigeration, weighing machines, scales, hygiene and quality standard equipment, all of which are relatively expensive.

3. Household energy

The main source of household energy is fuelwood, which constitutes almost 90 per cent of all energy consumed. Fuelwood collecting is not only a burden to women and children, but also time-wasting and leads to serious environmental degradation.

Other forms of energy used in the country include fossil oil (including kerosene), coal, natural gas, thermal and hydro electricity.

Given that wood fuel is becoming increasingly scarce and expensive, and that it accelerates deforestation, the government is taking the necessary measures to develop and promote indigenous renewable energy sources (hydro, biogas, wind, and solar).

3.1 Traditional stoves

These include three-stone stoves and the single-walled metal charcoal stoves (SIGILI) commonly found in East Africa.

The *three-stone stove* is found in almost all rural and peri-urban parts of the country (Fig. 5.6).

Fig 5.6   *Three-stone stove*

The stove is used for cooking and heating and in some cases it provides light. It is highly inefficient (useful energy utilization is about 19 per cent of

102

total energy stored in wood); much of the energy is dissipated into the surrounding air.

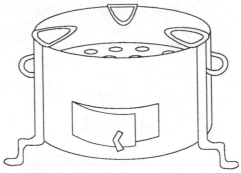

Fig 5.7   *Single-walled metal charcoal stove*

The *single-walled metal charcoal stove* (Fig. 5.7), mostly used in urban areas, is also very inefficient (useful energy utilization is 18 per cent of total energy stored in charcoal). Here much of the heat is radiated into the surrounding air through the metal wall.

3.2 Improved stoves
most of these stoves are adapted from designs originating from elsewhere. The improvement has mainly been in insulation to minimize heat losses.

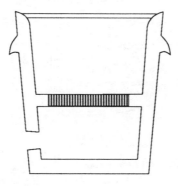

Fig 5.8   *Morogoro clay stove*

Clay stoves, made of fired clay, can be used to burn firewood or charcoal. Although the Forest and Energy Project of Gairo and Sharrif Dewji and Sons Ltd manufactured charcoal clay stoves in the past, their rate of reaching would-be users has been disappointingly slow. The Morogoro Stove Project, however, is making encouraging progress in this respect.

Fig 5.9   *Clay-liner stove*

Clay-liner stoves. Having been satisfied with the performance of the clay-liner stoves (Fig. 5.9), the Ministry of Energy and Minerals, with World Bank funding, is soon to undertake a pilot project of dissemination.

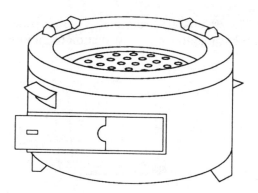

Fig 5.10   *Double-walled metal charcoal stove*

The *Double-walled metal charcoal stove* (Fig. 5.10), designed by UNICEF and originating from Kenya, where it is popularly known as 'UMEME JIKO', is well adapted to Tanzania (locally known as the Dodoma Stove). A number of local parastatal organizations, including SIDO and CAMA-RTEC, are producing this stove on a small scale and artisans mainly in Dodoma have also been trained to manufacture it. So far more than 2000 stoves have been produced and sold. Its metal sheet requirement is four times that of a traditional metal stove and therefore it is rather expensive.

Table 3 Tree-planting targets and achievements between 1982 and 1986

Year	1982–3		1983–4		1984–5		1985–6	
Region	Target	Achievement	Target	Achievement	Target	Achievement	Target	Achievement
Total	14,459	10,221	17,349	9019	20,818	9016	24,984	13,738
% achievement on target		−17		−52		43		35
% increase or decrease		−15		−12		−1		+53

Note: In 1985–6 a positive increase of 53% on the previous year's performance was achieved. This is in response to the intensified forestry campaigns undertaken by both party and government leaders at village and national level. Campaigns of Forestry Education to arouse the awareness of the local communities in tree planting should be accorded high priority.

Source: Forestry and Beekeeping Division.

3.3 Village Forestry Programme (Woodlots)

The Village Forestry Programme is being undertaken as an integral part of the rural development programme in order to maintain environmental stability and sustain the supply of woodfuel and of poles for building purposes.

'Village Forestry' was proclaimed a national programme in the Arusha Declaration of 1967. In implementing this programme, the Forestry and Bee Keeping Division (FBD) initially started to give seedlings to the farmers for planting communal woodlots. However, there was no follow-up on what happened to these seedlings.

After the decentralization reform in 1972, the regional, district, and divisional administrators became responsible for village forestry. In many areas foresters planted demonstration woodlots with the help of paid labour. These plots had some impact in areas where people were not used to planting trees, but it was often unclear whether the village or the district Forest Officer was the one responsible for their maintenance and use.

In 1980–84, the Institute of Adult Education, in collaboration with the Forest Division, launched a campaign, 'Forests are Wealth', in seven of the driest regions in the Central and North-Western parts of the country. The campaign used seminars, meetings, radio programmes, news articles, posters, women's wrappers (*khangas*), and other media to spread the message that people should plant trees. Tree-planting, measured by the yardstick of distribution of seedlings, did increase in those regions. According to the report of the campaign, the planting of trees increased from 4500ha in 1979–80 to 8500ha in 1980–81 in the seven regions concerned.

In 1981, the Village Forestry (VFU) of the FBD was formed and started some planting and evaluation of the Village Forestry Programme. It was found that schools and individual plots where women were more involved had better survival than communal woodlots, and gradually there was a shift of emphasis to them. Table 3 shows the summary of the success of the tree-planting campaign between 1982 and 1986.

3.4 Biogas

In Tanzania activities in biogas technology date back to 1974. Biogas is an inflammable gas consisting mainly of methane and carbon dioxide, produced through decomposition of organic materials (animal excreta, garbage, etc.). A good number of plants have been set up by individuals and institutions where the gas is used for cooking and lighting.

In 1985 CAMARTEC started the Biogas Extension Service (BES), which is being assisted by West Germany's GTZ through its affiliate German Appropriate Technology Exchange (GATE). By mid-1987 CAMARTEC had installed 61 plants. Though the main objective of the BES is to develop and disseminate family-sized biogas systems to small and medium farmers, the cost involved is very high. For example a $16m^3$ modified Chinese Fixed Dome costs about TShs100,000.

4. Domestic water supply

Traditionally the domestic water supply was, and still is in many cases, drawn from rivers, springs, lakes, wells, etc. Except for spring water, water from these sources would necessarily require some form of purification or treatment to be safe for human consumption. The work of fetching water is mainly done by women, and to a lesser extent by children, who in many cases are compelled to walk between 5 and 20 km per round trip. Depending on the size of her family, a woman may not be able to bring enough water in one trip for all her daily needs. Containers used to fetch water include earthenware or metal pots, metal tins, twenty-litre plastic buckets, etc. The twenty-litre buckets are about the largest containers used. Besides the women wasting a lot of time walking to and from the water sources, sometimes the yield can be very low, especially in the dry season. This would necessitate wasting more time waiting one's turn in long queues. The government has a development programme for rural water supply whose target is for everyone to have easy access to a public domestic water point, but this is still far from achievement.

4.1 Piped water supplies
 – Gravity water supply systems with surface and spring water sources.
 – Pumped water supply systems drawing water from either surface or sub-surface water sources.

Piped water supply systems distribute water to domestic points through networks of pipes. Distribution systems would invariably include distribution reservoirs, particularly in the case of pumped supply systems.

These supply systems, largely implied in the 1971 government target, are usually very expensive to install and operate, and to maintain in the case of pumped schemes. Until recently, these systems formed the greater proportion of the installed facilities.

4.2 Shallow wells
Shallow wells can be sub-divided, depending on the method of drawing water, into:
 – Hand-pumped wells.
 – Rope and bucket wells.

The latter are not very much used in Tanzania owing to inherent health risks associated with the method. Shallow wells fitted with handpumps currently receive top priority whenever a new supply system is envisaged.

4.3 Traditional technologies
Invariably these include hand-dug wells, infiltration galleries, etc. which need improvement of the traditional sources before considering any of the other technologies described here.

107

4.4 Rain catchment

In this system rainwater is directly caught over a relatively impervious surface and stored. During dry periods water would be drawn from storage for use. The capacity of a storage facility would depend upon length of dry period, per capita consumption rate, and number of users.

5. Rural transportation

Transportation in most rural areas falls primarily on women. Household transportation is mainly on foot with head loading. Ownership of the means of transport is rare and restricted to non-motorized vehicles. The most common vehicle is the bicycle, but the numbers are very low, and ownership is mostly by men.

The introduction of appropriate technologies such as wheelbarrows and carts in rural transportation will relieve women of the load burden and raise their standard of living in general.

5.1 Wheelbarrows

Wheelbarrows carry loads of up to 100kg. They are designed in such a way that the load is centred between the fulcrum and the effort, and the wheel reduces the amount of friction between the load and the surface. These factors reduce the amount of energy needed. CAMARTEC have developed a wooden wheelbarrow which uses timber for 90 per cent of its components. The few metal parts can be fabricated in simple workshops. It has been tested and proved to last twice as long as a metal wheelbarrow while costing only half the price. Maintenance and repair can be done in village workshops.

5.2 Carts

These are two- or four-wheeled machines which have hauling capacities ranging from a half to two tonnes. The single-axle, two-wheeled animal-drawn cart has proved capable and adequate in the field. CAMARTEC is concentrating on the production of this cart.

5.3 Bicycles and bicycle trailers

In some areas, both women and men own and can ride bicycles. The carrying capacity of a bicycle is limited to 50kg. However, bicycle trailers with a capacity not exceeding 150kg make a bicycle more appropriate for reducing rural transport problems. The trailer can be manufactured locally.

6. Factors influencing use of appropriate technologies by women

6.1 Institutional

A number of centres and individuals, both women and men, are involved in technological innovations and small-scale production of appropriate technologies. The efforts, however, remain largely fragmented and lack proper follow-up owing to lack of central co-ordination. In 1983, for instance, UTAFITI (Tanzania National Scientific Research Council) identified a planter devised by an individual, Mr Msigwa, which would have significantly reduced the drudgery involved in planting, but to date the planter has not reached smallholders and there seem to be no concrete plans for making it available for wide-scale use in the foreseeable future.

6.2 Financial

Prices of most appropriate technologies are in many cases beyond the means of most small farmers and more so of married women who, because of the bias of existing cultural conditions in favour of men, would normally own nothing of their own. Unfortunately, the present conditions of financial lending institutions make the majority of women, and certainly all rural women, unable to get access to credit facilities.

As a result, even the marketability of most appropriate technologies remains uncertain; consequently potential manufacturers, who would mainly be interested in investing in profitable businesses, shy away from undertaking production of technologies.

6.3 Dissemination

Dissemination efforts so far have remained sectoral. Extension Officers of different sectors, who are anyway too few to meet the needs, promote technologies relevant to their respective sectors. Many of the Extension Officers are male, and do not reach the women, owing to cultural inhibitions.

6.4 Flow of information and assistance

Most rural women are not aware of the improved technologies. Conservative attitudes have also had a negative impact on the adoption of new technologies. To the few who have access to various technologies, assistance in operation and maintenance of necessary spare parts are not readily forthcoming owing to the scarcity of technicians and lack of planning.

6.5 Development and design

Available evidence points strongly to the fact that technologies are designed without giving consideration to the would-be end-users. This situation arises mainly because R & D is carried out without seeking the views of intended end-users (men, women, and children). The oil press case study presented in Annex 2 is clear testimony to this claim: women failed to operate the machine because it was too heavy for them.

Annex 1 Food processing and energy preservation tools and equipments

No.	Tools/equipment	Local and registered manufacturers	Price/piece in Tshs	Capacity	Remarks
1.	Threshers (beans, sorghum, rice, and wheat)	TEMDO, KIDC		1000kg per day	Hand operated and portable operated by two people
				3000kg per day	Pedal operated and portable operated by two people
2.	Shellers (maize and groundnuts)	CAMARTEC, TEMDO, DHARMA SINGH	4500/=	750kg/hr	Power operated, can be owned by individual woman
				500kg/hr	Manual operated, can be owned by individual woman
3.	Winnowers	TEMDO, Dharam Singh	8,000/=	Up to 1000kg/hr	Power operated, can be owned by individual woman
4.	Hullers/Huskers	Dharam Singh, United Engineering, Umoja Engineering	90,000/=		Power driven, can be owned by women's co-operative through loan
5.	Hammer Mill	Mang'ula, Dharam Singh	90,000/=		Power driven, can be owned by women's co-operative through loan
6.	Hand-operated mill	SIDO	4000/=	10kg/hr	Too slow. Takes time to mill due to repeating to get fine flour

No.	Item	Source	Price	Capacity	Remarks
7.	Oil pressers	IPI, Themi, Dharam Singh	230,000/=		Too mechanical for women to operate
8.	Decorticators	Themi			Can be owned by women's co-operative
9.	Oil expellers	TEMDO		5 litres/hr	Power operated. Can be owned by women's co-operative through loan
10.	Milk separators	None	9500/=		Manual operated, can be owned individually
			10,500/=		Power operated, can be owned individually
11.	Fruit extractor	None	75,000/=		Can be owned by women's co-operative
12.	Kilns (Alton type)	Can be built locally			Smokes fish at a hygienic condition
13.	Fruit canning	None	4,000,000/=		Too expensive. Can be owned by village co-operative by loan Special hygienic conditions needed

6.6 Training

Much as it is appreciated that appropriate technologies hold a lot of hope for developing countries, formal training is not playing its expected role. On-the-job training remains the main vehicle for acquiring new skills. A review of curricula for training craftsmen, technicians, and engineers in East Africa in water supply and sanitation revealed their failure to address existing options for solving problems of development. Whereas reality dictates simple solutions like shallow and improved traditional wells and improved pit latrines, the curricula persisted in implementing complicated problem-solving techniques. Besides the inappropriate curricula, participants in most technological training programmes are invariably men. There is still a misconceived taboo against women taking up technical jobs.

6.7 Access to markets

Lack of transport to markets has discouraged women from producing surpluses, especially of perishable produce.

7. Recommendations

1. A regional Training Centre for Women's Appropriate Technologies should be established, responsible for exchange of information on existing technologies and curriculum development.
2. The possibility of manufacturing improved women's technologies for wider use in SADCC countries should be looked into.
3. Assistance should be extended to women to enable them to participate effectively in afforestation programmes.
4. A Regional Financial Facility to provide credit to rural women should be established.

Annex 2: Case Studies

Palm kernel oil extraction at Mwandiga Village

Kigoma women traditionally produce and sell oil from palm products. Two types of oil come from palm fruit: cooking oil from the pulp and kernel oil.

The case study involves the palm kernel oil produced by women of Mwandiga Village in Kigoma Region. The study showed how Mwandiga women's palm oil trade was jeopardized by an advanced form of technology which allowed the trade to slip into the hands of village men. This new technology was more productive and yielded a better income, but the women were not able to use the machines supplied.

After extraction of oil from the palm fruits, the hard inner nut was regarded as waste by the Mwandiga villagers and normally thrown on roads and floors as consolidating material. But the women of Mwandiga discovered that the palm kernel, which is oily like any other type of nut, has a very good oil content which can be used as body lotion as well as an ingredient for soap manufacturing.

Traditionally Mwandiga women extract palm kernel oil by first soaking the nuts in water, then cracking them with stones to extract the kernels. These are then sorted from the shells – it normally takes about 2 hours to extract 15kg of kernels – then the next stage is frying the kernels to obtain the oil. Frying 15kg normally took them 4 hours and this produced about 3–4kg of oil. The shells are used as fuel for frying. This extraction method is tiresome, wastes a lot of time, and the oil obtained is of poor quality and darkish in colour; this discourages purchases as a dark-coloured soap is produced from it. Another disadvantage is the choking smoke during frying, which can be a health hazard.

Through SIDO, as promoters of small-scale industries, with the cooperation of the University of Dar es Salaam, as designers and manufacturers, the European Economic Commission (EEC) financed a project to invent technology/machines which would improve and relieve these women's workload in extracting palm oil as well as boosting their efficiency and the quality of the oil.

A manually operated hydraulic system was introduced to the women, together with supporting accessories including:
- decorticator for cracking palm nuts with a capacity of 170kg/hr.
- clay bath for separating or sorting kernels from shells with a capacity of 40kg/hr.
- shredder for drying the nut flour ready for pressing.
- press for making the flour into oil, leaving hot cake as residue. This has a capacity of 20kg of oil per hour. The hot cake is sold as animal feed.

Though these machines had a much higher capacity than the traditional method, the press (last stage) was impossible for women in the village to use because of the muscle power needed to turn it. If the women could have used draught animals instead they could have run the machines themselves, but women at Mwandiga Village do not own animals. As a result, the men took over because they were strong enough to turn the press. But because of the effort involved, the village is now using the machine for the first 3 stages and then the nut flour is taken for pressing to the Kigoma Development Cooperative which owns a modern mill with the capacity to extract 350kg of oil per day.

Morogoro Fuelwood Stove Project

The Morogoro Fuelwood Stove Project (MFSP) was started in 1985. Housed at the Christian Council of Tanzania (CCT) centre in Morogoro, the project is funded by NORAD and run by women.

Aims and objectives

The aim of MFSP was to field test and disseminate two types of wood-burning stoves: a portable ceramic stove (Pangawe) and a fixed air-dried mud stove (Louga). The Pangawe Stove could be converted to a charcoal stove with the insertion of a ceramic grate.

The objectives of the project were to lower fuelwood consumption and to reduce time and labour spent on wood collection by women through the use of more efficient stoves.

For the MFSP activities a range of target groups was identified among villagers.

Training

The project's main target group has been the CCT's regular trainers (pastors' wives and other female church leaders) drawn from all over the country. The MFSP has conducted sessions on stove making and stove use and the focus has been mainly on Louga stoves.

GSP has also trained women potters during the CCT holidays. Under this programme, by mid-1987, MFSP had offered residential training to three groups of women (16 potters and 4 Community Development Officers).

Stove production

MFSP aimed at organizing ceramic stove production with village potters around Morogoro region. Since pottery is traditionally a female activity, the involvement of women was achieved automatically. Although the project established production of ceramic stoves in two areas, the quantity has not been sufficient to guarantee a supply to urban markets that would meet the objective of introduction of improved stoves on a substantial scale.

Initially, it was also planned to have the Louga stoves produced by users themselves. It was soon found that this was not the best solution, for although it is fairly simple, it took some experience to make a proper stove. Since the skill is used only once a year or less, it may be easily lost. At present, the aim is to have teams of stove-makers (women, preferably with pottery backgrounds) who can go around in their neighbourhoods and receive payment for their work.

Marketing

After training, the women go back to their respective villages to continue making the stoves, which are either sold to the villagers by the potters themselves or purchased by the MFSP and sold at the market.

Success and limitations

After 2½ years of running the project, MFSP staff discovered that few people regularly use both wood and charcoal. Those who had a reasonable access to a free supply of firewood preferred the traditional three-stone stove, whereas the situation was exactly opposite in areas suffering firewood scarcity. Thus, with time, the project started making two types of Pangawe Stove, the Morogoro fuelwood stove and the Morogoro Charcoal Stove.

The project leader admits that the fuelwood stoves are 'more trouble prone than they are worth' and is trying to make them more worth than trouble.

The Morogoro Charcoal Stove, on the other hand, after incorporating a number of improvements suggested by users, proved that it was fulfilling a genuine need among both users and producers. By September 1987, nearly 1400 stoves (annual average rate of 780 stoves) had been sold since December 1985, all in Morogoro town though a number of purchasers came from other urban centres.

Summary

This study has sought to demonstrate that the effectiveness of a particular approach in the diffusion of appropriate technologies is likely to be conditioned by the technical, economic, and social characteristics of the innovations. Those which require adaptation to users' needs, which entail a financial cost but provide marginal or no financial benefits, and which are aimed at economically and socially disadvantaged people, are unlikely to find ready acceptance through a market-oriented approach to promotion.

Adoption of technologies which require capital investment will inevitably depend on the purchasing power of the users.

Executive summary

Food security refers to the availability of food supply to the entire society at all times. It involves a cycle of land preparation, tilling, planting, weeding, harvesting, transporting crops from farm to house, storing, processing, marketing, preparation, and serving food in a hygienic manner. It has been revealed by researchers that women play a bigger role than men in this food cycle, contributing overall 71.6 per cent of the time. However, analysis of time used in performing different activities in a typical Tanzanian situation further reveals that much of the women's working time is actually spent on non-productive undertakings, as shown in Table 1. Fetching water, collecting woodfuel, and going to market alone consume over 60 per cent of their time. From the analysis, in which domestic chores are not included, it is clear that women only spend about 25 per cent of their working time in agricultural production.

In accomplishing all the above activities women are faced with two inter-related basic problems: they use inferior and strenuous technologies and consequently time and energy spent on the activities is not

115

commensurate with the output. Lack of improved crop processing and adequate storage facilities, for instance, cause enormous losses of the harvested crops despite the hard work and other effort women expend. One FAO report estimated post-harvest losses at about 30 per cent of the total harvest crop.

The need to introduce scientific production techniques and reduce women's workload, therefore, cannot be over-emphasized. In addition, there is an equally important need to introduce technologies which will cut down the time women spend on necessary but none the less non-productive activities so that the time saved can be invested in more gainful activities. Experience also shows that introduction of improved technologies makes men participate in more varied activities, even those which would otherwise be considered to fall entirely within the women's domain. Men are known to have taken over digging entirely where ox-ploughs were introduced; to fetch water where the supply source was within a short distance of the house, as in urban and peri-urban areas; in some cases they even became involved in preparing food where modern kitchen facilities were available. Participation by men in such activities, however, should not be looked upon as altogether relieving women of their burden.

It is well known that sometimes men have taken over women's activities because of their monetary value. For instance, they have taken over carrying grass to cattle in areas where zero-grazing is practised simply because of the commercial value of the dairy products, and subsequently pushed women into the more laborious non-productive activities. Sometimes the introduction of improved technologies has resulted in increased women's workload. For example, when ox-drawn ploughs are introduced, women's workload in planting, weeding, harvesting, and transporting the produce is increased unless improved technologies are also introduced in these other areas.

In order to guarantee sustained food security it is important that the continuity of technologies involved in performing various activities of the food cycle is maintained. It is of absolute necessity that technologies used can be operated and maintained by the users and above all that they are affordable. It is a common phenomenon in many developing countries, and Tanzania in particular, to adopt (usually imported) expensive technologies which do not benefit the nation much in so far as food security is concerned. Tractors, for instance, have sometimes been introduced en masse by the Government, but lack of spares, fuel, and technicians to maintain them have rendered their use short-lived and of very little benefit, if any at all. Furthermore, such technologies would only be accessible to very few people in the country, whose contribution to the food security problem is at best minimal. Much of the country's food security is dependent on small-scale farmers who are in general too poor to afford such technologies. To make matters worse, such small-scale farming is done by women who have

116

no access to credit facilities, as they would not be able to meet conditions stipulated by the existing financial lending institutions.

Although quite often appropriate technologies have been regarded erroneously as inferior in terms of productivity, examples are on record that they have contributed significantly towards agricultural productivity and hence to guaranteeing food security. The success of the agricultural revolution in China is mainly attributable to the successful introduction and utilization of appropriate technologies. Those technologies, however, are currently not well known to the small-scale farmers in Tanzania as they have not been advertised enough. The main agents of disseminating improved technologies so far are the few Extension Officers, who are mainly male. Furthermore, the manufacturing capacity of those technologies has remained very low despite the enormous financial resources and efforts being spent by government institutions and individuals on R & D. Another problem is that designers and manufacturers overlook women's special requirements. It is not uncommon to find a machine being given or sold to women who would finally fail to operate it because of its difficult mechanical construction or because it is too heavy as illustrated in Annex 2.

Thus, to guarantee food security in the country deliberate efforts need to be taken to alleviate most of the problems discussed. It is necessary at this juncture to look into educating women about the available technologies, manufacture enough to meet the needs, and create conditions which will allow their acquisition. There is need to provide credit facilities for women who are known to be poor. Increased efforts should also be taken to incorporate special design and construction requirements so that women can manage the technologies easily.

The two case studies, chosen from among many, illustrate situations where there was an improved technology and the means enabling its acquisition by an organized women's group with a known membership and management style. The women were involved at almost all the stages of the project – installation, operation, and maintenance. Although the potential benefits went to both group members and non-members in the community, the income accrued to the women group members.

Tanzania, like many other developing countries, cannot be self-sufficient in food without enabling women to acquire, own, and control improved technologies. This would increase agricultural productivity as well as reduce women's workload and release surplus energy for improved study and training. It is recommended that a SADCC centre be established for the development and dissemination of appropriate technologies suitable for use by women.

6
Angola

1. Introduction

Like their sisters in almost all other African countries, rural Angolan women are the ones who produce most of the food for the family's consumption and a fair share of the surpluses that are channelled out to be marketed. Moreover, it is generally their job to do the hardest farming work: sowing, weeding, harvesting, and husking, which during the busiest times take up almost all their daily working time. Almost 60 per cent of the women take part in agriculture from production to marketing.

Furthermore, they are also in charge of processing and preparing food so that it will keep or can be marketed. They often help transport produce over long distances.

Both in farming and in food processing (maize, cassava meal – the basic food commodity, especially in rural areas – palm oil preparation, salting, drying, and smoking fish from the sea, rivers, and lakes) women still almost exclusively use extremely rudimentary methods and implements. The picture is the same for cottage industries, e.g. basket making and utility pottery production (which has been on the increase in a number of provinces due to limits on imported manufactured products).

At the same time, peasant women also raise small farmyard animals for household consumption or marketing. In addition to taking part in the productive process, doing household chores (cleaning, cooking, and taking care of children), they do the heavy maintenance and repair work on their houses in the dry season, carrying thatch and kneading clay to make adobe bricks.

These tasks take up a large part (almost all) of peasant women's time and energy, especially if we consider that just to fetch water and collect wood they must travel long distances every day carrying heavy loads on their heads or backs.

It should also be pointed out that in the areas hardest hit by the war waged against us by the racist South African regime since 1975, there has been massive male emigration towards urban areas in addition to killings and the kidnapping of healthy men for forced recruitment into the ranks of bandit rebels.

Under these conditions, the position of rural women seems much more difficult, compounded by the burden of tasks and responsibilities that falls on their shoulders in producing food, keeping a stable atmosphere, and bringing up children.

For many years now, our country's institutions have paid particular attention to the problems of peasant women, especially as regards transforming production fundamentals in rural areas. Angola is an agricultural country: the most important organizational structures in rural areas are the Peasants' Associations and Farming Co-operatives. The goals of these structures are to integrate rural people, giving them effective support, and find collective solutions for marketing their produce and providing them with basic commodities.

Women in rural areas quickly rallied round the concept of farm co-operatives, taking on responsible jobs in the Management Commissions in co-operatives and associations though their numbers are still insufficient. There are 110 Farmer Co-operatives and 2502 Peasants' Associations under the authority of the co-operative movement: a total of 319,210 workers, 169,251 of which (53 per cent) are women. Out of a total of 4048 workers in co-operatives, 2823 are women. The Angolan Women's Association (OMA) is an active participant in the co-operative movement, guiding women's social work within the community.

But there are enormous educational limitations which hinder further professional training for peasant women and the change cannot come overnight. The Ministry of Agriculture and OMA have endeavoured to identify and develop projects sponsored by the international organizations. The aim is to improve the situation of rural women by introducing appropriate technology as a means of changing the fundamentals, thereby raising women's standard of living and helping them participate more in rural development.

Despite the magnitude of the effort that has been made in a context of almost constant external aggression, we cannot forget the following harsh reality: nearly one million women of working age live in rural areas and produce in family or private units without any kind of comprehensive support.

As a result of all the factors we have mentioned, it is necessary to modernize agriculture in order to guarantee better food security. This in turn means dissemination of innovations: practices, implements, and products developed by research centres that can boost productivity. In regions such as ours, where agriculture is mainly subsistence farming, the land is still worked with primitive methods. There is a shortage of financial and skilled manpower resources and it is of utmost importance to disseminate simple, easily applied, but efficient practices and implements that must be within the reach of available potential. Practices, implements, and products with these features constitute what is termed intermediate or adapted technology.

Intermediate or adapted technology is a set of techniques far superior to primitive ones, but at the same time low cost and more flexible than the ones that came out of the Industrial Revolution – something that takes local conditions into account. In societies such as ours which are poor in capital and rich in labour, the development of adapted technology must be promoted in the short-term future. It can be promoted by making traditional techniques more efficient, boosting their capacity and using them more skilfully. Farming operations such as ploughing, sowing, weeding, watering, and harvesting should no longer be done according to customary methods, but rather with the help of very simple machines especially designed and built for this purpose and using local materials.

2. Agriculture

Human muscle-power is used exclusively in most of Angola; animal draught power is used in only 30 per cent of the country and is, moreover, highly concentrated: over 80 per cent is found in the central highlands and surrounding areas. There are 240,000 households that regularly use animals, especially to prepare the land for farming (150,000 ploughs) and for transport. There is a fair number of carts in areas where livestock is raised, but the supply is considerably lower than the demand. This means that peasants must often use a sled-type vehicle, locally called a 'zorra'. All these implements are commonly used by women and there is no trouble in disseminating them, since people learn how to use them in their community.

In some areas in the north of Angola, the government is now attempting to intensify and widen the use of animal draught power. It is here that some difficulties crop up in using oxen as work animals, especially to prepare the land. In this type of situation we have systematically noted that men tend to monopolize the use of new implements which are related to social prestige, above all.

New implements have recently been introduced to help prepare the land for farming: the tropicultor and the cultivator. It is still too soon to evaluate their acceptance by the community. In the demonstrations held for peasant families an attempt is always made to give access to women, but for the reason given above it is not an easy job. However, we are convinced that as soon as the implements are fairly widely spread, women will begin to use them.

Manual sprays are used quite commonly for plant protection, but are in fact monopolized by men. New equipment (2000 units) has recently been introduced in cotton farming to control pests. In Angola today cotton-growing is confined to semi-arid areas where the shortage of water is a serious problem. The new spraying scheme needs no water and, as such, seems to be a suitable solution. We have noted that women who use the equipment have the same technical problems as men. Women use the equipment quite often since there has been marked male emigration from cotton-growing regions.

A programme is also under way to introduce husking equipment, especially for maize, beans, and groundnuts, but here, too, it would be premature to draw conclusions. Another programme is under way to introduce mechanically powered grinders for food processing. More than 500 have been sold in the past two years, but men have monopolized the management of these devices even though users are practically 100 per cent women.

As for equipment to clean (winnow) grains, there has been some decline in the country. Before independence, products lost value according to the amount of chaff and impurities, but now this task has been passed on by the producer to the consumer due to the deficit economy.

Women have fully mastered watering operations in areas where small waterways are chanelled off, or where the checkerboard system is used in areas with hydromorphic soils. Besides, women are excellent market gardeners; they are almost always in charge of the plots set aside for market gardening in peri-urban areas, and manage to get an income from this activity to cover their daily needs. As soon as watering operations begin to use mechanical energy with the aid of power-driven pumps, they also are appropriated by men. In the past three years, more than 3000 power-driven pumps have been introduced in rural areas, but only an insignificant number of women purchase them.

In colonial times the technique of making home-made soap was introduced quite successfully, but due to the severe restrictions prevailing nowadays in rural areas of Angola, this activity has practically died out.

3. Water and sanitation project

Originally planned for Luanda and Huambo in 1978, Subprogramme A of this project was then extended to Bengo Province and the northern border of Kwanza Norte Province. Plans were to cover Bengo, Kwanza Norte, and Uige provinces, but for a number of reasons – political/military in particular – operations in these provinces were suspended and drilling equipment was transferred to Cabinda.

By the end of 1986, 118 water-pump boreholes had been drilled in these provinces. From 1981 onwards, the project was extended to other provinces in Angola: Benguela, Bié, Zaire, and Malange (Subprogramme B). It was in Malange that the best results were obtained, particularly from 1984 onwards with the arrival of a UNICEF driller. By January of 1988, 3188 boreholes had been drilled and 309 pumps had been installed.

The main job is drilling the waterwells and installing manual pumps in proper sanitary conditions, particularly all round the pumps. With OMA's participation in intensifying awareness and mobilizing the communities, women have been/are being trained as waterpump monitors and take part in maintenance of the installations. With UNICEF's and OMA's assistance, the water supply programme is being extended to include disease control to eradicate diarrhoea and malaria.

Within the scope of Subprogramme C, that covers Namibe, Huila, and Cunene provinces, work was initiated in 1986 in Namibe, and by January of 1988, 15 boreholes had been drilled and 9 pumps had been installed.

4. Acceptability and accessibility of new technology to women, and dissemination

As mentioned above, in general the technology introduced in rural areas and taught through extension programmes is only used by women when it has gained widespread acceptance – that is, when women have access to it. There are historical and cultural precedents for sweeping women aside which continue to cast women in supporting roles, even though they take on all of the indirectly productive work and a good share of agricultural production.

In these programmes to introduce new technology, an attempt has always been made to involve peasant women more intensely. Success is achieved in regions where there is a high rate of male emigration, whether because the men are fleeing from the unrest or seeking a livelihood in or around urban centres. In these regions, women become the heads of families and of the family farming undertakings. They participate in community life and in the management of the various peasant organizations on an equal footing with men. A study carried out in Kwanza Sul Province in the municipality of Waki-Kungo showed 31 associations and co-operatives in 31 villages. There are 2500 members, 700 of whom are women. Until only a short while ago, they attended meetings passively and took no active part in discussion, whereas they now prepare for the meetings beforehand and elect a spokeswoman to present women's consensus on the topics discussed, which are of the greatest interest to them and have an impact on their daily lives.

The choice of the topic, object, or technology that will be introduced and how it will be introduced is extremely important, since those that entail higher esteem for women's role in the family and community are bound to be accepted and quickly show more visible results.

If it has been recognized that there is no significant difference in the level of acceptance and assimilation between women and men in extension programmes that do not contain any particular angle designed specifically for women, why not use this experience to launch concrete programmes addressed directly to women? Given that each introduction of new technology is a revolution in rural areas, why not envisage a much broader programme aimed at a 'revolution' in the way people think? It could include a series of actions that would enable peasant women to free themselves gradually and move away from the domination exercised by men through cultural values, tradition, etc. In this connection, there is room for action in birth control, day-care centres in the villages, and other types of social welfare such as

122

meals services or 'rural canteens', laundries. . . These are all actions that would promote women's role in the family and community and open up (egalitarian) horizons as regards access to new technology – a necessary step if new technology is to be a success, since rural women have much more impact on daily life than their city-dwelling sisters. Though this list of actions may on the surface seem irrelevant to improving women's access to technology, it is in fact crucial, since it conditions all promotion actions in terms of professional training that may be defined in the most varied areas in integrated rural development projects.

The complement to the actions referred to above can be found in projects carried out concurrently or in successive phases in other areas, such as installation of water pumps, planting of small woodlots with fast-growing exotic species for fuelwood, introduction of improved seed, fertilizer, and weed control through market gardening programmes, for example. As mentioned above, market gardening is traditionally women's work and, as it runs no risk of male competition, positive results would be guaranteed from the outset in upgrading rural women's professional skills and promoting greater participation in family income.

In processing and preserving produce (areas where women play the leading role) there is also room to introduce new techniques in small-scale transformation of maize and cassava into their many end-products, maintaining or even improving on standards of quality while significantly reducing the time and effort spent by women on these tasks. The same approach could be envisaged for extraction of palm oil or other types of food processing.

This discussion gives us the opportunity to address the question of accessibility and acceptability of technology to peasant women, but in the context of genuine physical/intellectual receptiveness won as the result of women's promotion in the family and community, a challenge to those who argue worldwide that women are genetically inferior in their learning capability, in particular.

The development of draught animal power, introduction of motorization/mechanization, and innovations in food processing and preservation, women's effective participation in managing peasants' associations, their active participation in choosing and distributing the industrial goods earned by sale of farm surpluses, are all perfectly feasible and practicable with the same degree of difficulty as if the target population were men, as long as the conditions are created which make women truly receptive to change. This stage will be attained slowly as women's prestige is enhanced in the family and community context.

Instead of entering into direct confrontation with traditional values, which would only stifle initiatives, we believe that the right answer is to discern mechanisms to raise the status of women's family, social, and community work, thus achieving their increasingly effective participation in the different phases from conception to realization of a given project, and enjoyment of the commodities produced or exchanged.

5. Future prospects

It is obvious that the absence of programmes specifically designed for women makes it more difficult for them to have access to technical innovations and to use the technology that can help improve standards of living and ensure their effective participation in national food security programmes.

A major step was taken when OMA organized a study centre, which will not only examine the role of Angolan women in depth, especially rural women, but also co-ordinate and promote programmes specifically designed for women. From a practical viewpoint, given the serious limitations we have in our country, we intend to take an objective stance in drawing up programmes that respond to concrete situations and are feasible. We have therefore selected the following:

Reafforestation and tree planting. Our intention here is to make fuelwood more accessible – it is the main energy source in rural areas – and also to improve the diet of the population. Plant nurseries are currently being established throughout the country which will enable implementation of this type of programme. It will sometimes include fuelwood-producing trees. We know that there are countries in our region such as Swaziland, Lesotho, etc. that have a good deal of relevant experience and it would be very useful if we could co-operate with them in this activity.

Better productivity in weeding. We all know that this is the most arduous chore in farming and that women are the ones who do it. This programme will be very restricted in scope, since in the first phase we will be testing the adaptation of implements and equipment produced in other regions. We are planning to introduce the use of herbicides for some crops.

Food processing. We will pay attention especially to maize, cassava, and tomatoes, since they are the usual products from the gardens that women are normally in charge of. There are heavy losses every year. Our idea is to teach simple methods of making preserves such as tomato jam, etc.

Farming techniques. In many villages OMA has been organizing farming plots, but generally along traditional lines. We would like to take advantage of this practice to introduce technical innovations, especially relating to soil fertility.

Access to water. Our intervention will mainly address management and maintenance of water supply points. Since women are in charge of providing water to the household, they are the chief users of the water schemes that are being implemented in the country. Often from ignorance, women damage these schemes or make them non-operational. We already have some experience and hope to broaden it.

Ocean fishing. A new type of communal fish-smoking oven was constructed in Ibendua (Bengo). This model increases fuelwood consumption but also increases production of smoked fish tenfold while maintaining quality. The drying-through-salting method has been upgraded by distributing implements required for salting, such as plastic receptacles, baskets, and filleting knives, and techniques have been improved. These new methods and implements have been extended to fishermen's associations.

A number of studies has been carried out, among them:
1. Improvement of rural fish drying technology.
2. Traditional fish curing technology.
3. Semi-hot curing technology.
4. Hot curing and fish curing.
5. Storage.

6. Energy problems and their social consequences in the People's Republic of Angola

Aggregate figures on the energy crisis do not give a meaningful idea of what it is like not to have enough energy to cook and heat with. In rural areas in developing countries most or all of the households are without gas or electricity, and kerosene (paraffin oil) is practically inaccessible. Fuelwood is the basic fuel for over 94 per cent of the rural population and over 83 per cent of the peri-urban population. When fuelwod grows scarce, women and children (who are the ones in charge of gathering wood for space-heating and cooking) are the first to suffer. They have to travel long distances to gather the minimum amount of wood they need to subsist. In peri-urban areas, they must wait for delivery of wood that comes from sites farther and farther away. In Luanda, for example, fuelwood and charcoal are already brought in from over 30km. The situation has worsened with the increase in population density in the major urban centres in the country, more particularly near the coast.

Difficulties in getting enough fuel, because of distance or cost, cause hygiene and nutrition problems. Among the main food crops in developing countries, there are very few that can be consumed raw. And if there is not enough fuel to cook them, the daily ration of proteins is curtailed. In a number of areas, families can eat only one cooked meal a day instead of two. The effects of fuelwood shortage go beyond the individual household. The shortage sets off a chain reaction which affects the very essence of rural society, its agricultural base and environmental stability.

In rural areas the problem is not so severe, since rural dwellers use dead branches and agricultural wastes. In peri-urban areas fuelwood and charcoal become more expensive, so much so that an average family of six has to spend close to US$365 a month, i.e. the equivalent of two minimum monthly salaries or nearly 1/3 of the maximum monthly salary. Alternatives are not easy, due to the lack of appliances to burn other fuels and the distorted or even non-existent systems for distributing kerosene and LPG (bottled gas).

Given this energy crisis situation, the Ministry of Energy and Petroleum, by means of its Department of Renewable Energy, has been developing a number of projects along with the Organization of Angolan Women. The goal is to try to overcome or minimize the problem of household fuels, thus also helping to improve women's standard of living while assisting the move towards food security.

Some of the projects implemented, being carried out, or under study are:

6.1 Solar fish dryer
This project will be set up in a settlement some 15km from Luanda. The community lives by small-scale fishing and by processing fish through salting and drying, using very rudimentary methods.

A series of surveys was carried out among the community to characterize it and enable later analysis of its socio-economic and technical features.

There are some 23 fishermen in the community who own their boats and around 20 paid employees of boat owners.

Fish is processed by the women: 15 of them are married to fishermen who have their own boats and seven of them are married to men with other economic activities. It should be noted that fishermen's wives buy fish from their husbands.

The average age of the fishermen is 48: the oldest is 87 and the youngest 16. Among the women who process the fish, average age is 36: the oldest is 59 and the youngest 20. The average number of people per household is seven.

The following data illustrate some of the community's socio-economic features (US$1=Kz30.214):

- 16% of the fishermen have another livelihood, mainly subsistence farming.
- 55% of the fishermen's wives process fish.
- 25% of the fishermen live in huts lacking even minimum conveniences.
- 81.5% of the fishermen use fuelwood for cooking. They consume an average of 54kg per month, corresponding to the equivalent of Kz26,000 per household/month.
- 85% of them use kerosene for lighting. They consume an average of 22 litres/month, corresponding to some Kz785. They have no kerosene lamps, but improvise with a tin can and a wick that they use both at home and out at sea.
- 77% of the fishermen use official medical services, and 63% have children enrolled in the official school in Cacuaco.
- 68% of the women who do the fish processing are married to fishermen; 32% are either single or are married to men with other livelihoods.

- 55% live in huts in the community; 11% have running water at home and 78% have no running water.
- 64% of the women use fuelwood for cooking and consume an average of 80kg per month, the equivalent of Kz40,000 per household/month.
- 100% of the women who do the fish processing use kerosene for lighting and consume an average of 18litres/month.
- 100% of the women use official medical services, and 64% have children in school – an average of two children in the official school.

The objective of the project is to build a solar fish dryer, thus reducing drying time by one half and giving a better quality product. Further plans are to build fish salting facilities to create better working conditions for the women who do this job. Ultimately, the goal is to boost the supply of dried fish to the community, thus guaranteeing its food security.

Within the scope of this project a health post will be established as a joint activity with OMA. This will provide first-aid and will have a doctor on duty twice a week. There are also plans for a literacy centre that can serve as a school for the children, and a centre for extension work to teach the community about primary health care, nutrition, and sanitation.

6.2 Improved stoves
The main objective of this project is to study, design, and disseminate a type of improved stove that will contribute substantially to reducing the domestic consumption of fuelwood and charcoal. This in turn means reduced fuel costs, and less time spent gathering wood.

6.3 Supply of drinking water to the population
Three solar pumps and two wind-powered water pumps have been erected in rural areas in the south. They supply drinking water for the people as well as for their economic activity: livestock raising and farming. Some positive results have already been noted, such as reducing water collection times.

A project is also under way to erect ten more wind-powered pumps in the region, as well as to survey and repair all existing wind pumps installed during the period before independence.

More than 9000 peasants, women and men, benefit from these projects.

6.4 Community reafforestation
In 1988 a woodfuel reafforestation project was being implemented some 70km north of Luanda. The major objective is to supply fuelwood and charcoal to two villages as well as fodder for the goats that are raised in the area. It should be pointed out that woodfuel is so scarce in the region that the situation is already considered serious.

This project will benefit more than 5000 people. It is an experimental project whose results will enable new schemes to be formulated in other areas.

127

Many other projects could be carried out to improve women's standard of living, especially in rural areas, if it were not for the war situation prevailing in the country, the funding difficulties for this kind of project and the lack of qualified personnel for this type of technology.

7. Women's participation in SADCC energy sector regional programmes and projects

The SADCC Energy Sector Technical and Administrative Unit (TAU) has been working in the various energy subsectors towards a concrete definition of strategies, programmes and projects within the scope of a five-year plan.

The SADCC energy ministers have approved the strategies, defined in the areas of petroleum and woodfuel. As for women's participation, it is believed that in this phase women can be more effective in the woodfuel subsector.

The following is a summary of woodfuel strategy, whose chief objectives are:

- to ensure a sustained supply in rural and urban areas;
- to reduce or arrest the depletion of resources in order to ensure sustainable growth.

To facilitate attainment of the objectives, a total of 7 broad programmes was initiated with indication of possible project areas as outlined below.

Programme	Possible project areas
A. Increased supply potential of woodfuel	– Afforestation efforts in rural and urban areas – Agro-forestry – Improved management of existing natural forests and trees – Species selection and provision of seeds – Assessment of supply potential, i.e. yield and stock
B. Improvement of efficiency of woodfuel and consumption surveys	– Improvement of charcoal production techniques – Introduction of improved charcoal and fuelwood stoves – Improvement of woodfuel end-use efficiency in rural industries – Household and non-household woodfuel consumption surveys

C.	Intensification of mass awareness (education)	–	Use of mass media channels, audio-visual aids, seminars, workshops, and household visits in educating the public on woodfuel issues
		–	Establishment of a printing unit and documentation centre at TAU to facilitate dissemination of information
D.	Training and strengthening of planning capacity	–	Training of woodfuel experts in specific fields
		–	Assisting member states in formulating national woodfuel strategies and plans
E.	Assessment of environmental impacts of woodfuel consumption and production	–	Assessment of negative effects and their underlying causes, and extent of the problem
F.	Fuel switch	–	Development of fuel alternatives
G.	Development of woodfuel energy techniques	–	Gasification
		–	Steam engines and turbines

7.1 Regional project ideas

A total of 12 project ideas has been developed under the headings outlined above.

The project ideas are:

1. Development of improved charcoal production techniques.
2. Development and dissemination of improved charcoal stoves.
3. Improved end-use efficiency of woodfuel in rural industries.
4. Household woodfuel consumption surveys and afforestation.
5. Development of regional and national programmes to increase awareness of woodfuel issues.
6. Development of micro-printing centre and dissemination of information.
7. Development of national woodfuel strategies and plans.
8. Assessment of the role of non-governmental organizations (NGOs), women and children in woodfuel production and utilization.
9. Assessment of environmental and socio-economic impacts of woodfuel scarcity.

10. Development of fuel switch opportunities.
11. Development of wood-powered power plants.
12. Woodfuel manpower assessment.

These project ideas can be developed as concrete proposals for funding.

The TAU requires technical and financial support to define and implement projects. We would welcome any contributions from countries and internal or external organizations that might want to join in the SADCC region's efforts.

7

Mozambique

1. Introduction

Women constitute more than half of the population of Mozambique (13,991,547 according to the 1975 census) and of these, 8090 live in rural areas with farming as their main source of livelihood. The Government's agricultural programme aims for self-sufficiency in food, the provision of raw materials for national industry and a guaranteed level of exports. Its activities concentrate upon rural development including the introduction of socialized health and education.

In recent years, the country has experienced major economic and food crises and a reduction in agricultural output as a result both of natural disasters (the floods of 1977 and 1978, followed by drought in 1981 and 1983) and the war with South Africa. It has been calculated that some 5 million people have been displaced in addition to the destruction of centres of production, electricity lines, bridges and farming land.

The country must now consolidate its independence by establishing peace and overcoming underdevelopment. With the aim of eliminating hunger, illiteracy and economic backwardness, the Government launched its Programme of Economic Rehabilitation in 1987. Its results have been encouraging, and economic decline has been halted. Clearly the rural population – and, in particular, women – must occupy centre stage in this development process.

The rest of the paper provides a description of the activites of those agencies involved in the reconstruction programme.

1. The South African Transport and Communications Commission (SATCC)

SATCC was established shortly after the historic Summit Meeting of 1 April 1980 in Lusaka, where the member states of SADCC committed themselves to pursue policies aimed at the economic liberation and integrated development of their national economies.

A prerequisite for such development must be a reliable and efficient transport and communications system and has been accorded the highest priority by the SADCC states. However although the SATCC Programme of Projects has been well supported by the international community, the financing of its implementation has been slow. It is to be hoped that the process will be speeded up in order to assist the SADCC countries in their efforts to gain greater economic independence and so reduce their trade dependence on South Africa.

1.1 Objectives

The priorities as regards capital investment projects have been defined by the policy organs of the Commission, and endorsed by SADCC, as follows:

- the rehabilitation and/or upgrading of existing facilities;
- the establishment of adequate telecommunication links and civil aviation facilities;
- provision of new transport facilities where deemed necessary and viable by reliable studies;
- initiation of feasibility studies for further additions to the regional infrastructures.

It can be seen that the first priority for SATCC is the proper maintenance and effective use of existing assets, rather than provision of new ones. These aspects have been identified as major problem areas in the region.

SATCC places much emphasis on the operational co-ordination and development of training and, in particular, co-operation and management of programmes and projects, which include:

- roads;
- railways;
- ports and water transport;
- civil aviation;
- telecommunications;
- meteorology;
- postal services.

In all these fields, the programme includes projects concerning capital investments, operational co-ordination and training.

The capital investment projects concerning surface transport modes, (road, rail, ports and water transport) are grouped according to a corridor approach, providing connections to the five regional ports, Maputo, Beira, Nacala, Dar es Salaam and Lobito.

The SATCC programme covers the infrastructure, navigational and traffic operations aspects of civil aviation. In telecommunications it covers both terrestrial and satellite connections, and in the meteorological field the national capability to make adequate primary observations and the use and dissemination of useful information. The postal services programme aims to speed up the service and regionalization of mail.

1.2 Organization

The basic organizational structure of SATCC comprises:

- a Committee of Ministers;
- a Co-ordinating Committee;
- a Technical Unit (TU).

The TU functioning as the Commission's secretariat working under the responsibility of the Chairman of the SATCC Co-ordinating Committee has, until recently, been staffed by technical assistance personnel from the Nordic countries and Italy. In the past couple of years the work load of the TU has expanded, particularly in areas of operational co-ordination, the preparation of documentation for studies, projects and meetings, and the increasing supply of information and advice to organizations, institutions and individuals within and outside the region. While this has put pressure on the unit, it has to be seen as increasing recognition of SATCC's central role and competence in the co-ordination of regional transport and communications.

In response to this challenge, the TU has been strengthened, beginning with the 'regionalization' of professional staff and the arrival of a Zambian telecommunications expert as the ITU representative with the TU. Also, increased co-operation of SATCC with United Nations agencies and other partners is being reinforced. Documentation and information has in the past year received particular attention in the unit's organization and work. The importance and need for a systematical and organized handling of information has been recognized and the establishment of the SATCC Documentation System started in 1986. This is a computerized referral system containing a bibliographical and project data bases. Transport statistics and postal and telecommunications statistics data bases are also in progress, and a corresponding document system is being implemented; a regional documentation expert is at present being recruited in order to ensure appropriate manning of the documentation function in the future.

The system at headquarters is designed to provide information retrieval for all groups and SATCC sub-sectors in member countries; to ensure regular input from member states one liaison officer from each country has been appointed.

1.2.1 Operational co-ordination
SATCC aims to:
- improve capabilities in the member states to manage, operate and maintain their transport and communications systems and facilities;
- eliminate institutional obstacles to movement of traffic;
- promote bi- and multilateral agreements on operations;
- route traffic through regional ports;
- stimulate co-operation between airlines;
- increase use of regional resources and know-how.

While the investment projects aim at rehabilitation and improvement of the physical infrastructure and facilities, the purpose of these complementary activities is to ensure their efficient operation and use.

Working groups consisting of representatives of all member states have been established, meeting on a regular basis in the following fields:

- Road Infrastructure
- Road Traffic and Transport
- Railway Administration
- Civil Aviation Administration
- National Airlines
- Port Administration
- Shipping, Clearing and Forwarding
- Telecommunications
- Meteorology
- Postal Services

Under the auspices of these working groups, several regional studies have been completed and others are in progress, the groups acting as steering committees. The members are charged with follow-up of implementation in their respective countries, endorsed by higher SATCC/SADCC organs as required.

1.2.2 Training

A major part of SATCC work related to training and manpower development has so far consisted of studies and surveys on the principal SATCC subsectors concerning training needs and capabilities of existing institutions to meet those needs.

The focus is now shifting to implementation. The SATCC programme includes more than 20 separate projects ranging from subject-specific courses and preparation of training programmes to comprehensive manpower development plans for major organizations (like TAZARA) and physical facilities (such as the Port School in Maputo).

The working groups in operational co-ordination are actively involved and several have established training subgroups.

SATCC's training-related activities are co-ordinated by the Regional Training Council (RTC). SADCC's capital investment projects normally include training components, especially on-the-job training with the guidance of technical assistance personnel.

1.2.3 Surface transport systems

The overseas trade of SADCC member states, excluding coastal states but including Zaire, is currently (1987) estimated at 4.5–5 million tonnes, and including coastal states is 8–9 million tonnes per annum.

Once the current projects have been completed the railway and port capacities in SADCC member states will be adequate to handle this and future traffic. Work is already in progress to re-open the Nacala–Malawi, Beira–Malawi, Maputo–Zimbabwe and Lobito routes.

The main problem areas affecting the operational capacity of railways are shortages of rolling stock and skilled manpower. Projects aiming at improvement in these respects are therefore of highest priority. The railways carry the bulk of the regional traffic flow and the roads have a supporting role. Problems related to the road infrastructure are due more to poor condition than to inadequate capacity.

SATCC has developed a comprehensive development plan for the transport system, showing the inter-linkages and priorities of the various components and projects. This approach was first applied in 1984 when a 10-Year Development Plan for TAZARA was prepared, and a Technical Co-ordination Conference with financiers was held in 1985. A similar plan for the Beira Port Transport System was prepared in 1985 and a conference was held in 1988.

1.2.4 Civil aviation

Several airports have been completed or renewed, such as Dar es Salaam, Kilimanjaro, Kilongwe, Gabarone, Maseru and Matsapa – whilst others at Harare, Maputo, Lusaka and Beira will soon require modernization. The number of flight connections between member states has increased in recent years due to on-time scheduling co-ordination monitored by SATCC.

Further activities aim to co-ordinate use of aircraft maintenance facilities and also their fleets. A study is to be carried out on the joint utilization of wide-bodied aircraft and regional airline co-operation.

The expected increase of air transport in the region means that the highest priority must be given to aeronautical telecommunications, to bring the safety regulations up to accepted international levels.

1.2.5 Telecommunications

Considering that telecommunications are one of the basic needs for economic growth, SATCC has promoted projects with specific regional significance, such as the PANAFTEL terrestrial microwave radio systems, earth stations, international telephone and telex transit switching centres and telecommunications related to other transport and communication sectors.

The main strategy is to reduce dependence on South African transit facilities for SADCC intra-regional traffic. Lesotho and Swaziland still depend to a large extent on such facilities, without the use of satellites.

Angola and Mozambique will continue to have no or limited PAN-AFTEL connections to the other SADCC countries until the end of 1991 at the earliest.

SATCC's objectives are to promote maximum links within the region in order to create full diversity on as many routes as possible. Presently it is limited by the fact that the earth stations are spread between the Atlantic Ocean and the Indian Ocean satellites.

It is envisaged that full international subscriber dialling will be realized among SADCC countries when the satellite connection, PANAFTEL microwave radio systems and international gateways are fully implemented and completed towards the end of 1991.

135

The feasibility of introducing postal giro services to bring banking facilities within easy reach of the whole population is being looked at.

The main emphasis at the monent is to route mail through regional channels, especially the development of a regional sorting centre in Harare and of the Beira postal terminal.

A Technical Co-ordination Conference on Telecommunications was held in Lusaka in April 1987 to discuss the SATCC document on the 10-year Telecommunications Development Plan for the SADCC countries, which recommended the evaluation of the large investments made in the PANAFTEL network in terms of the level of intra-regional traffic, traffic routed via South Africa, operational reliability and tariff structure conducive to traffic growth.

1.2.6 Meteorology

Meteorological services are intensively used by Civil Aviation and Maritime Services. Further telecommunications play an important role for transmission of meteorological data. On these grounds the Council of Ministers decided in 1984 that meteory shall be included in the SATCC work programme.

The prime aim of the SATCC Meteorological Programme is to improve the region's capacity to:
- make correct and timely observations;
- maintain the measuring equipment;
- collect and disseminate observed data; and
- provide manpower development and training.

In the meteorological system, telecommunications play an important role. Therefore, 2 of the 10 capital investment projects are directed towards the up-grading and development of regional as well as national telecommunications facilities. It is intended to improve the storage and accessibility of data by transfer from paper to micro-computers and suitable software.

The planned Drought Monitoring Centre in Harare will be equipped with more powerful computer systems capable of receiving large amounts of regional data as well as making advanced statistical calculations.

It is anticipated that the SATCC Meteorology Programme will greatly improve the region's abilities to prepare and issue more user-oriented information, and so involve it more fully in the worldwide system of weather observation and forecasting.

1.2.7 Postal services

Postal services provide means for communication between and outside the member states, and there is an urgent need to develop services further.

Preliminary work concentrated on identification of problems and the development of postal projects.

136

SATCC hopes to further improve services by:
- routing regional surface mail via Veira;
- better sorting organization and more speedy handling of mail;
- giving mail conveyance the highest priority by transport enterprises; and
- introducing Express Mail Services (EMS) in all member states.

2. The National Institute for the Development of Light Industry (NIDLI)

In order to understand the actual situation of light industry in the country, it is necessary to start by making a brief analysis of our situation since National Independence on June 25 1975.

At independence, the majority of the Mozambican people were illiterate. The major part of the population lived in the countryside and were agricultural workers, with only a small number of working class or unskilled people. The commercial network was entirely in the hands of foreigners, mainly Portuguese and Indian.

With the Portuguese exodus, between 1974 and 1977, their numbers dropped from 250,000 to 200,000 and created an enormous need for technicians and professionals, since this was the only group that had had access to medium and higher levels of education.

As they left they destroyed and sabotaged machines and equipment they could not carry out.

2.1 The creation of NIDLI

The National Institute for the Development of Light Industry was created by the Ministry of Industry and Energy in 1984. At its IV Congress, the Frelimo party called on the Government to develop small industry at a local level, giving priority to the countryside to encourage the development of consumer goods and production means for the population, and rehabilitate and activate the existing infrastructures.

2.2 Objectives, management and functions

Whereas large-scale industry – which is confined to Maputo and Beira – is dependent upon the supply of raw materials, equipment and technical assistance from abroad, the growth of light industry is seen within the perspective of local, autonomous development based upon the needs of the rural population and making use of appropriate technology.

NIDLI's headquarters are located in Maputo although there are plans for other regional branches. The Institute has an independent administrative and financial structure and is managed by a Council of Administrators representing both the private and co-operative sectors. The Council is responsible for the presentation of annual rural development plans in areas such as civil construction, engineering, finance and banking. This is done in close co-operation with local authorities and other organizations. It also promotes research undertaken by the Investigation Department at the University.

The Institute concentrates upon providing support for the activities of small entrepreneurs and co-operatives in the form of external financing, the application of new technologies, installation of equipment and training of personnel. It is particularly concerned to stimulate the use of appropriate technology.

The introduction of new technologies will raise both the level of competence and national utilization of local resources, and also – through the production of consumer goods – satisfy basic needs, increase employment, provide social stability and reduce dependence upon external support. The rural population will gain in confidence and capacity and will be actively involved in improving the quality of their lives.

2.3 The role of local authorities

The local authorities provide NIDLI with detailed information on such diverse subjects as:

- agriculture, forest, hydraulic and mineral resources;
- communication networks and transport;
- potential future projects in new areas of development;
- demographic statistics, food habits and production techniques;
- agricultural production and cattle breeding.

The emphasis throughout is upon the promotion of self-sufficient development.

Projects are presented in plan to the Provincial Directorates of Industry, who have the task of analysing technical viability. The national bank also plays an important role supporting small industrial enterprise activities, through a concessional credit system.

Once a project is approved, implementation begins. Here the role of the Institute differs from case to case, and either a project is constructed wholly by its own beneficiaries, or the Institute installs the equipment and provides technical training. In all cases the main responsibility remains with the beneficiary – private or co-operative.

In the Economic Rehabilitation Programme, development of small industry is a factor of great importance, not only to complement large and medium industries, concentrated only in Maputo and Beira, but to form a new nucleus of development; with the creation of the Institute, it is hoped that the development of small industry will promote rural development, good organization and networking at the local level.

2.4 Completed projects

So far the Institute has supported the following projects: 20 schemes for the extraction of vegetable oil, 15 for soap making and 18 for the installation of grinding mills.

These projects are installed mostly in rural areas and communal villages.

One with most impact in the life of women is the installation of grinding mills, which reduce the work load in preparing the family food, maize.

Centres for repair and maintenance have also been set up.

2.5 Conclusion

The experiences of the past show us that co-operation in the field of small industry is beneficial and that transfer of technologies among the women of our countries will play a significant part in the growth and development of economic and social life. Promoting the growth of organizational and communications networks will provide a foundation for rural development, and the role of women in the exchange of this information is becoming recognized.

3. National Directorate for Rural Development (NDRD)

Of the total population of the country, 80 per cent live in rural zones dedicated to agricultural activities. Sectors distinguished here are the dominant state sector, the private, and family sectors which together account for 36% of commercialized agrarian production.

The peasant woman plays a leading role, as out of the total Mozambican population 51.4% are women.

The NDRD within the Ministry of Agriculture is the structure responsible for the integration and development of the small-scale economy in order to make it more profitable and more equitable.

3.1 Objectives

The NDRD is committed to:
- the creation and development of the communal villages, peasant associations and co-operatives.

3.1.1 The Rural Extension Services

The Rural Extension Services are the executive organ of the NDRD. They gather and supply information and give technical training, creating a link between the State structures and the peasants.

The Rural Extension Services work with 1100 workers, of which 250 are various technicans and 850 are fitters.

The extension network is now a real fact in all the provinces of the country, although it has not yet reached all districts and localities. At the end of 1986, 2227 communal villages corresponding to a total population of 3,200,000 inhabitants (about 300,000 families) were covered.

The activities have the following objectives:
- to encourage planning for efficient production;

- to promote and develop agricultural production (for example the selection of seeds);
- to promote and develop social infrastructure and conservation of natural resources;
- to co-ordinate co-operatives, etc.

Obviously there are essential factors to be considered, such as transport, communications, the existence and functioning of a training centre, teaching material and equipment. To date the supply of these services cannot meet the enormous demand.

It is also planned to:
- promote development programmes and rural groupings and organize requests for land attribution to family aggregations, co-operatives and other integrated organizations;
- co-ordinate and ensure distribution of tools and other resources;
- introduce techniques to increase productivity and hence growth in economic capacity of those sectors;
- develop scientific and agrarian techniques for integrated rural development;
- organize rural extension schemes; and
- encourage small rural industries to use local resources.

The Directorate pursues its objectives within two fundamental parameters of action. Firstly it aims to integrate branch activities of the agrarian sector at the rural level, and to identify priority activities for each locality and region within overall planning targets. Within this context, there is a specific project for study of the women in 6 provinces, in order to assess the existing programmes to permit a greater integration of women.

3.1.2 Problems and perspectives

The extension and rural development programmes also consider other activities that equally contribute to rural development – for example, rural transport, communications channels, social infrastructures linked to the health and education programmes, field water supply and commercial networks. The programmes cover all this, not only the transmission of new production techniques to the poor. The Directorate still encounters great problems in financing such vast programmes. The financing tends to be linked to specific projects, which is a limiting factor to general development.

Moreover, the results are not immediately visible from one campaign to another, and require time and patience. The war conditions in which our country is living make even the involvement of the peasant more difficult.

The plans laid out up until 1990 include:
- improving the direction of the rural extension network;
- revising and defining of priorities at regional and local levels;

140

- analysing and approving the projects;
- promoting training;
- promoting a system of co-operation between agrarian associations and co-operatives;
- promoting and co-ordinating easy acquisition of production factors.

To support such a vast programme, the Government has set up the latter with the ability to grant long-term credits not only to agriculture but also to fishing, small industry, agrarian commercialization and to rural transport sectors (for example the funds for rural progress, hydraulic agriculture, the agrarian credit fund and rural development).

4. The Co-operative and Green Belt Movements

Following independence, a nationwide movement of the peasants formed collective agricultural work groups and co-operatives of cattle breeding, in response to the policy of Frelimo and the Government.

One of the most valuable experiments began 6 years ago on the outskirts of the capital, Maputo. Women played a dynamic role in this co-operative movement.

4.1 Oganization

The aim of this co-operative programme was to safeguard food supplies to the city. In 1980, the Government created the 'Office for Green Belts', which had the task of training, organizing and assisting the co-operatives with market production and finance.

To represent the movement at the central level, a 'General Union of Co-operatives' was established, composed of one president and two deputies.

For each group of 15 or 20 co-operatives, there exists a local structure called the 'District Union', and the choice of the leaders is made by the workers themselves. This structure refers to provision, storage, accounting, agriculture, cattle-breeding and social services such as day-nurseries and social centres.

4.2 Training

One of the characteristics of the co-operative movement has been its dedication to training and encouragement of initiative. This enthusiasm can be harnessed in many areas – agriculture, cattle-raising, accounting and administration, literacy and childcare. Traditional prejudices about the role of women in society must also be overcome.

The supporting system is effective and the enthusiasm of the co-operative members increased from year to year.

The personnel to be trained were self-selected from the co-operatives. More than a thousand women have been trained.

Additionally, in the area of small technology twenty women are now working as biogas system operators.

4.3 Development of the co-operative movement

The co-operative sector has grown rapidly as a result of the creation of organizational structures and the provision of training. Today there are about 200 units with 10,500 members of whom 957 are women.

In the first phase the workers received no wages. However, with the money gained from the market, they were paid a small allowance. For the first time in their lives, peasant women opened bank accounts.

Within the co-operatives, women participate in the management and making of decisions, and enjoy equal benefits. Their involvement in co-operatives has definitely broken the social basis of women's inferiority, acknowledgement of their economic importance and their demand for participation has resulted in women assuming more powerful roles.

The co-operatives have also transformed the life of the peasant woman. For example, there are more than thirteen day nurseries, for over 2000 children, supply centres and proper refectories, and training centres. These free the women from physical workloads, freeing them to fulfil intellectual potentials, and improving family relations.

Being socially recognized, the woman is no longer only a 'family human being' but also a 'social human being'.

8

Lesotho

1. Introduction

1.1 Demography and population

Lesotho is an independent state situated in the south-eastern part of Southern Africa. The Head of State is King Moshoeshee II, a descendant of King Moshoeshee I. The country is about 30,355 square kilometres in area and lies about 1300 metres above sea level. Thirteen per cent of Lesotho's area is arable, the rest is range and heavily eroded expanses of land unsuitable for any form of agricultural development. Temperatures range from 26°C in summer to −7°C in winter. The landscape has four regions, i.e. mountains, foothills, lowlands, and the Sengu River valley. The highest mountain is Thabana-Ntlenyana which is 3482 metres high. The climate is monsoon under normal circumstances, with good rains in summer and autumn, but weather conditions have become unreliable with occasional long dry periods followed by heavy rainfalls. Temperature readings are inconsistent, with occurrence of frost in mid-summer especially in the mountains and foothills. These climatic variations are catastrophic to the country, as the economy is based on agriculture.

The country is divided into ten districts for administrative purposes: Mokhotlong, Butha-Buthe, Leribe, Berca, Maseru, Thaba-Tseka, Mafeteng, Mohale's Hoek, Quthing, and Quacha's Nek. The capital city is Maseru. The country is completely surrounded by the Republic of South Africa, with every district sharing a common border with the Republic.

The population is about 1.5 million, growing at 2.6 per cent a year. The capital's population is 106,000, about 16 per cent of the total. The population of males is 746,000, while females number 790,000. The death rate is 14.9 per 1000 for males and 12.7 per 1000 for females. Life expectancy is 49.3 years for males and 52.7 years for females. Death rates coupled with life expectancy for the sexes accounts for the higher population of females at any particular time.

1.2 Economy

The economy is based on agriculture. Summer crops include maize, beans, vegetables, and fruits. Winter crops are wheat, peas, vegetables, and deciduous fruit trees.

2. The problem

Lesotho has failed to feed its inhabitants for a number of years. There are justifiable causes which are quoted for low agricultural production in the country. Statistics on imports indicate indirectly the very discouraging picture of low food production. Imports range from grain products, fruits, vegetables, to livestock products.

Table 1 Value of imports by commodity, 1983, in M000s	
Product	Value
Live animals (chiefly for food)	133,428
Meat and meat preparations	10,333
Dairy products and poultry eggs	9139
Fish and fish preparations	3780
Cereal and cereal preparations	47,470
Vegetables and fruits	19,520
Sugar and sugar preparations	15,461
Coffee, cocoa, tea, and spices	5755
Animal feed	4689
Miscellaneous edible food	7650
Crude animal and vegetable materials	653
Domestic energy	1162
Electric energy	4135
Animal and vegetable oils and fats	4017
Chemicals and related products	43,038
Manufactured goods	117,412
Agricultural machinery and equipment	16,256

The following have been cited as causes for low agricultural production:
(a) Climate
(b) Low and unreliable rains
(c) Soil erosion
(d) Drought
(e) Frosts
(f) Hail
(g) Lack of proper technological innovation
(h) Pests – diseases
      – insects
      – animals
      – theft by human beings
(i) Credit facilities

144

The climate is changing rapidly. It has been observed for the last ten years that the seasons are sometimes delayed. In 1987 the country experienced heavy snow and frost in spring and summer, especially in the mountains. This caused the worst crop failure and livestock losses ever. In the lowlands there was heavy rainfall that checked land preparation and seeding. Seeded lands had poor germination rates because of rotting seed.

Table 2 Estimated areas of crop failure by cause and by districts, 1983–4 (hectares)

	Frost	Hail	Drought
Lesotho (total)	000	345	28802
Butha-Buthe	–	–	1765
Leribe	–	153	2914
Berea	–	81	3634
Maseru	–	–	2741
Mafeteng	–	21	3624
Mohale's Hoek	48	–	5184
Quthing	–	–	2715
Qacha's Nek	–	6	2104
Mokhotlong	355	2	1130
Thaba-Tseka	6	63	991

Source: From Annual Statistical Bulletin 1987, p. 56.

It has also been observed that the acreage under crop production has been decreasing. This may be due to drought and soil erosion or lack of relevant technology. Though there are periods of drought, there are big rivers which could be exploited by irrigation schemes on lands adjacent to the river. The country is sunny most of the year and the sun's energy could be harnessed and be used for development.

Soil erosion is a major cause of reduced crop area, with 20 tonnes/ha/year being lost. The erosion is caused by floods, wind, animal, and human factors. Women have been mobilized to undertake control projects which include terracing, grassing, waterways, tree plantations, gabions. Pests, in the form of insects, animals, and human beings, have also reduced agricultural production.

Animal power has been used to supply energy for agricultural operations. Ox-drawn implements were once common, designed specifically for men and not for women. Men left their homes for work in the towns, and in the Republic of South Africa after the introduction of the tax system. There arose a need to devise technology suitable for women, as most of the agricultural work became their responsibility as did fodder production, livestock structures, livestock feeds, storage facilities etc. Animals kept at home include cattle, sheep, goats, pigs, poultry, donkeys, horses, etc.

Table 3 Estimated number of cattle, sheep, goats, pigs, horses, donkeys, chickens, 1973–4 to 1983–4

Year	Cattle	Sheep	Goats	Pigs	Horses	Donkeys	Chickens
1973–4	465,500	1,556,900	279,030	–	114,000	99,900	–
1974–5	512,400	1,577,400	246,000	36,000	114,000	104,800	875,400
1975–6	502,400	1,519,700	226,800	35,700	100,300	92,700	694,300
1976–7	485,500	1,128,000	175,300	29,200	104,100	89,400	752,400
1977–8	526,181	942,833	164,284	32,746	104,331	86,014	812,105
1978–9	560,407	973,996	179,626	25,660	101,687	87,867	659,992
1979–80	593,929	104,556	241,242	21,888	101,123	88,017	826,312
1980–1	590,021	1,160,404	233,348	24,370	100,090	104,922	729,887
1981–2	562,372	1,337,448	274,541	42,795	103,114	97,540	814,551
1982–3	537,517	1,279,400	261,105	20,022	104,426	11,893	1,051,868
1983–4	529,175	1,280,975	249,700	18,250	113,475	120,725	924,075

Source: From Annual Statistical Bulletin 1987, pp. 59–60.

It should be borne in mind that most of the animals kept by farmers are traditional animals of poor quality. A lot of them will have to be culled and the remaining ones to be improved. These animals are the principal cause of soil erosion in the country. Women are left with weak animals to use as farm power and are not trained in their harnessing and proper maintenance.

There is need for technology for use by women in the following areas:

(a) Crop production

(b) Animal husbandry

(c) Pest control

(d) Storage of food

(e) Cooking and hot water provision

(f) Cleaning

Women are multipurpose workers and technology has to be developed that will render them efficient in time management. Each job needs a time specification.

A married woman is by law a minor and as such is not credit-worthy. She has no collateral. A woman gains access to credit/loans by being a member of a Co-operative Society. Lesotho Agricultural Development Bank (LADB) gives loans/credit to every male farmer. Other banks need collateral and the husband's permission for a wife to acquire a loan. Problems of female farmers include the following:

1. Technology

2. Access to credit/loans

3. Land

4. Non-participation of women farmers in policy formulation on food security

5. Legislation.

It is difficult to design a constructive and systematic policy on development of technology for women participating in food security because the actual number of women is unknown. An effort has to be made to collect data on everyone engaged in food security in the country. The target groups should be stratified by age and gender. The most active group could be involved directly in policy formulation, project and programme designs, monitoring, and evaluation.

3. Objective of the paper

The major objective of this paper is assessment of women's access to relevant technology on food security in Lesotho.

Areas to be addressed are:

(a) Government policy on food security.

(b) Government policy on credit/loans.

(c) Availability of technology for food security, women's access to such technology.

(d) Constraints on the use of such technology.

(e) Recommendations to improve women's access to such technology.

The emphasis of this paper is *women's access* to technology on food security and *not the existence of* such technology in Lesotho.

4. Research methodology

Questionnaires were designed whenever deemed necessary. These were useful in seeking for information from normal programmes of the Ministry of Agriculture and Appropriate Technology Section of the Ministry of Interior, Chieftainship Affairs, and Rural Development. The researcher decided to use questionnaires so that information could be recorded for use in future technology improvement. They were delivered by hand to the relevant bodies, with whom they were discussed in detail. The respondents were given two weeks to complete the questionnaires.

Special projects were visited and asked to give details of their programmes. Site visits gave the researcher an opportunity to see equipment and technology used, provided first-hand information, and made possible the viewing of actual field problems. On such trips the researcher talked with women using the technology to find out if they were comfortable or could suggest any modifications.

Effectiveness and efficiency of the devices were assessed by calculations of proportions and percentages of areas covered. This helped give a picture as to how many years it will take for the technology in question to reach a larger population or all women, if other things like capital, infrastructure, education, and health facilities are provided.

A literature review of relevant publications was conducted. The data were analysed to indicate historical trends in technological innovations; the potential for technological developments in food security; the publicizing of technological devices and innovations and education in their use. An assessment of publicity campaigns on appropriate technology by various mass media (radio broadcasts, brochures, and newspapers) was made.

5. Literature review

Very few publications exist which have written material on the Appropriate Technology Section of the Ministry of Interior, Chieftainship Affairs, and Rural Development. The Appropriate Technology Section (ATS) releases a regular newsletter with articles on appropriate technology in food security. Contributions are acquired from the National University of Lesotho, ATS, and other governmental and non-governmental agencies.

In a 1985 *Litsoakotleng* newsletter, it was reported that one woman had used empty beer/soft drink cans to construct a dwelling house. She was planning to build a cafe using the same materials. Empty beer/soft drinks cans can also be used for the construction of food storage devices. One man was reported as having made containers for carrying provisions, and bins for storing wheat flour and maize meal.

On page 9 there was an advertisement for a stove which saves wood and coal, the Mabotle Wood and Coal Stove. On page 15 there was a report on achievmeents on Itakeng Basotho Women's Group which was involved in Women in Development (WID) activities. The group had constructed stoves, paolas, and houses. On page 16, we read about women of Thabana-Morena who had started brickmaking for constructing a poultryhouse.

Transport is another factor that inhibits equitable distribution of food materials. It was encouraging to read of women's involvement in building a bridge in Likhakeng. There was a good advertisement on VIP toilets. It is a well-known fact that food security is part of an integrated rural development. Toilet facilities are essential elements in food security.

Control of plant pests is crucial to food production. On page 28, there was an article on aphids, codling moth, and fruit fly. It stipulated precautions to be taken when using chemicals/pesticides and the risks involved. A description and drawing of each pest was presented. Methods of control were well detailed, with an interesting account on the control of aphids through the use of nicotine from cigarette stubs.

In the question and answer slot, page 31, a teacher enquired about pig farming. Here we learned of pigs with three legs. The teacher was also keen to learn about skills to construct stoves and biogas systems. The reader was promised that relevant articles would appear in the following issue.

The second publication of *Litsoakotleng* gave instructions on how to construct a grass grain storage unit (Sesiu). Instructions were accompanied by photos on page 6. Page 7 advertised a stove and solar-energy equipment. There were also advertisements on VIP toilets (page 19), and Scotch carts (page 23). On page 22, there was an article on the proper pruning of fruit trees. Illustrations were presented.

In *Litsoakotleng* issue No. 1 of 1986 there was an article on clean water storage systems. It was stated that water can be stored in corrugated iron tanks and underground cement devices. Materials for constructing cement tanks are available throughout the country. Corrugated iron tanks can be purchased from retailers and wholesalers. Pictures of storage devices were also presented to support written accounts. Advantages and disadvantages of both storage systems were listed.

On page 9 of the same issue was an article on the hot seed-bed for an all-year-round production of vegetables. In Letters to the Editor, readers advised each other on various development issues of interest. There were paragraphs on young farmers. On page 21 there were advertisements on VIP toilets and solar-energy. There was an advertisement for Scotch carts on page 28. The address of the supplier was given also. An interesting account of blight disease on tomato appeared on pages 34–5. Precautions on prevention of the disease were given and early and late blight symptoms discussed. Symtoms on the tomato fruit and plant leaves were illustrated. Dithane M45 was recommended for cure. Simple, improvised means for measuring and mixing the chemicals were given. Materials to be used were pictured in the article, i.e. 500ml oil tin, lid of a litre bottle of coke, a one-litre coke bottle, and a piece of wire.

Milk is a good source of protein. Basotho farmers are beginning to show great interest in dairy farming. On page 41 there was a good acount of dairy farming in Quacha's Nek. At the time of writing of the article there were 30 members of a dairy association with 32 dairy cows. One farmer reported expenses of M56 and turnover of M300/animal/month. One old farmer had a dairy cow which produced 20 litres of milk at every milking.

Clean water is essential to a healthy and productive life. In *Litsoakotleng* No. 2 of 1986, pages 4–10, is a detailed account of constructing a clean well. Ten steps are given on the procedures to be followed. These are accompanied by good pictorial demonstrations, photos, and drawings. On page 12, Letters to the Editor, the following were reviewed or were topics of interest: poultry production, procuring rabbits, and pig farming.

On page 24 there was an advertisement for solar energy and VIP toilets. On page 32 there is a pictorial lesson on a credit union movement. One of the major objectives of credit unions is to increase agricultural production by providing farmers with credit and training on management techniques and farm equipment.

Litsoakotleng No. 3 of 1987, pages 5–8, gave a good demonstration on the skinning of cattle and a method to preserve the skin. Photos and drawings were used. On page 15 there was an advertisement for fruit and vegetable seedlings. Prices and places of purchase were indicated.

Food security and family planning go hand-in-hand. On pages 32–33 there was a lesson on family planning.

The ATS of the Ministry of Interior, Chieftainship Affairs and Rural Development publishes a newsletter, which educates the public on appropriate technology devices. As an example of the usefulness of the newsletter we can inspect Volume 1, No. 3 of June 1987. On page 2 there was an article on 'Resources and Technology Course for Lesotho's Development'. The course is offered by the Department of African Development of the National University of Lesotho. Practical problems addressed include scarcity of fuel, declining food production and food security, soil erosion, deforestation, overgrazing of rangeland, water shortages, malnutrition and ill health, and the need for alternative employment opportunities. Among the solutions were listed: renewable and non-renewable sources of energy, large- and small-scale irrigation schemes and dams, large and small industries, the Green Revolution, the tourist industry, primary health care, and infrastructure such as transport and communication and housing.

The article further explained that 'in each area of study, the resources available in Lesotho are identified in conjunction with the various goals'. It was also pointed out that traditional technologies were recognized as extremely useful for cultural, psychological, and practical reasons. An integrated approach to development was emphasized. The article pointed out the co-operation between the university departments themselves and the governmental and non-governmental organizations in teaching this particular course.

Other articles disseminated knowledge on mudstove construction (page 3) in an interesting article entitled 'ATS Cares for Rural Women'. The writer emphasized the fact that women had shown interest in appropriate technology devices, with most interest in fuel-saving. At the time of writing ATS was planning to conduct a course for 25 women from different organizations at the Mazenod Conference Centre. Demonstrations would be part and parcel of the course.

Another article on page 3 was on growholes: 'Dissemination of growholes at Plenty-Ha Makoae'. It was reported that a local villager was sent to a course at ATS on building a growhole among other things. In 1986 growholes were introduced to communal gardens and schools.

On page 4 there was an eye-opening account of 'Biogas Production in Lesotho'. The article gave the principle on which the system works. Various types of biogas production systems have been installed at the National University of Lesotho, and three other schools. Diagrams were given on pages 4 and 20. The devices publicized are the Indian Digester, the Chinese Digester, the Plug-flow/Fry Type, and the modified Chinese Digester.

Biogas will be used in energy production for, among other uses, food production, and food preservation.

Page 5 advertised the ATS Mabotle stove, a fruit and vegetable dryer, and the growhole. Page 6 gave advice on 'How to care for your Nursery'. The article was divided into the following topics: why start a nursery, collecting seed, nursery site, growing seedlings, time of sowing seeds, and planting a tree. This advice was for a woodlot nursery. The article was related to the topic on page 7, 'The Potential for Agroforestry in Lesotho'. Advantages and disadvantages were stated, and the interdependence of trees, land, livestock, people, and crops illustrated diagrammatically.

Page 8 enlightened readers about the establishment of the 'Renewable Energies Committee – A Brief on the Purpose and Activities for the Committee'. In introductory remarks the article gave a brief history of energy generation. The paper pointed out that the pioneer in exploitation of renewable energy was the Ministry of Agriculture – the Rural Technology Unit's Solar Energy Project in Thaba-Tseka. Other government ministries had subsequently taken an active interest. The efforts failed due to lack of 'liasion and co-ordination between organizations engaged in renewable energy activities'. Hence the committee was set up to co-ordinate all energy activities/programmes. It would also promote networking and co-operation between all departments and agencies interested and involved in renewable energy and formulate policy in close consultation with the Department of Energy. Membership of the committee was: the Department of Energy, Biogas Unit of the Ministry of Agriculture, the Architects' Department of the Ministry of Works, the ATS of the Ministry of Interior, Chieftainship Affairs, and Rural Development, and the Public Health Section of the Ministry of Health, Senakangoeli Solar Systems, NUL and Lesotho Housing Corporation and Lower Income Housing Company. At the time of writing two more members from a government department and a private company were expected to join. An account of the activities of the committee was given. Constraints were also stated.

Page 9 gave a well-illustrated account of 'The Use of a Growhole'. Page 15 gives another account of fuel-saving devices. In this publication we can read the following: 'The Energy Efficient House', 'Women in Appropriate Technology', ATS mailbox, drama of the Mabotle stove and the address of the supplier.

All the ATS newsletters are interesting. ATS also publishes a booklet on the retained heat cooker. Aspects treated are: what is the retained heat cooker, advantages of use, how to make one, how to make the two pillows, important points to consider in making the cooker, insulating materials, how to use the cooker, maintenance and care, cooking hints, recipes, foods that can be cooked, other uses, definition of terms and bibliography.

151

Agricultural information newsletters do occasionally have articles on appropriate technology. Research Division also have articles on technology used in food security.

In all the literature reviewed statistics on women involved are rarely given, except page 17 of the ATS newsletter Volume 1, No. 3 of 1987.

5.1 Lesotho Women in Development (WID) project

There is a report by Juliana Rwelamira on 'An Exposition of Basotho Rural Women in Development Project' published in January 1987. Juliana Rwelamira was the Project Technical Adviser of the Basotho Rural Women in Development Project. In the introductory summary the writer gave the historical background of the project. Implemented in 1984, it was a joint Lesotho Government/UNICEF scheme. Its main stress was in problems of rural unemployment and participation of rural women in development. The project was nationwide and was organized in two Phases. Phase One dealt with four districts and Phase Two with six districts. Selection of areas in the districts was based on the following points: they must be rural, have active women and/or groups, support integration of national development efforts, have nutrition assistants (NAs), be accessible for monitoring and have expressed interest in seeking help for development. Women participants had to have the following qualifications: have dependent children, be willing and able to work on a regular basis in the community, not be participating in another income-generating project, be willing to make a commitment to equipment purchase in cash or with a Credit Union loan.

5.1.1 Objectives

The broad objectives of the WID project are as follows:

Impact objectives
1. To help rural women to generate income so as to improve the situation of children and that of their families in rural Lesotho.
2. To promote self-sufficiency in agricultural production.
3. To generate local employment through income-generating activities.
4. To introduce appropriate food preservation and time/energy-saving devices to reduce the amount of food losses and to relieve women of some of their daily burden.
5. To upgrade the capacity of the Government to deliver services.

Output objectives
1. To provide skills to 560 rural women in 28 areas which will promote self-sufficiency in agricultural and other products, and facilitate storage and marketing of items for local use, using local resources where possible. These figures were arrived at using the ANP experience by the Nutrition Section.
2. To create income-generating activities which will generate employment for about 560 women in 28 areas.

3. To increase the number of appropriate technology workers from 4 to 9 to ensure national coverage.
4. To ensure proper field supervision and on-going monitoring of appropriate technology activities.
5. To increase the number of AT courses involving 15 people each, to at least two/worker/quarter ensuring that women participating in income-generating projects receive priority.
6. To increase the number of AT devices from three to ten including those for food preservation and time/energy-saving devices. The Village Level Food Preservation Programme was used as a basis for estimation.
7. To ensure effective management and implementation of the project.
8. To promote co-ordination by the Women's Bureau of activities for rural women to open and maintain channels of communication between National Steering Committee, District Agricultural Offices, Project Management, Area Project Management Committee, and Village Leadership.

The implementation strategy indicated co-operation of all involved. Each group of participating women elected a management committee. The major project activities were: training of project management, nutrition assistants, and participating women; credit management for women; input procurement, delivery, and distribution; establishment of income-generating small businesses by women's groups; demonstration and construction of appropriate technology devices. An important aspect of the project was the element of 'Credit Arrangements for Women'. The project document had stipulated that after skill training, productive equipment and materials would be available to women. The assumption was based on women's groups qualifying to join credit unions and getting credit services from the Lesotho Co-operative Credit Union League (LCCUL). Qualifying conditions of LCCUL required that the women should have undergone training in credit union philosophy and should have saved with LCCUL before they could borrow money. All groups qualified except the Molumong of Mokhotlong district.

Their problem was solved by the UNICEF Procurement and Assembly Centre (UNIPAC) offering credit services to the groups. The women were given a period of grace after which they repaid the loans. In page 23 of the report, 'Future Solution in Pipeline', it was revealed that UNICEF and ACOSCA entered into an agreement whereby UNICEF would provide funds to develop a model credit project using an established national savings and credit co-operative system to facilitate UNICEF's assistance to women.

Achievements of Phase One (page 24) were that 10 women participated in poultry (eggs) and 21 women in vegetable production. In Phase Two 49 women were involved in poultry production (eggs and meat), 10 in dairy farming, and one women was engaged in a bakery. In total, there were 59 women in poultry, 10 in dairy, 21 in vegetables, and one in a bakery.

Appropriate technology is another important area of emphasis. Seventy-eight women were trained on the construction of growholes, hot box cookers, stone paolas, water jars, and solar dryers.

The SADCC Co-ordinating Unit responsible for soil and water conservation and land utilization programmes publishes a quarterly newsletter called *SPLASH*. The newsletter is published in English and Portuguese. Reports on seminars and workshops, staff, and consultant studies are carried. Fourteen articles have been published in the 1985 to 1987 editions.

5.2 Conference on Another Development for Lesotho
In the Conference on 'Another Development' for Lesotho, a group working on an endogenous, scientific technological base for the country put forward the following recommendations:

(a) enhance technological capability in the citizens;

(b) provide forward and backward linkages and supportive infrastructure for enlarging and deepening productive capacity;

(c) optimally utilize every aspect of national resources keeping in view both the short- and long-term national interest;

(d) involve people at every step to build up their faith and confidence in the national plan.

The group made a total of nine recommendations. The trend of thought was that Lesotho should tap its own materials and manpower resources, in the interests of self-sufficiency, before applying for foreign assistance.

5.3 Food and Nutrition Co-ordinating Office (FNCO)
The activities of FNCO were deduced from the 1986 bulletin Volume 1, No. 8. This gives data on rain-fall, crop and vegetable production, livestock, producer prices, consumer prices, sales, and disposals by producers, purchases by households, miners' remittances, commercial food imports, food stocks and storage capacity, total food supply and self-sufficiency, water and sanitation, nutritional status, morbidity and mortality, and statistics on numbers of beneficiaries. All the above topics are essential components of comprehensive food security programmes.

The bulletin indicated that Lesotho had to import food items, as commercial food imports and food aid (tables 8.1 page 35 and 9.1, 9.2 pp. 37–8). It gave a picture of the country's potential capability for food storage. Facilities were classified as Food and Management Unit (FMU) stores, Co-op Lesotho stores and depots, ex-Senqu project stores, ex-Thaba-Besiu project stores, Basic Agricultural Services Programme (BASP) stores, ex-Khomokhoana stores.

At the time of reporting, there were 12 FMU stores with a capacity ranging from 34 to 2641 tonnes; 29 Co-op Lesotho stores with a capacity ranging from 900 to 15,000 sq. ft; 7 ex-Thaba-Bosiu project stores; 8 ex-Senqu project stores; 45 BASP stores with a capacity ranging from 373m to 1238m; 6 ex-Khomokhoana project stores. Storage facilities are provided in urban centres and rural areas. A lot of the rural stores are not used due to a decline in domestic food production and the poor distribution system. The report gave statistics on numbers of people provided with clean water and sanitation, complementary activities in food security programmes.

FNCO reported traditional and modern food storage devices. Devices for storing grain were listed as 'Lisiu', modern cement-built structures, sacks or hessian bags (big and small), plastic bags and bins. Those for storing fruits and vegetables were listed as bottling, drying, and burying. In meat and fish preservation bottling, drying, smoking, and immense fat preservation were common. Women's voluntary organizations use the devices. Membership is reported to be about 10,000.

6. Results

Various government and non-governmental organizations have programmes which emphasize food security. These include bodies involved in food production, food preparation, food processing, energy for food security, and other devices used in the home to make it a suitable environment enabling women to participate in food security programmes effectively and efficiently. The list of organizations carrying out activities on food security are the following:

1. Appropriate Technology Section (ATS) of the Ministry of Interior, Chieftainship Affairs, and Rural Development.
2. The Ministry of Agriculture
    (a) *Crops Department*
    (i) Horticulture Section (Fruits and Vegetables)
    (ii) Food Self-Sufficiency Programme (FSSP)
    (b) *Livestock Department*
    (i) Poultry
    (ii) Dairy
    (iii) Beef
    (iv) Small Livestock
    (v) Fishery
    (c) *Extension Department*
    (i) Home Economics
    (ii) Agricultural Research
    (iii) Agricultural Information (newsletters)
3. Projects
    (a) Phuthiatsana Integrated Rural Development Project.
    (b) Thabana-Morena Rural Development Project.

(c) Plenty (Quthing–Makoae).
4. Co-operatives
    (a) Co-op Lesotho
    (b) Phela-U-Phelise (Butha-Buthe)
5. Parastatals or private concerns
    (a) Lesotho Agricultural Development Bank (LADB)
    (b) Catholic Relief Services (CRS)
    (c) Lesotho Steel
    (d) Basotho Canners (Masianokeng)
    (e) Senakangoeli – BEDCO

6.1 Responses to Questionnaires

6.1.1 ATS
Responses by ATS to the questionnaire designed specifically for it were satisfactory. ATS was able to report 453 women involved in designing and use of appropriate technology devices, including stone paolas, metal stoves, retained heat cookers, food dryers, growholes, and mud-stoves.

Table 4 Number of devices constructed by district and type

	Stone paolas	Metal stove	Retained heat cooker	Food dryer	Grow-hole	Mud stoves
Butha-Buthe	32	24	40	11	9	–
Leribe	16	17	11	6	11	–
Berea	50	33	12	11	13	–
Maseru	28	62	100	30	28	4
Mafeteng	60	10	35	14	20	–
Mohale's Hoek	30	16	16	5	20	–
Quthing	35	36	18	5	15	3
Qacha's Nek	30	30	15	10	10	–
Mokhotlong	250	38	80	40	40	15
Thaba-Tseka	61	30	8	1	4	3

ATS also reported that Save the Children Fund has built 1400 stone paolas in 412 schools. It reported that 11 courses were conducted and 500 women had participated in such courses. Participants were trained in skills needed to build food dryers, growholes, stone paolas, while 30 women were trained to build mud-stoves.

6.1.2 Ministry of Agriculture
(a) Crops Department
(i) Horticulture Section

There were five questions for the Horticulture Section, dealing with irrigated vegetables. The first question was 'What irrigation devices are in use in Lesotho?' The answer was sprinkler and mechanized sprinkler systems. The second question was 'What devices are available to women?' The response was sprinkler irrigation (manual, semi-permanent, and small-farm mechanized systems). The third question was 'What devices are unavailable to women?' The response was the mechanized systems which involve heavier equipment. The fourth question was 'If some are unavailable to women, what are the constraints?' The response was some equipment may be too heavy to be moved by women. The fifth question was 'What is the distributive pattern of the devices in Lesotho?' The answer is given as Table 5.

Table 5 Distribution of devices by districts

District	Device	Number of women having access to the device
Butha-Buthe	Manual sprinkler and semi-permanent	30
Leribe	Manual, semi-permanent and mechanized systems	280
Berea	Manual sprinkler, and semi-permanent	100
Maseru	Manual and mechanized systems	180
Mafeteng	Manual and mechanized devices	250
Mohale's Hoek	Manual sprinkler and semi-permanent and mechanized devices	200
Quthing	Manual sprinkler, semi-permanent and mechanized devices	240
Qacha's Nek	Manual sprinkler	10
Mokhotlong	Manual sprinkler	20
Thaba-Tseka	Manual sprinkler	–

Irrigated and rainfed vegetable production

The Ministry of Agriculture has a project called Lesotho Agricultural Production and Institution Support Programme (LAPIS) whose main objective is to increase agricultural production, with a section involved in vegetable and fruit production. LAPIS reported that there are 101 farmers involved in vegetable production on 56 hectares of land. Two farmers' associations are producing irrigated vegetables. Twenty-two hectares of this land are under feasibility studies.

It was also reported that there are 45 farmers producing fruit trees. The area under production is 12 hectares. Total number of fruit trees under production is 7014. In addition there are five nurseries producing 43,000 seedlings. The tree nurseries are produced by the fruit and vegetable cannery, Government of Lesotho, CARE, CIDA, and Hololo Valley. It was further reported there are 19 orchards under feasibility studies and 4558 trees are planted in the new orchards.

Marketing of fruits and vegetables is one of the concerns of LAPIS. Four marketing sheds have been ordered for installation at selected sites in rural areas. Two sheds have been erected so far.

It was also stated that 94 farmers are involved in production of vegetables and fruits at home and home gardens are under feasibility studies. It was pointed out that 78–80 per cent of fruit and vegetable farmers are women. Extension services are provided by the Ministry of Agriculture and technology used is available nationally. Ox-drawn and tractor-drawn implements are used for land preparation and weeding. Seeding, weeding, and harvesting is by hand. Maintenance tools include knives, pruning shears, chemicals for control of pests and diseases.

(ii) *Food Self-Sufficiency Programme*

There were 8 questions classified under land preparation, seeding, weeding, and harvesting designed for the FSSP.

(*a*) *Land preparation*

The first question was 'What equipment is used for land preparation?' Please list?

(*a*) *Primary operations*

The answer was spades, hoes, and ploughs, which are 1029 in number.

(*b*) *Secondary operations*

Planters – 286

Discs – 286

Drills – 200

Harrows – 400

Cultivators – 300

The second question was 'What power is used to drive the equipment?' The answer was oxen and tractor for both Primary and Secondary operations. Question three was 'Is equipment for land preparation available in Lesotho?' The response for both Primary and Secondary was tractor-drawn with equipment for primary operation 1029, devices for secondary tillage 876. Question four was 'Where do farmers purchase this equipment?' The answer was:

(*a*) Animal-drawn – Co-op Lesotho and local traders.

(*b*) Tractor-drawn – local garages and foreign firms.

The fifth question was 'How many women have access to the following implements according to districts in Lesotho?' The response is listed in Table 6.

Table 6 Number of women having access to tractor-drawn implements

Butha-Buthe	3181
Leribe	9964
Berea	3361
Maseru	5720
Mafeteng	3893
Mohale's Hoek	2937
Quthing	1275
Qacha's Nek	1125
Mokhotlong	1575
Thaba-Tseka	900

N.B. No figures were given for animal-drawn implements.

No figures were given for animal-drawn implements.

(*b*) *Seeding*

Under seeding the question was 'How many women have seeding equipment?' The response was:

Type of seeding equipment	Number of women
Animal-drawn	–
Tractor-drawn	+ 33,930
Other	–

(*c*) *Weeding*

The question was 'How many women have weeding devices?' The answer was:

Type of weeding device	Number of women
Hand-weeding	+ 33,930
Animal-drawn	–
Tractor-drawn	–
Herbicides	100

(d) *Harvesting, Threshing and Winnowing*

Equipment for	Type	No	Number available to women
Harvesting	Combine	30	30
Threshing	Slattery	20	20
Winnowing	Slattery and combine	50	50

(b) *Livestock Department*

(i) *Poultry*

The first question under poultry was 'How many chickens are kept by farmers in Lesotho?' The answer was half a million per year, of which half are reared in Maseru district. At any particular season there are 15,000 broilers and 200,000 layers. Three hundred farmers were reported to keep poultry, 270 of whom were women.

Question two was 'What is the capacity of the poultry plant?' The response was that there are 7 houses which keep 2000 chickens and annual production is 30,000 chickens to point of lay. It was also added that as a result of women's participation in poultry production, the Unitarian Service Committee of Canada (USCC) became interested in poultry production and 16 Egg Circles were constructed. It was also reported that the programme will be expanded by two houses which will house 6000 chickens with annual production of 24,000. Question five: 'What systems are used in keeping poultry in Lesotho?' – cage and deep litter systems are used. Question six was 'Are women farmers able to procure the systems?' The answer was positive, indicating that the systems can be obtained by women.

(ii) *Fisheries*

Eight questions were laid down for this section. Question number one was 'What is the approach to fish farming in Lesotho?' The response was that farmers are encouraged to form rural communal fish pond associations. The second concern was 'How many rural fish pond associations are functional in Lesotho?' There are 29 associations in operation. Question three was 'What is the membership of the associations?' There are 580 farmers involved in fish farming. Question number four was 'How many women are members of the associations?' The answer was 464, 80 per cent of the membership.

Question five was 'What equipment is used for constructing fish ponds?' The response was hand tools, that is, spades, shovels, and wheelbarrows. Grass was planted on the borders of the ponds to control soil erosion. Question six was 'Are fish feeds available in Lesotho? What feeding system is used?' The fisheries section used to encourage farmers to use fish pellets but now recommends fish-cum-duck complex. Question seven was 'What problems are faced by the associations?' The answer indicated:

(i) Management problems due to lack of individual commitment and initiatives in communally owned schemes.

160

(ii) Fish farming is regarded as a secondary farming activity.

(iii) Lack of capital and of credit facilities. LADB does not offer credit/loan facilities to fish farmers.

Question eight was 'What solutions do you recommend?' The following were suggested:

(i) Individual ownership of ponds.

(ii) People to be trained to manage their ponds well so they can be profitable.

(iii) LADB to be asked to finance fish farmers. A project proposal to be written up and sold to donors for financial assistance as is done with other farming activities.

National Abbatoir and Feedlot Complex (NAFC)

This is a facility that serves as a marketing outlet for livestock. It was reported that it deals in cattle, sheep, goats, and pigs. The complex has fattening and slaughtering facilities as well as 420ha land for fodder production. By the end of 1987, 6746 head of cattle, 21,206 sheep, and 1055 pigs were slaughtered for sale. There are no figures as to number of farmers using the facility as a marketing outlet.

It was also reported that there are 50 women employed at the complex. It can be deduced that women benefit from its services as most women in Lesotho are farmers.

Efforts to start rabbit farming

The head of the Fisheries Section reported that he is carrying out pilot schemes on rearing rabbits for meat production and skins. There are eight districts where rabbit farming has been started with success; 84 farmers and 22 institutions are involved.

Table 7 Rabbit units by districts

District	Institutions	Farmers
Butha-Buthe	1	6
Leribe	1	20
Berea	3	10
Maseru	12	30
Mafeteng	1	7
Mohale's Hoek	1	7
Quthing	1	4
Qacha's Nek	–	–
Mokhotlong	1	–
Thaba-Tseka	1	–
Total	22	84

Most farmers are women

Plans are highly advanced for Maseru district wool growers associations

161

to diversify their activities by rearing rabbits. This is an effort to reduce pressure on limited range and eroded grasslands. The potential for keeping rabbits is great as reported by the head of Fisheries Section.

Wool Growers' Associations (WGAs)

The Livestock Department sponsors and promotes the establishment of viable Wool Growers' Associations. The main activities of the associations are breeding of wool animals, proper feeding, management, and marketing of wool. The department assists by training, loans, and extension services. It was reported by the head of Small Livestock Section that there are at present 89 associations. Membership is 4234 of which 847 are women.

In the 1986–7 breeding season, 1058 merino rams and 656 angora rams were purchased by WGAs, as well as 274 angora ewes.

Leribe Dairy

The researcher visited the dairy plant in Leribe run by the Dairy Farmers' Association. Membership of the association is about 28, and 9 of these farmers are women. The association has a communal cooler with a capacity of 2000 litres.

It sells milking equipment to the members, including milking cans, strainers, strip cups, and milking buckets.

Farmers produce fodder for feeding. Supplementary feeds are sold by the association. These are calf starter, growth meal, and dairy meal. The Veterinary Clinic supplies all medication at reasonable prices. Farmers can get loans to purchase production stock.

Pig Industry

Information on pig farming was extracted from a paper written by the Senior Pig Technical Officer for the Maseru District Livestock staff conference. Objectives for pig production were listed as:

(*a*) Supply of protein source to Basotho people.

(*b*) Income generation.

Production figures were given from 1977 to 1985.

Table 8 Production figures in pig farming by year and type

Year	Sows	Boars	Finisher pigs
1977	18	4	216
1978	4	10	182
1979	12	7	344
1980	52	21	434
1981	176	24	1281
1982	173	28	1407
1983	156	27	1112
1984	91	21	1217
1985	102	12	1632

The pigs are housed in individual or communal pens. Feeds used are ultra grow, pig finisher, and breed more. Co-op Lesotho is the major supplier.

Medication is administered in the form of iron injections, and vaccination against worms. Animals should be washed at least once a month.

Equipment used for maintenance includes buckets, wheelbarrows, tooth clippers, knives for castrating males, ring applicators, and hoof trimmers. For housing, local materials should be used, i.e. stones, mud; bricks and cement can be used if funds permit; for roofing, grass or corrugated iron can be used.

(c) Extension Department

(i) Home Economics

Five questions were designed for this section. Question number one was 'What appropriate technology devices are designed for women in order to achieve food security in Lesotho?' The following were cited: solar dryers, grow-holes, hot box cookers, mud-stoves, and stone paolas. Question 2 was 'What are the purposes of the above-mentioned technologies?' The answer was organzied thus:

Food-dryers – to encourage and promote food preservation.

Grow-holes – facilitate proper environment for plant seedlings in winter.

Hot box cookers – conservation of fuel/energy.

Mud stoves and stone paolas – conservation of fuel/energy.

It was reported further that the devices relieve women of the multiple burdens characteristic of the home. Question 3 was 'What is the distribution pattern of the technologies in Lesotho?' The response was as in Table 9:

Table 9 Number of women having access to device

District	Technology or device	Number of women having access
Butha-Buthe	All devices are	148
Leribe	distributed evenly	1206
Berea	in all the districts	159
Maseru		186
Mafeteng		214
Mohale's Hoek		140
Quthing		333
Qacha's Nek		200
Mokhotlong		147
Thaba-Tseka		54

Question 4 was 'Are there any problems that hinder women's access to the technological devices?' The answer indicated there are. Question 5 was

'If there are problems, state them.' The response indicated financial problems and shortage of staff.

(ii) *Agricultural Research*

This section was given the same questionnaire which was sent to Food Self-Sufficiency Programme (FSSP). Question one was 'List equipment used for land preparation in Lesotho.' Question 2 was 'What power is used to drive the equipment?' The answers were:

(*a*) Primary   – Mouldboard plough (ox- and tractor-drawn)
              – Disc plough (tractor-drawn)
(*b*) Secondary – Cultivator (ox-drawn)
              – Harrow (tractor/ox-drawn)

Question 3 was 'Is equipment for land preparation available in Lesotho?' The answer indicated availability of:

(*a*) Primary   – Animal drawn
              – Tractor-drawn
(*b*) Secondary – Animal-drawn
              – Tractor-drawn

Question 4 was 'Where do farmers purchase these implements?' The response was organized thus:

(*a*) Animal-drawn – Frazers
                  – Co-op Lesotho
                  – Lesotho Steel
(*b*) Tractor-drawn – Co-op Lesotho
                  – Private companies
(*c*) Tractors   – Private companies
                  – Rental service from Technical Operations Unit (TOU)

The answer to question 5, 'How many women have access to the following implements according to districts in Lesotho?' was unknown.

On seeding, question 1 was 'How many women have seeding equipment?' The response, based on number of farmers not women, was most farmers and they could rent if they lack the equipment.

On weeding, question 1 was 'How many women have weeding devices?' The response was not satisfactory, that is:

Type of weeding device	Number of women
Hand-weeding	All
Animal-drawn	Some
Tractor-drawn	Few
Herbicides	Can rent

On harvesting, threshing and winnowing, question 1 was on the availability of equipment for:

Activity	Type	No	Number available to women
Harvesting	Combine	100	Can rent
Threshing	Combine	100	Can rent
Winnowing	Hand	–	–

Rural Structures Unit (RSO) of Agricultural Research Station

The head of the Unit was asked to describe its background, its objectives and activities. It was reported that the Unit was set up in 1982 as a special tripartite project of the Government, FAO, and SIDA. It is responsible for construction and design of low-cost farm buildings for small-scale farms. It also builds demonstration structures in the districts and at the Research Station. Research on these structures will provide information for improving the designs.

At first the emphasis was on grain storage. Twenty-eight cement/brick silos were constructed for demonstration in seven districts. The structures were successful and farmers have expressed a desire to acquire the knowledge and skill to build them and plans are under way to hold courses for local builders and farmers. The Unit is also conducting a survey of crop loss in storage in 1987–8. Two insecticides are being tested, phostoxin and malathion.

The Unit is experimenting on adapting the Kenyan maize crib, with slight modifications to suit national conditions. The walls are made of chicken wire instead of wood and the uprights are made from locally available poplar. The structure has not been tested but will be used this year. It is hoped its viability will be confirmed and information provided on its drying and storage potential.

The other structure of interest is that for potato storage. This will be another adaptation of the Kenyan design to national needs. Thatching grass and chicken wire will be used for its walls instead of wooden offcuts. RSU is co-operating with District Agricultural Offices, Extension Section of Research Station, and Extension Agents. RSU would like to put up storage facilities for water, water filters, farm houses, village stores, chicken houses, milking parlours, and pig houses. It is true the number of women having access to demonstration structures is not yet determined.

The nutrition section of the Agricultural Research Station is undertaking studies on sorghum use. Work carried out at present includes a survey on the national use of sorghum as a food compared to other food grains, i.e. wheat and maize, in three prototype areas (Siloe, Nyakosobu, and Molumong in Maseru and Mokhotlong districts respectively). The report stated that research is being carried out with use of sorghum as a staple food, as porridge, and as a weaning food for babies/children. The information gained will be a basis for improvement of sorghum as a major part of the Lesotho diet (for adults and infants). This research will eventually benefit women.

Other areas of interest are fruit tree production and fruit preservation. The great potential to develop the industry was indicated by the number of farmers and farmers groups involved in planting trees.

Table 10 Initiator and the number of trees planted

Initiator	Owner	Village/ward	Orchard size No. of trees
	The Queen (backyard)	Matsieng (Maseru)	164
	The Queen (commercial)	Matsieng (Maseru)	322
	The Queen (vineyard)	Matsieng (Maseru)	260
	Josef Mapule	Pulane (Berea)	48
M. Malebo	Communal orchard	Ha Ntsuba (Berea)	3600
	Research	LAC (Maseru)	1300
	L.A.C.	LAC (Maseru)	340
Association of Women's Affairs	E. 'Mota	Pulane (Berea)	170
"	Women's Association	Ha Mokhothu (Berea)	350
"	Women's Association	Matsieng (Mafeteng)	600
	Communal Orchard	Majara (Berea)	250
	Col. S. Letsie	Thabana-Li-Mele (Maseru)	230
	Col. N. Tŝotetsi	Lancers Gap (Maseru)	210
Irish Project	Communal Orchard	Hololo Valley (B. Buthe)	450
Chinese Project	Communal Garden	Mejametalana (Maseru)	475
	Patrick 'Mota	Communal Nursery	400
Chinese Project	Communal Nursery	Leshoele (Leribe)	125
Irish Project	Communal Nursery	Hololo Valley (Leribe)	1000 seeds
	Government Nursery	LAC (Maseru)	1000 "
	Cannery Nursery	Cannery (Maseru)	14000 "
ISC Project	CIDA Nursery	Mohale's Hoek	6000 "
	CARE Nursery	St. Michaels (Maseru)	2000 "
	Mahlabaheng Communal Garden	Maama (Maseru)	?

N.B. Statistics on these are included in the section on irrigated and rainfed fruits and vegetables.

Nutrition section of Research Division of MOA

The results of the survey on the utilization of sorghum will lead to the development of technology for its production, storage, and processing. Such technology will address women's issues. The Government, through the FSSP, is increasing sorghum production in the country. Three districts in the south, i.e. Mafeteng, Mohale's Hoek, and Quthing, are concentrating on sorghum production. Technology is offered by FSSP through a rental scheme; last year a total of 7694 acres was planted.

Variety trials by the Research Station of the Ministry of Agriculture

The Agriculture Research Station has completed basic research work on variety trials and plant protection. Fodder sorghums and Sudan grasses have been tested also. Traditional technology in land preparation, sowing, weeding, harvesting, threshing, and winnowing is still utilized. Threshing is done using clubs, and threshed sorghum is stored in jute sacks. Some of the grain is used for brewing beer (*joala*) and the rest is ground by hammermills spread all over the country; women have access to these hammermills, which are owned by co-operative societies or commercial traders/individual farmers.

The Research Station is also working hard to find a technology to improve the acceptability of sorghum as food for human consumption (for adults and as weaning foods). Articulation of this principle has been indicated by holding fairs. The dehulled whole grain and hard porridge (*papa*) prepared from dehulled meal were found to be acceptable among those attending. Participants expressed a need for dehulling technology to be made available.

In future, research efforts will be involved in:

○ a project by SADCC Food Security through which funding will be secured for a two-year pilot project to improve utilization of sorghum;
○ foods from processed sorghum;
○ sorghum as composite flour;
○ commercial production of very fine sorghum flour for porridge making;
○ weaning foods from sorghum-based products.

Forestry Department

There was a questionnaire designed for the Forestry Department of the Ministry of Agriculture, consisting of five questions. The first question was: 'How many villages are establishing woodlots?' The answer was that more than 300 woodlots have been established all over the country. The second question was: 'How many tree seedlings are planted?' The response to this question was 2925 million seedlings are planted annually. Question three was: 'What types of trees are planted?' The answer was eucalyptus species and pinus species. The fourth question was: 'What equipment is being used?' The response to this question was that mattocks, picks and planting trowels are used for ground preparation and planting. Question five was:

167

'What equipment is available to women in terms of distribution and number of women using the particular equipment?' The response is organized in Table 11:

Table 11 **Distribution of equipment accessible to women per district**

District	Type of equipment used	Number of women using the equipment
Butha-Buthe	Equipment listed	311
Leribe	in question	892
Berea	distributed	480
Maseru	equitably in all	1574
Mafeteng	districts	274
Mohale's Hoek		263
Quthing		310
Qacha's Nek		90
Mokhotlong		81
Thaba-Tseka		75
Total		4521

Special projects

There are various national projects which emphasize food security. The technologies involved range from simple traditional or cultural devices to modern, complicated structures.

(a) In the FSSP tractor power and tractor-drawn implements are used, as reported earlier on. Devices used, and the number of women having access to the devices, have been indicated.

(b) Phuthiatsana Integrated Rural Development Project (Berea District). The researcher visited the project area and was informed of the activities of the programme. Two irrigation projects, namely the Lebina and Mapoteng Irrigation Schemes, are involved.

It was reported that equipment used for land preparation includes a land leveller, a plough and a disc; for seeding and hand-sowing, tractor-drawn planters are utilized; and for weeding and hoeing cultivators are used. Chemical weeding is not used. Harvesting is by hand for beans and vegetables; machines are used for harvesting wheat and lucerne.

The harvest is stored in the homestead and in barns, especially grains. There are no market problems. Produce is sold directly from the field and from nearby commercial centres. Maize is normally sold as fresh cobs/green maize. A cold storage for vegetables is being constructed under the assistance of the Unitarian Service Committee of Canada. It will be run and controlled by farmers, and all farmers in Berea district will have access to the facility.

Table 12 Types of crops, membership of groups and number of women involved

Name of scheme	Crops grown	Total membership of farmers	Number of women	Area
Lebina	Maize Beans Wheat Vegetables Lucerne	17	14	30.4 ha
Mapoteng	Maize Beans Wheat Vegetables Lucerne	11	10	14.2 ha

(c) *Thabana-Morena Integrated Rural Development Project*

The researcher asked for the latest report of the project and the annual report for the period January–December 1987 was released, from which the relevant data were extrapolated. The total number of participants is 360, 313 of whom are women (87 per cent of the total). The total population of Thabana-Morena is 13 600. In the project women number 3316, while the male population is 3137.

Project activities include fodder, vegetable and poultry production, bakery and cottage industries. A hammermill has been installed for food processing. Clean water is essential. The Village Water Supplies Section of the Ministry of Interior, Chieftainship Affairs, and Rural Development provides services to the project area. Eleven boreholes have been installed.

Support services in the form of extension, training, and marketing are the backbone of the project, and participants are directed and guided by three extension agents. Training is divided into three areas, for trainers, general membership, and leadership.

Resources at the disposal of participants include equipment for land preparation, seeding, weeding, harvesting, and winnowing. Machines can be tractor- or animal-drawn. Services can be provided by the mechanical section of the FSSP.

Conventional technology is used for livestock production. For fodder production, tractors and implements are rented from the FSSP. These include ploughs, disc harrows, seeders/planters, bacterial innoculants (for lucerne), harvesters, and balers; shelling and winnowing are manual.

d) *Phela-U-Phelise (P-U-P) Co-operative*

The researcher visited P-U-P and received an interesting account of the scheme. Phela-U-Phelise provides services to 3–4000 members. It is situated in Khukhune, Butha-Buthe and is basically involved in agricultural production and input distribution. Agricultural activities include field-crop, vegetable, and poultry production. It was reported that the area under vegetable production is 66 acres, with 64 women involved. Equipment used may be tractor- or oxen-drawn, and hand tools such as spades and digging forks are used. Tractor-drawn equipment is rented from the FSSP while farmers buy the oxen-drawn tools. Equipment is available to all women without discrimination. Financial problems exist, however.

In poultry farming there are 90 women farmers. Vaccinations are available through the input store. Poultry may be kept on deep-litter or in cages. Feeds are supplied by the input store.

Table 13 Materials used per year

Input		Quantity
A.	Fertilizer	
	2.3.0. (21) + ZN	4728 packets x 50 kg
	2.3.2. (22) + ZN	5506 "
	3.2.1. (21) + ZN	4210 "
	LAN	474 "
	MAP	181 "
B.	Seeds - Maize	
	PNR 473	608 x 10 kg
	RO 419	709 "
	CG 4141	3327 "
	TX 14	70 "
	TX 382	362 "
C.	Herbicides	204 litres
D.	Insecticides (granular)	5988 kg
	Insecticides (liquid)	560 kg
E.	Vegetables	Sprinkler irrigation used
F.	*Implements*	
	Matlama Complete Set	6
	Yoke	40
	Scotch-carts	10
	Total	56

Site visit: Co-op Lesotho

Co-op Lesotho is an apex co-operative society. It is also involved in food processing in the rural areas of the country. The manager of Co-op Lesotho reported that twelve diesel engines and thirteen electric hammermills were distributed to eighteen co-operative societies throughout the country.

CARE Lesotho

There are five areas where CARE was involved in spinning wool and mohair. When the spinning programme stopped in the early 1980s CARE started diversifying the activities of these areas. Participants are former members of the thirteen Primary Co-operatives. The members are now involved in agricultural production, mainly of crop seedlings, fruit trees, vegetables, and firewood; making cement blocks for building houses; and knitting.

Table 14 Areas and numbers of women involved

Area	Number of women
Peka	10
Ramokotjo	10
Moitŝupeli	10
Mpharane	10
St Michael's	10
Total	50

The equipment used in agricultural enterprises includes very few machines. Instead spades, shovels, rakes, wheelbarrows, and hoes predominate.

Site visits: Plenty Lesotho

The researcher took a study tour of Plenty Lesotho Project site at Makoae's in Quthing district on 21 May 1988. The Project Manager, a local Mosotho man, elaborated on the objectives of the project:

A. *General*

To optimize the use of available land and rainfall in the Quthing River Catchment area. This will be achieved by:

i) Institutionalizing research and extension services to further help the farmers to help themselves through increasing the production of traditional crops and the growing of soya and other annual leguminous crops, and further indigenizing these services.

ii) Improving nutrition by advocating and demonstrating food products made of soya and developing its production/marketing cycle, especially by introducing soya flour in combination with traditional foods in the context of overall nutritional education.

B. *Specific*

1. To continue to research, test, and demonstrate varieties of sorghum, cowpeas, white haricots, maize, sugar beans, wheat and soya, as well as other crops that are suggested by the Ministry of Agriculture or that are seen to be appropriate, including groundnuts (peanuts) and pigeon peas.

171

2. To provide extension services to 30 villages over the two-year period, directly benefiting 300–400 farmers.

3. To rehabilitate and improve existing communal gardens and develop three new ones, one in the first year and two in the second, on the basis of local input. To develop low-cost and easily maintained systems of irrigation for these gardens.

4. To work closely with schools and other extension officers in the project areas and to collaborate with the Ministry of Agriculture and NGOs.

5. To further develop acceptable soya products. To demonstrate and promote these products, especially soya flour supplements, in conjunction with government services and also in conjunction with Plenty's overall nutrition education programme in the area.

6. To train local counterparts for the management and implementation of the programme and explore means of increasing local inputs through integration with government services and mutual aid associations so that a self-reliant support and management structure is built on local need and input.

7. To generate employment, particularly through training and the use of local inputs.

8. To further engage Canadian volunteers in solving development problems and thereby build up their skills and understanding in locally directed, integrated rural development. To further collectivize and share experiences with government services, NGOs, the public, and international agencies in Lesotho and Canada.

9. To further integrate agricultural activities with projects providing woodlots, orchards, water, and education in nutrition, socio-sanitation and environmental control.

10. To implement the projects in such a way that the local women feel comfortable with their involvement and are able to express their leadership roles within the schemes.

The project is financially supported by Plenty Canada and the Lesotho Government. It is an agricultural development programme designed to focus on the poorer, less prosperous areas of the south (Quthing and Qacha's Nek). It emphasizes the participation of youth and women in the socio-economic development of Lesotho. It also stresses watershed management and soil conservation with great emphasis being placed on grassroot participation of villagers. Lesotho's Five Year Development Plan (1984–90) greatly supports Plenty's efforts.

Plenty has been active in Lesotho since 1979. The Quthing River Valley was incorporated into its programmes in 1980. It advocates integrated rural development involving village water supply, afforestation, sanitation, orchard establishment, education and training, and agricultural production.

The programme had two phases:

Phase One
– basic research on legumes, including soya beans
– communal gardens (vegetables)

Phase Two
– use of Phase One data to consolidate the potential for improved income production and nutrition in the area

Makoae is the resource centre from which Plenty activities are extended to other parts of the country.

Protein deficiency is one of the main problems facing the Basotho today. Soya bean production and processing is of vital importance in trying to redress this situation. About 90 women are involved in Quthing Valley, 15 women in Mafeteng district (Qhoqhoane), ten in Berea district (Thupa-Kubu) and five in Leribe district.

The technology includes conventional equipment used in field crop production, namely oxen-drawn implements. In the soy bean dairy the following devices are used:

– traditional grinding stone (*leloala la Sesotho*)
– casseroles
– buckets for soaking beans overnight
– cloths for sieving
– press for making soy cheese/tofu
– a clock.

Another programme is the community garden at Quthing Valley where 12 women participate in vegetable production. Forestry establishment is also emphasized. It consists of the nursery (fruit trees and trees for firewood). There are 6000–7000 fruit and firewood seedlings ready for planting.

Special projects

7.1 Taung-Phamong Integrated Rural Development Project
This is a project of the Lesotho Government and CIDA (Saskatchewan, Canada). It is involved in village water supplies, soil conservation, water harvesting, rural roads, and communal gardens. The project is implemented in Mohale's Hoek in the southern part of the country.

Technology used includes piping, stone and cement water tanks, picks, spades, shovels, wheelbarrows, rakes, digging forks, seeds for vegetables, trees (fruit and forestry), fencing materials, and Scotch carts.

Table 15 Population benefiting from the project activities and having access to technology used

Project activity	Number of women
Village water supply	3098
Soil conservation	340
Water harvesting	85
Rural roads	450
Communal gardens	240
Total	4213

7.2 Lesotho Agricultural Development Bank (LADB)

This Bank provides credit/loan facilities for agricultural-based enterprises. All Basotho entrepreneurs who satisfy the following conditions are eligible:

(*a*) Mosotho national.

(*b*) A married man.

(*c*) A married woman with her husband's permission.

(*d*) A widow/divorcee/spinster with a chief's letter of approval.

(*e*) Payment of an application fee of M10 and security/collateral equal to 50% of the credit/loan amount requested.

(*f*) Availability of the market.

(*g*) Knowledge of the technological device in question.

(*h*) A new mill has to be purchased.

(*i*) The applicant has to open an account with LADB.

(*j*) The entrepreneur should inform the Bank of problems faced during the operation.

Interest rate is 12% on the loan. Repayment of the loan will be after five years from the initiation of the project.

Husbands are ready to give permission for their wives to procure LADB services. This is due to the fact that farming activities remain the responsibility of the women during the absence of the men who are working in the mines in the Republic of South Africa. Chiefs have always given credentials to widows/divorcees/single women who have proven credibility to run their household and national responsibilities effectively and efficiently.

LADB has given loan assistance to Basotho to enable them to purchase hammer-mills.

These mills are installed in the rural areas, implying that the mills are at the disposal of women, who represent about 60 per cent of the rural population. Figures on women having access to hammer-mills could be given.

LADB provides services to co-operative societies involved in food production. Seasonal, medium- and long-term loans are provided. Services for short-term loans cover the following: working capital, repairs, diesel fuel, rabbit-farming, pullets and broilers, poultry and livestock feeds,

174

Table 16 Hammer-mills loaned to farmers by year and numbers

Year	Number of hammer-mills loaned to farmers
1985	10
1986	3
1987	33
1988	10

feedlotting, bulk purchasing of agricultural implements, ox-drawn implements, insurance premiums, draught oxen, and tractor reconditioning. Medium-term loans cater for second-hand tractors, tractor implements, poultry units, hammer-mills, poultry equipment, breeders, livestock, pig units, commercial trucks, dairy cows, irrigated vegetable production, wool and mohair production. Long-term loans are for tractors and implements, orchards, irrigated lucerne production.

Table 17 Assistance given to Basotho farmers by LADB and type of loans in 1987, by month

Month	Short-term		Medium- term		Long-term	
	Co-ops	Indivi-duals	Co-ops	Indivi-duals	Co-ops	Indivi-duals
January	–	3	–	1	–	2
February	–	6	–	3	–	2
March	–	10	–	4	–	0
April	–	13	–	10	–	0
May	1	11	–	10	–	4
June	–	11	–	7	–	2
July	–	11	–	16	–	2
August	–	19	–	15	–	6
September	10	52	–	27	–	9
October	36	108	–	21	–	14
November	39	162	–	24	–	7
December	11	87	–	6	–	1
Total	97	493	–	144	–	49

Total membership in co-operative societies is 3965 of which 80–90 per cent are women.

7.3 Seforong Women's Integrated Rural Development Project
The main emphasis of this programme is provision of services to the rural

175

community of Seforong in Quthing District. The donors are the Lesotho Government and USCC. The project started operating in 1983 and is benefiting about 1166 women and 999 men (533 households). Activities include the following: water supply, health clinics, sanitation, transport and road improvement, agriculture (poultry, vegetables, forestry, co-operatives), primary school improvement, Hareeng High School improvement, and a women's sewing brigade.

The project is administered by the Interministerial Steering Committee with the Women's Bureau as the Chairman of the Steering Committee. The functions of the committee are to:

(*a*) set up policies to guide implementation.

(*b*) review goals and objectives and set up targets and new directions (through quarterly meetings).

(*c*) consider the quarterly budget.

(*d*) evaluate and appraise sub-projects and initiate requests for funding of these etc.

Equipment used includes spades, shovels, wheelbarrows, rakes, tape (for measuring), fencing. Locally available materials are used whenever possible, for example, water storage tanks are built of cement and stone. Piping is used to convey water throughout the project area. Ventilated Improved Pit (VIP) latrines are made of planks and corrugated iron.

There is one operational communal garden and two poultry co-operatives, for layers and broilers. The broiler co-operative has three members. Poultry farmers use the following equipment for their enterprises: fencing, nesting boxes, perches, waterers, and feeders. Nesting boxes and perches were built by the farmers themselves.

Forestry establishment and fruit-tree planting programmes are progressing well. Over 400 trees were sold in early 1988 for establishing fuelwood lots.

7.4 Thabana-Li-Mele Training Centre for Women

This is a tripartite project of the Lesotho Government, SIDA and UN-VFDW whose first phase was implemented in 1982. Its objectives are:

Long-term: To encourage the self-sufficiency of rural women.

Immediate: To establish relevant structures for training rural women including the following:

(i) Agriculture and agro-based activities.

(ii) Handicrafts.

(iii) Appropriate technology.

(iv) Management.

(v) Daily life skills (sanitation, family planning, health, etc.).

The present researcher was interested in appropriate technology, in which 150 women were trained. Devices emphasized were water jars (85); solar dryers (125); and stone paolas (100). In food production techniques

1625 women were trained. A total of 1775 women received training in technology for food security. Among these, 291 received training in leadership.

Phase One of the project has elapsed and negotiations are being conducted on Phase Two, whose objectives are:

Long-term:

(i) National self-sufficiency in those areas where this is possible. There is no doubt that the improvement of womenpower will lead to a partial realization of this objective.

(ii) Local-level formulation, implementation, and evaluation of development plans. It is through a wholesale improvement of the socio-economic status of women that this objective can be realized.

(iii) The formulation of effective policies that will integrate women in productive and income-earning activities with a view to curbing rural–urban migration, and reduce the negative effects of unemployment, particularly among young women.

(iv) Continuous analysis of problems facing women and the design of model plans and programmes for integrating them in development, both locally and nationally.

Immediate:

(i) The strengthening of the Women's Bureau enabling it to formulate short- and long-term policies on women, and in particular facilitate the incorporation of women's issues in sectoral plans and programmes.

(ii) Carrying out baseline surveys/studies to assess the needs of women and recommend ways in which these needs can be met.

(iii) Based on identified needs, the design of practical curricula that will emphasize practical skills and improve women's income-earning capacity.

(iv) The isolating of laws that adversely affect women and the drafting of amendments for consideration by policy-makers.

(v) The establishment of a Women's Resource Centre and a system of information, dissemination, and publicity on the rights of women.

(vi) The setting up of administrative systems at the Thabana-Li-Mele Centre and the establishment of effective programmes in the Women's Bureau.

(vii) Short- and long-term fellowships for both the Women's Bureau and Thabana-Li-Mele staff.

(viii) Assisting groups of women to develop their own businesses by identifying at the national level economic sectors suitable for self-employment initiatives, providing training opportunities, identifying openings at the local level, providing technical and credit support.

(ix) The setting up of a viable marketing system for products of women's groups.

(x) Improvement of the management systems of the revolving fund and provision of technical services to projects so funded.

(xi) The establishment of a women's counselling service in the Women's Bureau aimed at improving gender relations and helping women realize their potential.

Phase Two will emphasize the establishment of a physical framework as the resource base for skills training. At Thabana-Li-Mele women will be trained in skills necessary for self-sufficiency, that is, food production, storage devices for food, appropriate technology for processing and preparation of food, and firewood production.

7.5 Catholic Relief Services (CRS)

CRS runs health clinics in Catholic Church premises throughout Lesotho. Supervisors of the clinics realized women need cash in order to provide for household services, and so CRS started a pilot project of oilseed production and oil extraction from sunflowers. The project was initiated at five centres, namely, St Ann (Peka), St Rose (Peka), Ts'akholo (Mafeteng), St Rodrique (Mafeteng), and St James (Mokhotlong).

The programme is suffering a setback since the promoter went for training. CRS is making efforts to revive the schemes, for Lesotho has proven great potential for sunflower production.

Technology used for land preparation, seeding, weeding, harvesting is the same as that used in other field crops. In the processing of the sunflower seeds for oil extraction the following devices are used:

(i) Power Husker 'LO'.
(ii) Hand Grain Winnower.
(iii) CECOCO Oil Expeller.
(iv) CECOCO Filter Press.

These devices are imported from Japan and cannot be purchased from local suppliers. This poses maintenance and repair problems.

7.6 Basotho fruit and vegetable canners

This is a special facility that markets fruits and vegetables. It preserves foodstuffs and packs them for the local and international markets. It is situated at Masianokeng, 15km from the capital Maseru. The complex deals in asparagus, peaches, beans, and peas. All farmers can send their produce to the cannery, but it does not have mobile units to collect produce. Plans are underway to involve other districts.

7.7 Matlama farmers' equipment by Lesotho Steel

Lesotho Steel started the construction of Matlama Agricultural Implements in 1985. The main purpose of the project was to design versatile farm implements specifically to suit national conditions. The implements, designed for primary and secondary operations, can be pulled by animal and tractor power. The important breakthrough of Matlama is the construction of a single, green, high-grade steel frame which is the base to which a plough, cultivator, harrow, and planter/fertilizer can be attached. The system has been tested in other parts of Africa and has been adapted to national conditions. A number of implements has been introduced.

The project manager reported statistics on Matlama's achievements.

The implements are distributed to all districts of the country. The devices are supplied by private traders and government projects/programmes. Most farming activities are run by women, so it is safe to say that women have access to these implements. Actual figures on women's access could not be given.

Table 18 Yearly production

Product	1981–2	1982–3	1983–4	1984–5	1985–6	1986–7	1987–8
Asparagus in brine		15,154	13,159	28,000	26,252	32,853 (460g) 799 (410g) 89 (tube can)	46,934 (460g) 725 (410g)
Asparagus soup						4836	
Green beans in brine						2581	3042
				4349	4890	(cuts) 6	(cuts) 115
Peaches		2939	798		475	82	
Beans in tomato sauce	8967	6054	12,600	19,300	1025		

Table 19 Annual asparagus yield records

Year	Number of farmers	Acreage harvested (ha)	Total yield (tons)	Yield per hectare in tons
1976	96	19.58	5.8	0.30
1977	61	12.30	9.50	1.30
1978	141	24.84	39.90	1.60
1979	229	39.00	85.50	2.20
1980	290	53.78	107.00	3.50
1981	266	48.61	170.00	3.50
1982	257	47.22	181.00	3.80
1983	245	45.30	158.00	3.50
1984	260	50.50	231.00	4.60
1985	289	54.54	255.40	4.70
1986	383	77.20	422.00	5.50

Table 20 Type of equipment designed (annual achievements)

Type of equipment	Numbers produced
Multipurpose all-in-one frame	311
Ox-yoke	416
Cultivator	76
Plough	81
Harrow	56
Planter	166

7.8 Senakangoeli Solar Energy Project

Senakangoeli specializes in harnessing the sun's energy for cooking, heating water, and drying food (fruits and vegetables). The system for heating water for household needs consists of a water tank, insulation, glazing, housing and base plate, and absorber. The working principle is based on convection currents, namely, that heated water rises and cold water sinks. Heated water is sent into the house by means of convectional pipes. Two food dryers have been sold to Lesotho, one to a farmer in Maseru district and the other to Plenty Lesohto at Makoae's in Quthing district. Eight solar fridges were sold to women in 1987. There is great potential for the use of solar energy. Plans are underway to develop the following devices:

(i) Solar stove – steam combustion stove

(ii) Solar sewing machines

(iii) Solar lights which will be used at night.

7.9 People's Participation Project

This is a joint Government/FAO project. Its main objective is to encourage integrated rural development to improve the life of people of Ramabanta, Tiali, and Raleqheka areas in the Maseru district. Activities include a piggery, poultry (layers and broilers), knitting, sewing, communal gardens, and crop farming. The project caters for 355 households, each of six members. That implies that the total number of people involved is 2130. Female participation is 95 per cent, 2024 women.

Poultry is kept in deep litter systems. Local materials are used for constructing the poultry houses (wooden poles and mud for walls). Poles and corrugated iron are used for roofing.

Training is emphasized in agricultural techniques, leadership, and co-operatives. There are 22 co-operatives registered in the area of operation. The participants have credit facilities. The repayment rate of credit has been recorded as 67 per cent. A better repayment rate would result if members formulated their own credit policy. The project has carried out education campaigns on credit administration.

A problem is lack of training facilities for the groups at the project site. Lack of transport is another constraint.

7.10 Village water supplies

This is a project conducted and funded jointly by the Government and USAID. Its main purpose is provision of clean water for village households, and water for communal and individually owned gardens. The project started operations in 1981. At the beginning about 14.1 per cent of the rural population had been served with clean water supplies; by December 1986, this had risen to 38 per cent.

In 1986, 459,810 women were benefiting from the project and 34.4% of the total population was receiving clean water for home use by December 1986. New technologies used were simple spring protection, gravity hand pumps, and power pumping, alongside picks, pipes, and water tanks. Training in their maintenance and proper use is vital. In most cases the majority of people working on installation are women. The 1986 figures were an increase from the 146,160 women involved in the use of clean water in 1981.

Table 21 Population served with clean water indicating improvement from 1981–86

District	Number of villages served		Total population served		Total population		% served	
	1981	1986	1981	1986	1981	1986	1981	1986
Butha-Buthe	32	85	16,200	44,600	76,400	89,000	21.2	50.1
Leribe	53	107	29,500	84,400	201,800	253,600	14.6	33.3
Berea	52	138	22,900	75,500	140,900	159,500	16.3	47.3
Maseru	54	161	23,700	78,900	202.600	199,400	11.7	39.6
Mafeteng	48	155	17,900	78,300	153,800	186,100	11.6	42.1
Mohale's Hoek	33	150	9600	71,400	137,700	164,600	7.0	43.4
Quthing	36	56	10,500	28,200	89,000	106,300	11.8	26.5
Qacha's Nek	47	56	12,900	18,100	37,400	46,000	34.5	39.3
Thaba-Tseka	23	44	6,800	15,900	37,000	45,000	18.4	35.3
Mokhotlong	53	62	12,400	15,600	75,400	89,000	16.4	17.5
Total	431	1041	162,400	510,900	1,152,000	1,338,500	14.1	38.2

8. Results, analysis, conclusion, and recommendations

Activities in food production and food security have been of major importance in Lesotho since time immemorial. Traditional methods of food production involved the use of simple home-made devices; seeding, harvesting, threshing, and winnowing were manual operations.

In the early 1930s there came the age of simple farm machines – steel ploughs, planters, cultivators, chemicals for pest control, and maize shellers. The devices were ox-drawn. The period from the 1930s till now witnessed the development and use of complex farm machines drawn by tractors. At present there are ox- and tractor-drawn devices.

Food processing and food preservation have also experienced changes. Traditional methods included food drying, grinding, simple cooking, etc. Modern processes are canning (tins and bottles), and the replacement of many manual operations by those performed mechnically by large plants of agro-industries (the Cannery, Lesotho Flour Mills, and the Maize Mill). Food drying is now done by solar dryers and air blowers (for grains in grain storages).

Government and non-governmental organizations have realized that most individuals fail to acquire large, expensive, and complicated technological devices. This fact prompted these agencies to develop policies on provision of appropriate technology, which it is expected will be installed at the homestead to facilitate women's access.

The research results indicated that about 56,070 women (7 per cent) have access to the technology used in food production, food storage and food processing. It is also realized that the actual percentage of women having access to appropriate technology is only 1 per cent. Supportive services like village water suplies, sanitation, and storage facilities are also crucial to food security programmes. It is reported by the Village Water Supply Section of the Ministry of Interior, Chieftainship Affairs, and Rural Development, that 510,900 rural people had been provided with clean water by the end of 1986, 90 per cent of whom were women; of the total population, 30 per cent, and 58.2 per cent of all women, receive clean water.

A FNCO report indicated that there are storage facilities for food grains throughout the country. These can be used for storing food aid supplies, agricultural inputs, and implements. It is safe to say that the total female population (790,000) has access to stores reported to be available nationally. The only constraint is distance.

Table 22 Summary of services and facilities accessible to women

Facility/infrastructure	Number of women having access to device	Percentage of total women's population having access to device
Appropriate technology	7900	1
Technology in general	56,070	7
Village water supply	510,900	64.7
Sanitation	N/A	N/A
Storage facilities	790,000	100

The implication is that all women have access to some form of technology either for storage, provision of essential services, or general purposes. Very few women have access to appropriate technology devices.

It is clear from the literature review that very few publications have articles on technology for food security. ATS publishes in English, not in the local language. A lot of information does not reach the greatest part of the female population who speak and understand Sesotho only, or better than English.

The coverage of the newsletters by Agricultural Information is very limited. They are written in Sesotho and are free, but are normally sent to areas easily reached by the extension agents of the Ministry of Agriculture. There is no systematic method for their distribution to village, ward, and district development councils. It is worth noting that the articles in newsletters, newspapers, and brochures are well illustrated with diagrams and pictures or photographs. Very little publicity on technology for food security is done through radio or newspapers. Little training for women in construction skills and use of technological devices is conducted.

Greater efforts have to be taken to devise a systematic policy on technological development for food security. Women will have to be incorporated at all the stages of proposals, planning, implementation, monitoring, and evaluation of technological development and innovation.

SADCC Co-ordinating Unit publishes a quarterly newsletter on soil and water conservation and land utilization. They fail to reach the largest part of the rural population, since the medium of communication is English and not Sesotho. The newsletters address the technocrats only.

8.1 Recommendations

1. The Renewable Technology Committee should be reactivated and publicized.
2. A survey on endogenous and traditional technology should be conducted with emphasis on its strengthening and improvement before promotion of foreign technology.
3. Policy on technology for food security should be formulated with immediate effect. Women to be involved in proposals.
4. Publicity, education, and training on technology for food security to be emphasized strongly in the next two years to cover about half of the female population in Lesotho. Articles to be written in English and Sesotho.
5. Educational and training institutions should include courses on technology for food security with immediate effect (especially institutions for women). Both official languages to be used as media of instruction.
6. Exhibitions on technology (traditional and modern) on food security to be carried out regularly at all development levels with rewards for the most appropriate devices.

7. Subjects on technological devices for food security to be included in curriculums and syllabuses for all levels of education up to technical institutions and University.
8. National and international networking to be promoted for staff in Government and non-government organizations involved in technological devices and women as the potential benefactors.
9. Manpower Development Secretariat to organize scholarships for higher education and training on technology for food security.
10. All organizations involved in food security to keep proper statistics on beneficiaries or target groups as a basis for planning, implementation, monitoring, and evaluation.
11. Serious efforts have to be carried out to develop a major national construction industry for the manufacture of technological devices for food security. The distribution of such devices should be so well-planned that they are within easy reach of every Mosotho woman at:
   – village level
   – ward level
   – district level
   – national level
   Devices for home use should be produced in large numbers so that every woman has access. Promotion of locally produced devices to be conducted effectively.
12. Storage facilities for food, agricultural inputs, and implements at all development levels is needed, especially at village level.
13. Thabana-Li-Mele Training Centre for Women should emphasize skills training in appropriate technology and recognize the existing traditional technological and scientific base.
14. A national task force/technological council to be formed consisting of educated and grassroots members which will be responsible for promotion of technological development.
15. Credit/loan policies to be revised and reformulated to provide women with funds to purchase the technology that will enable them to participate effectively and efficiently in comprehensive food security activities (food production, preparation, preservation, distribution, storage, and energy).
16. An effort should be made to establish an efficient marketing network.

9

Swaziland

1. Introduction

This paper will try to address the conference topic in general, and specifically how and for whom technology should be used in the developing countries.

In discussing the issue of women in Southern Africa we should bear in mind that they are part of a whole and their situation should be viewed as such. We must therefore discuss science and technology in education, agriculture, and industry. Then we must consider the grass-roots approach to technology for development, taking account of local technical ability and the social forces needed to set up appropriate technology institutions, after which the case of Swaziland will be reviewed.

From Swaziland's point of view, the paper will describe the government's agricultural policy and whether it addresses the needs of women farmers or not; the tools used for agricultural purposes; preparing the land and ploughing; types of irrigation schemes; fertilizers; pre-harvest problems and pest control; harvesting operations and the division of labour; grain ring methods and the division of labour; pest problems and control; threshing/shelling methods and the division of labour for threshing, winnowing, and loading the store; storage methods for shelled grain and the division of labour for construction, purchase of storage containers, pest problems and control; homesteads selling grain and division of labour in bagging, transport, and marketing of produce; forest land use; livestock; and energy.

Women's participation in agriculture is a topic of major concern in most developing countries of the world. While it is true that traditionally women are mainly responsible for tasks around the home, there is enough evidence to support the fact that women also play a very important role in farming. Yet their participation in agricultural activities has not been addressed specifically in national development plans or in SADCC programmes, and is only implied in the general formulations. The concern has been the development of self-sufficiency in food production without improving the lot of the producers in the rural areas, who are mostly women.

When discussing the topic of Women and Technology we must study agricultural production as a whole and identify the areas in which women could intensify their production efforts.

To increase production by small-scale producers developing countries need simple, cheap, and effective technology which may be met by specifically designed 'intermediate' techniques. Another obvious approach, when one thinks of it, is to recycle surplus equipment from the throw-away

185

societies of the industrialized countries, equipment which, although in perfect condition, is no longer used merely because it has been outmoded by new fashions and designs.

Therefore, SADCC needs a factory to recycle all the equipment now not in use in member states in order to develop the needed machinery. This would be less expensive than manufacturing from scratch and spare parts would be readily available. There is also a need for a regional central supply agency. Technological dependence is incompatible with cultural, economic, and political independence, but there is no need for everyone to invent the wheel. However, it must also be remembered that a technological environment can be hostile to social development and that tinkering with nature can be dangerous.

For technology, whether derived from home or abroad, to be compatible with development, each country should formulate a comprehensive and coherent national science and technology policy designed as part of its national plan to contribute to the achievement of its development objectives.

The aim of our meeting here is to look into the role played by women, to take stock of the tools they use and how these can be improved in the food cycle so that food self-sufficiency can be attained. We have to make sure that the political will and commitment from our governments are forthcoming so that recommendations are put into practice.

When we talk about 'appropriate technology' we understand that this is a substitute for and not a complement to the establishment of a new international order, where there is socio-economic and political change not only in relations between different states, but within states in both the developed and the developing countries, changes which should be ordered, coordinated, and of benefit to everyone.

1.1 Applying science and technology to development

Science and technology are a means of understanding and action which enable human beings to alter their surroundings. But, like any tools, they can be used well or badly.

The technology that we as women talk about is that which will make us live better and meet our priority needs for food, clothing, housing, as well as energy, transport, and communication. Science should broaden our horizons, enrich our imagination, and continue to stimulate innovation. Scientific methods used fully, not as a key to separation but as an element of relations between things, can give human beings safer and wiser means of working in harmony with their environment and with one another.

Scientific and technical knowledge has long been the province of specialists; it must be opened up to everyone. There is a need for technical know-how at all levels, the transmission of traditional skills being a vital component, as they are an integral part of technological solutions as a whole and make progress a richer process.

We in developing countries need to create an endogenous capacity for innovation at the national level, so as to avoid massive imports of foreign technology, which are harmful to development in the long run. This capacity for innovation involves:

- training technicians with a general grounding and enough technical and scientific skills to deal with the interaction between the scientific, technical, and social problems they encounter in industry, crafts, and agriculture;
- making the whole population aware of what is involved and introducing them to the problems, at various levels.

Education, therefore, as a public service, should be able to provide pupils and students, and the whole of the population, with the means they need to deal with the main problems posed by the rapid development of science and technology. 'Emphasis should be given to the development of technologies for small-scale and agro-based industries, which are essential for rural development.'[1]

Technology is not new in Africa. Traditional technology has been used for different reasons in differing situations. Many of these techniques have been supplanted or simply fallen into disuse and been forgotten. In most cases, foreign conquest and occupation were accompanied by the importation of more advanced technologies (i.e. more mechanically elaborate techniques) which apparently allowed societies who adopted them to respond more efficiently to their members' basic needs.

Most of the goods produced by the new techniques were available only through purchase and as societies became more firmly integrated into a monetary economy, the decreasing values of their agricultural produce, as related to prices of manufactured goods, meant a lowering of real income and of access to such goods for a large percentage of the population.

Cultural and economic domination has led to a general ideological context in which indigenous technologies are often regarded as irrational, or even uncivilized and primitive. Only those techniques and sciences which follow the disciplinary structures of European or American schools are regarded as valid, although these disciplines developed at the same time as, and to a great extent because of, the needs of the social groups which control economies which dominate the world today. In some cases, the belief in the power inherent in large-scale imported machines, the techniques, and their accompanying technicians to 'develop' society appears almost fetishistic and serves to hide the increased economic dependence which often results.

This ideological domination has led to valid endogenous technologies being ignored or even pushed out of collective consciousness (although they well be revived if people are questioned) and little or no time has been spent in attempting to improve them. Unless this is done rapidly, will not many of these valuable techniques and their technologies disappear with traditional society itself?

1.2 The grass-roots approach to technology for development

'Traditional technologies must be better known, must be improved upon and not blissfully admired just because they are traditional.'[2]

Governments should make sure that when policies of autonomy in food production are planned and implemented in order to counter the declining nutritional levels of the poor, they should not turn to the type of exogenous technology which leads to a further alienation of the poorer rural people. This can occur through loss of land rights (particularly true for women in settlement schemes) and increased economic dependence because of the need to import vast quantities of fertilizer, agricultural implements and spare parts, petrol for machines, cement and steel for the silos and factories, and the technicians themselves to make the whole thing work.

Without doubt, patterns of development are necessary which will respond more closely to people's basic needs and take into account their value systems and the type of society in which they wish to live. In order to achieve this, alternative development strategies of self-reliance will have to be worked out.

If inventiveness and creative work are to play their full part, the conditions for their development must exist.

- Care must be taken that the creativity of a few is not stimulated at the expense of the majority.
- The increased use of environmentally sound and appropriate technologies will not come about by spontaneous growth; the ideas and their applications must be borne by different social groups in society.
- Institutions at grass-roots and community levels, such as women's groups, must be built up to allow techniques, technology, and science to be used towards achieving the goal of increased self-reliance. They should have varied aims, different functions, and be active at different levels of society, e.g. in market gardening, backyard poultry-raising for income generation and providing better food for their children, or by the community building a dam for irrigating their plots of land.

Other institutions would be more concerned with integrated health, education, agricultural and livestock production, cottage industry, and soil protection.

1.3 Local technical ability

Awareness of existing technical capacity will probably be a first step to effective control of new technologies. This means helping people to become aware that they already possess a considerable amount of technology:

- Traditional technologies, together with more recent endogenous introductions and inventions, must become better known and improved upon.
- Direct exchanges between development groups facing similar problems will become necessary and should take place throughout the subregion.

188

- Another type of institutional structure would be charged with assisting village and work groups active over a fairly small area of rural extension services (e.g. agriculture, home economics, community development) under a unified command or more technically specialized units working on a larger scale.
- On an even larger scale – national, sub-regional, and regional – it will be necessary for institutions to collect and disseminate information on the use of technology in progress in order to encourage and stimulate existing groups and support units to reply to specific queries. These groups should work on general integration of technical themes, or be more specialized as we are here.
- There is also need for research, research-development, and technical experimentation in real-life situations by institutions.

A co-ordinating body formed by the users to control any disjunction between research interest and development problems is necessary.

1.4 The social forces needed to set up appropriate technology institutions

'An overall choice of a self-reliant development strategy at country level will obviously facilitate institutions – building for the effective use of environmentally sound and appropriate technologies. A political institutional framework which will allow and actively encourage local initiatives (rather than merely tolerate, ignore, or even suppress them) is a necessary prerequisite for the effective use of environmentally sound and appropriate technologies on a large scale in any country.'[3]

Administrative structures in general should be geared to undertaking grass-roots action. These structures always standardize production and social control, not as a result of the necessity felt by the grass-roots development institutions, but through bureaucratic habits, centralized technocratic processes, acting from technical rationality and taking away initiative in technical decisions from the people's own institutions.

2. Swaziland Government policy on agriculture

The government policy on agriculture is to assist farmers to achieve higher productivity and income and to become more market oriented. However, the government has always viewed the natural areas in Swazi National Land (SNL) as subsistence farming with maize as the major crop.[4] In this sector family labour and draught animals are employed. 'Such practices definitely lead to low productivity levels.'[5] Agriculture on SNL contributes only 7 per cent to GDP. The land tenure system has been said to be probably the major cause for low productivity in SNL.

Eighty per cent of the total population depends on agriculture and approximately 75 per cent of the female population lives in the rural areas and is directly responsible for the production of all foodstuffs for domestic consumption. The tasks which women perform in the agricultural sector are many and often require hard physical labour. Jobs such as slashing, burning, clearing, and ploughing are mostly done by women in addition to such typical 'female' jobs as planting and transplanting, sowing, weeding, and sorting, as well as feeding and tending animals. Often women are also responsible for food processing and storage and the transportation of farm produce to collecting points.

In a survey on the roles, tasks, needs, and skills of rural women undertaken in 1978–9 it was discovered that 29 per cent of women are involved in the preparation of land, 74.5 per cent in hoeing, and 61.6 per cent in weeding.[6]

2.1 Tools used for agricultural purposes
The evaluation of output levels for different operations has enabled an appreciation of the muscular power available and resulted in the design of various hand tools (principally hoes and cutting blades/knives) whose weight distribution takes maximum advantage of the posture adopted by a human using them and has reduced the arduousness of many manual tasks. The Dutch hoe and the weighting of knives used for sugar-cane chopping are evidence of this new approach.

The survey on the roles, tasks, needs, and skills of rural women mentioned above showed that 6.7 per cent used hoes, 1.2 per cent used spades, 61.6 per cent used ox-drawn ploughs, and 18 per cent used tractors, but the ox-drawn ploughs were mostly operated by men.[7]

Tractor-drawn equipment of the soil-engaging type has also been modified through a greater understanding of the mechanics of the interaction between the implement and the soil, while the quality of work produced has been maintained at much higher operating speeds than those achieved by draught animals. The development of implements and equipment to suit minimal tillage and stubble mulch techniques, which reduce the power and fuel requirements of crop establishment while reducing soil and soil water losses, afforded the farmer a means of instituting a resource-conserving production system at a time when the droughts and cyclones of the 1980s were making the potential productivity of Southern African agriculture based on climatological data an increasingly risky proposition.

With respect to field power sources, 1971 saw the birth of the Tinkhabi tractor (a mechanized system) which could replace draught oxen for all field operations requiring a pulling source without involving a great cost penalty but providing superior work quality and work rates. The system could be easily adapted for water pumping and irrigation, sawing wood, transportation of field inputs and produce. The design simplified most controls to the level where no formal training in tractor or vehicle driving is required to operate the unit in the field. The tractor featured hand-cranking for starting and was initially produced without an electrical system because of the difficulty that many rural workshops or mechanics face in maintaining vehicle electrical systems. The unit has developed to produce an engine output and work capability comparable to a modern agricultural tractor but still does not require formal driving training to operate it. Of all the innovations available to small-scale agriculture, the Tinkhabi mechanized system offers the greatest potential of overcoming the production bottlenecks caused by dependence on animal draught power, at an affordable level.

Small tractors of conventional design have had their productivity improved through the introduction of turbo-charging, which enables a large increase in the power of a diesel engine of a given size with a small penalty in terms of fuel consumption. The availability of four-wheel drive (commonly called front-wheel assist systems) has enabled these higher powered tractors to improve the amount of engine power they generate into a pulling force without making the tractor so heavy as to cause soil compaction and soil structural damage when the tractor has to work in relatively wet conditions. Modern agricultural tractors now offer spring seat design which reduces vibrational and bump effects; by protecting the operator from severe bumping the incidence of spinal and kidney-related ailments is greatly reduced. The modern tractor presents less of a health risk than tractors of the sixties, particularly with respect to the larger vehicles which feature cabs which isolate the driver/operator from heat, noise, and vibration as well as reducing the possible contact the driver/operator has with potentially harmful chemicals during spraying. Modern tractor cabs feature air-conditioning, radio and tape systems, and ergonomically designed controls which reduce the stress level imposed on the driver/operator during the course of a normal day's work in dusty and hot field conditions; this has been shown to improve productivity significantly.

However, 6.7 per cent of the women still use traditional hoes for ploughing, either because they cannot afford to hire ploughs from those who own cattle or tractors, or because neither of these is available in the neighbourhood. Women have always expressed concern about the lack of funds to purchase modern implements such as tractors, in whose operation and maintenance they need to be trained.

2.1.1 Preparing and ploughing the land

Although preparing and ploughing the land is more of a male activity, the survey revealed that 34.7 per cent of women are involved in felling trees and clearing the land, and 39.7 per cent in fertilizing the fields. The male involvement, however, was found to be reasonably high: 54.6 per cent were responsible for preparation of the land and 61.9 per cent for ploughing. Some husbands who are away send remittances home for hired labour.[8]

191

Table 1 Task distribution by age/sex adult males/females over 16 years in percentages (1983)[9]

Activity	Adult males	Adult females
Ploughing	40.7	18.1
Planting	26.6	34.5
Weeding	4.8	48.7
Harvesting	4.4	45.9
Herding	27.8	18.8
Fencing	73.9	10.7
Milking cows	42.1	15.1
Cooking	1.3	77.7
Grinding mealies	1.8	67.7
Collecting firewood	2.3	66.4
Collecting water	1.1	63.4
Selling produce	17.5	70.6
Handicrafts	4.8	90.1
Agricultural work for neighbours	22.6	43.8
Child care	3.3	83.1

As far as agriculture is concerned women spend most of their time weeding (48.7 per cent), followed by harvesting (45.9 per cent), 43.8 per cent of their time doing agricultural work for neighbours, and 34.5 per cent planting. It can be seen from Table 2 that hoeing and weeding are traditionally done by rural women.

Table 2 Assistance in agricultural activities (percentage)[10]

	Husband	Children	Relative or neighbour
Preparing land	19.6	37.3	35.1
Fertilization	25.3	47.4	22.1
Ploughing	21.1	35.1	26.3
Planting	30.4	37.8	25.9
Hoeing	22.6	40.9	29.6
Weeding	12.6	40.8	41.7
Harvesting	23.4	48.1	24.7
Sorting and storing	42.9	23.5	30.3
Preservation	3.2	35.4	61.3

Women are 88.5 per cent responsible for hoeing and 91 per cent for weeding while 12.6 per cent of the time assisted by their husbands, 40.8 per cent their children, and 41.7 per cent by neighbours. The preparation of the land before ploughing was found to be the responsibility of women 34.7 per cent of the time and men 54.6 per cent. This is a very strenuous activity which may involve felling of shrubs or trees, slashing the grass, removing stones, and tilling the soil before fertilization. The women obtained assistance from husbands 19.6 per cent of the time, children 37.3 per cent and relatives/neighbours 35.4 per cent. The survey revealed that in ploughing, planting, hoeing, harvesting, sorting, and storing, women obtained more assistance from children, because most activities take place during the schools' summer and winter breaks. Hired labour for the above activities was found to be higher as compared to assistance for domestic activities because those women who cannot afford the cash for hired labour use crops from their previous harvest to pay for the labour. Weeding, however, took 48.7 per cent of women's time.

The 1975 report on *The Role of Women in Rural Development*[11] stated that 'the efficient use of women in rural development working together with their men is one of the primary means by which improvement in some aspects of agriculture can be brought about, namely, food production, animal husbandry, the land tenure system, physical environment of the area or village'. As shown in the above tables, the agricultural labour force has become predominantly female; the reasons are:

(*a*) more young men are away from their home areas, looking for wages in the urban areas;

(*b*) older men have stopped working and have left their tasks to their young wives;

(*c*) school drop-outs have also migrated to towns for jobs and better living conditions.

2.1.2 Crops grown by women

Although ploughing and crop growing were the best established agricultural male tasks, it is interesting to notice the change in this position. Of the women that took part in the 1978–9 survey, more than 50 per cent were found to be involved in crop growing for consumption as well as for cash.

Crops grown by women are maize, beans, pumpkins, sweet potatoes, sorghum, cotton, tobacco, and vegetables.

The thrust to improve the productivity of small-scale agriculture has included, *inter alia*, the introduction of hybrid seeds and the use of chemical pesticides. The modern raw crop planter (both animal and tractor drawn) available to farmers at this level of production provides for the application of a starter fertilizer at the time of planting and is designed to ensure that fertilizer is not deposited directly alongside the seed but some distance away to reduce the possibility of scorching.

Alternative ways of increasing or improving agricultural production on SNL could include planting at the appropriate time, careful use of pesticides and fertilizers, and the use of high-yielding varieties.[12]

Modern farming has been advocated by many experts as the answer to the problem. The commercialization of agriculture on the SNL entails land capability assessment and proper land use, irrigation and drainage, use of fertilizers and pesticides.

2.2 Irrigation and drainage

Irrigation is a major support of agricultural activity.[13] The dry Middleveld and Lowveld have very erratic rainfalls, therefore crop production in these regions needs irrigation.

The total irrigated area of the country is estimated to be about 37,000ha or about 4 per cent of the cultivated land area. Of this, 35,000ha is given over to large-scale commercial production. The major crops in this sector are sugarcane and citrus, with smaller areas of beans, cotton, and other crops.[14] However, irrigation has not yet gained much ground on SNL. In 1983–4 only about 900ha of land on this subsector was under irrigation, or 0.8 per cent of the total crop area.[15]

2.2.1 Types of irrigation schemes

Furrow irrigation is the dominant system in the country, followed by sprinkler irrigation. The development of drip systems offers a means of high-efficiency use of water in those conditions where supply is limited, while tied ridging offers an opportunity for the ponding of water which would otherwise run off following severe storms. While both systems are still at an evaluation stage for Southern African agriculture, they show a great deal of potential.

Nkambule states that if commercialization of crop production is to be realized on SNL, irrigation should be seriously considered. There are a number of constraints to the acquisition of irrigation equipment by farmers in this subsector. The land tenure system does not give enough security to the farmer so that she/he can take the risk of making investments, particularly when the farmer does not own the land. The Fourth National Development Plan stated that those farmers who took the risk have improved their production tremendously. A lot of encouragement is necessary to persuade other small-scale farmers to follow suit.

Another problem facing the farmers on SNL is lack of access to credit facilities. They rarely have the security required by banks in the country, and those who own cattle are reluctant to risk losing their stock.

The establishment of such schemes as Vuvulane Irrigated Farms and KaLanga Irrigation on unused arable land, with facilities such as tractors made available to the RDAP, may provide the answer to such problems.

However, certain improvements will be necessary, including:
- Self-motivation and farming ability must be the major criteria in the selection of farmers, unlike what was done at Vuvulane where these were treated as advantages rather than criteria.[16]
- Giving priority to those farmers who take the initiative to establish private schemes but are limited by financial resources. The interest in such schemes was demonstrated by on Vuvulane Irrigated Farms.

194

– Farmers should be enabled to buy land in instalments, as was done in part of Vuvulane. With more security perhaps more farmers would be willing to make investments and the individual/private irrigation schemes, which are considered to be a success, would flourish. Women would form co-operatives and invest in such schemes.

Nkambule argues that such a proposition implies the introduction of private ownership on SNL; but how else can the message be conveyed to farmers that their children will not be able to get more land and that they must improve the productivity of what they have, protect the land from degradation and plan their family property?

There is evidence of improved crop production as a consequence of irrigation in Swaziland. However, irrigation, like all other modern agricultural activities, is not without risk. For example, inefficient management may lead to the wastage of up to 90 per cent of the water obtained at great cost from specially built dams[17] such as the Mnjoli and Sand River dams. The use of canals might have negative effects promoting vector-borne diseases.[18] Bilharzia is considered endemic in Vuvulane, while malaria and diarrhoea are common.[19]

There is need for individual and collective efforts to educate the community about the dangers of misusing irrigation water. Such water should be treated, in addition to providing clean water in the areas.

Soil degradation is probably the most serious negative effect of irrigation and may be irreversible.[20] 'Irrigation of soils ill-adapted to those methods and irrigation accompanied by drainage that is insufficient to leach out salts or to prevent their surfacing along with rising water tables already naturally at a high level may lead to salinization of the soil and/or water.'[21]

Irrigation of steep slopes and furrows may cause serious erosion of the land. It may also be a major cause of groundwater depletions where the resource is tapped to the limits of aquifer capacity and at rates exceeding that of recharge. However, considering the expenses involved in tapping underground water for large irrigation schemes it is not expected that the use of this source is going to develop into a serious problem.

Therefore, the protection of land from harmful effects of irrigation needs education on technical skills as well as the introduction and enforcement of legislation.[22] Such technical information could be disseminated through workshops, seminars and conferences, demonstrations, and an effective extension programme.

2.3 Fertilizers and ameliorants

Fertilizer use and improvements of agricultural production are inseparable entities.[23] The trend in the use of fertilizer has been said by Nkambule not to be clear. In 1980–81 about 47,500 tonnes were used, but in 1985–6 the figure fluctuated.[24] However, the fourth National Development Plan implies an increase. The commercialization of agriculture demands the use of fertilizers. Land high in fertility will be 'exhausted' and there is going to be a need to use substantial amounts of inorganic fertilizers.[25]

The effective use of fertilizer can make it possible not only to increase yields but to concentrate production on the most promising lands and by so doing bring relief to marginal lands where cropping might cause ecological dangers.[26] Therefore, the use of fertilizers should be encouraged but not without due consideration of their possible impact on the environment, in particular:
- The efficiency with which they are used by crops.
- Possible contamination of streams and rivers.

2.4 Pesticides

The behaviour of pesticides used in agriculture is of practical interest from two standpoints: they are essential in order to maximize returns from their use and, just like fertilizers, form an integral part of improved food production. Without them crops would be ravaged by disease, insect pests, and weeds, and these would lead to severe loss of food production.

The development of the ultra low volume (ULV) sprayer has enabled many farmers to carry out their spraying programmes even when water is not readily available. This lightweight sprayer uses chemical formulations that do not require further dilution, and the width of action of the sprayers allows 2-3 rows of crop to be treated at a time because it makes great use of natural air currents to drift spray. Droplet size reduces the periods in the day when the sprayer needs be used in order to maintain some control over the extent of spray drifts. This sprayer represents a technological breakthrough because of the lack of mixing of chemicals (which is potentially dangerous), and because of the sprayer's ability to reduce the amount of field time allocated for spraying and the fact that water is not required for the operation. The ULV sprayer uses ordinary torch cell batteries to run a small electric motor which drives a disc at high rotational speeds (10–15,000 rev/min), to atomize small amounts of spray concentrate fed to the spinning disc at a low flow rate.

The light weight of the sprayer makes for a very easy operation compared to having to carry a knapsack sprayer weighing 20–25kg and to pump it at the same time to maintain pressure.

It has not been possible to quantify the benefits accruing to the use of pesticides in Swaziland because:
- their use and that of high-yielding varieties are being adopted simultaneously;
- such a project would require experts and substantial funds, two things the country does not have.

Of the major crops grown in Swaziland cotton is the one on which most pesticides are used. Sugarcane, vegetables, pineapples, and maize may be considered the other major beneficiaries of the technology. Insect control

196

may raise yields by 100 per cent in rainfed cotton and over 600 per cent under irrigation.[27] Weed competition in the initial stages of crop growth can be so severe that the final yield would be a small fraction of the crop's potential on a piece of land. Most of the weed control in the country is done manually, and is not only enslaving but also time-consuming. In the commercialization of farming modern techniques must be adopted.

The only alternatives for farmers are mechanical cultivation and the use of herbicides. The latter has the advantage of making possible the practice of minimal or no tillage. The use of herbicides like paraquat, followed by direct drilling of the seed, would not only save fuel but would reduce the severity of erosion and conserve soil moisture.

Pesticides are also used to control ectoparasites in domestic livestock. Without their use meat and milk production would seriously decline. Dipping is the main control measure against ectoparasites. To counter the resistance developed by ticks to arsenicals, alternatives such as triatix are used.

DDT and Dieldrin do not conform to the attributes of ideal pesticides. DDT is a great problem because it is said to accumulate in the fat of animals and humans without decomposing, is toxic to birds and fish, and eradicates beneficial insects. The treatment of aphids and spider mites with DDT may eradicate the natural enemies of the pests and thus lead to outbreaks in subsequent years.[28] This pesticide has been banned in other countries and Swaziland has to follow suit. Dieldrin has all the attributes of DDT except that it is less persistent. The two chemicals can be substituted by other chemicals even though the substitutes may be more expensive.

Among the herbicides a chemical called 'Hyva' used by pineapple growers may pose a danger of desertification.[29] Where the herbicide has been used it is difficult to grow other crops such as maize and cabbages. Hyva is also suspected to remain for long periods in the soil.[30]

Today pesticides are accepted as a component of an integral control approach in which all available techniques are blended to minimize the damage caused by pests with the least disturbance of the environment.

2.4.1 Pre-harvest problems and pest control

Such problems occur when insects damage the crop, and include weevil infestation as well as stalk-borers. Mould and rat damage result from delayed harvesting because it is done by hand.

Insect problems seem significant in the middle and high veld and in Lumombo, but mould and rodent problems taken together have been observed as more serious. Late rains cause damage by logging a late-sown crop and rotting the cob where late harvesting occurs in early-sown crops. Bird attack is regarded as minimal but cattle sometimes stray into the field.

2.5 Harvesting operations – division of labour

Delays in harvesting occur due to shortage of labour and the dependence of the women on the labour of children. As a result crops remain in the fields long after they are mature and harvesting is spread over a long period of time (up to 3-4 weeks), with portions of the field being harvested as time permits. Harvesting may be done by cutting the plant and stooking it in heaps with the cobs in the sheath attached to the stalk.

Another method is to de-husk the cob in a standing crop and heap the exposed cobs in a convenient spot in the field. This heap is then covered with a few plant stalks. If transport is not readily available to take the harvest to the homestead, and the field is a long distance away, the maize cobs may remain exposed to the weather and pests for several days.

Damage results from rodents, rain, ground moisture, termites, etc. Moulds, often *Fusarium* spp, multiply. The burden of harvesting rests mainly with the women and the task often exceeds the capacities of the female members of a household; as a result relatives or neighbours come to help. Black-Michard and Simelane, in their study of small farms in the Central RDA,[31] indicate very high labour inputs for harvesting and shelling, often exceeding those for other tasks like planting, fertilizing, and pest control.

2.6 Grain drying methods, division of labour, pest problems and control

Drying is done on either a covered or uncovered platform ouside the hut. These are the traditional methods of drying grain, i.e. maize, sorghum, and even legumes.

At the farmstead level, the introduction of improved, rodent-proof maize cribs has reduced the level of loss encountered in storage of the crop, while improved maize sheller design has limited the degree of fungal and pest infestation that can occur through seed breakages. The introduction of the sprung suspension system to traile design will reduce the amount of bruising that soft-skinned agricultural produce encounters in a rural environment. These areas are still under investigation at the Faculty of Agriculture, UNISWA.

2.7 Threshing/shelling methods, division of labour for threshing, winnowing and loading the store[32]

Shelling is usually done in May/June in the Lowveld and dry Middleveld and Highveld. In general, grain is rarely left on the cob after this time. Thus, although part of the harvest will already have been consumed during the drying period, a substantial portion remains and this is shelled or threshed by removing the kernels from the cob by hand or using a small hand-held stone to strip the grains off the cob.

The cobs are also placed in a heap on a hard floor and beaten with sticks so that the bulk of the grain is removed. Further stripping may be done by hand. In a few cases machines are available and surveys indicate that these are predominantly in the Highveld.

The labour requirements for threshing are quite considerable and this job is the prime responsibility of the women with substantial help from the children. Women and children are similarly important in winnowing and cleaning the grain, but the greater assistance obtained from men when loading the store could be explained by the larger proportion of homesteads using metal tanks to store the crop.[33]

The Women in Development Project was established in 1978 to train women in income-generating activities. It was necessary that some devices were tested to help them save labour, time, and energy. The following were proposed and also disseminated to the rural communities:
- 1300 cement grain storage jars.
- over 700 water jars.
- 370 sink tables.
- brick stoves, used by 540 families.
- solar driers, used by over 400 families.
- maize shellers, used by over 800 families.
- groundnut shellers, used by over 100 families.
- wooden washing machines, used by 20 families.

2.8 Storage methods for shelled grain, division of labour for construction and purchase of storage containers, pest problems and control[34]

In Swaziland when shelling is done at the end of the dry winter months the grain moisture is below 13 per cent and insect infestation is low. The grain can then be put into an enclosed container, most commonly the metal tank. This is modified from a water tank by the provision of filling and emptying hatches. Walker[35] indicates that their introduction occurred before 1940 and that their popularity increased from then onwards, with the 1–2 tonne size being the most common although containers range from ½–12 tonnes.

The second most popular container for shelled grain is the hessian or jute sack which is more easily obtainable and generally cheaper than the traditional *silulu* (plural *tilulu*). The *silulu* constructed from grass (*Eragostic* sp.) has not entirely lost its popularity, especially in the Manzini Highveld and the Lubombo Plateau. It does not have much advantage over the sack, except perhaps that, if coated with mud, it is more difficult for rodents to attack, and also that a single container can be constructed for up to half a tonne of grain.

Underground pits of approximately 2-tonne capacity are still available in the Lowveld and Lubombo Plateau. However, their actual use has declined considerably. They are generally built in the cattle kraal and their precise location hidden. They were important when concealment from enemies was necessary, but are rarely constructed nowadays and when a pit is filled it is not opened for several months.

199

Other containers used are the 200-litre and 20-litre oil or diesel drum, 15kg tins, clay pots of 30–40kg, and mud tanks (a framework of wattle twigs plastered with mud) of 0.5–3 tonnes. In a few cases the cribs are also used to store the shelled grain after it has been put into another smaller container. Many homesteads use more than one method of storage and grain is often transferred from a larger to a smaller container as its quantity decreases during the storage period.

Of the storage containers that can be constructed at the homestead level, cribs are generally made by the men with assistance from older children. Women may also be involved in construction. The *silulu* is woven only by the women and generally with outside assistance from others more experienced. Mud tanks are usually built by men with assistance from women.

Containers that have to be purchased, like metal tanks, tins, bags and drums, are generally acquired by the men although women are becoming involved in their purchase.

2.8.1 Pest problems in storage[36]

The type of pest problem obviously varies with the container used. Insects are generally considered more of a nuisance than moulds except in the Hhohho, Lowveld, and the Manzini Middleveld. Rodents are a significant problem especially in the Lowveld and Lubombo Plateau and may be associated with the higher levels of storage in sacks or *tilulu* in those areas.

A greater proportion of the farmers use fumigants to control their pests in sealed tanks or drums while some use an insecticide dust (Malathion 1.5 per cent, blue cross) when storing in ventilated containers. Generally 50 per cent or more of the homesteads in the Middle and Highveld carry out some form of pest control of shelled grain.

In the Lowveld fewer farmers treat their grain because most have a very small harvest which can be consumed before pests become serious. Those farmers treating would have purchased their grain from the sale of cash crops like cotton. Some homesteads use an insecticide dust on shelled grain, and of those storing in bags and *tilulu* less than a quarter adopt pest control.

The relationship between homesteads owning a metal tank and those using a fumigant is very good, with nearly 82 per cent of those storing in tanks using a fumigant. The main fumigant used is phosphine and the unavailability of the tablets releasing this fumigant may account for the low use especially in parts of the Lowveld. Liquid carbon bisulphide may sometimes be used, but Walker[37] indicates that it is generally less effective than phosphine.

Milling of grain is done by hand by grinding on a stone or using a local hammer-mill. Milling is generally the responsibility of women, in some cases assisted by older children.

2.9 Homesteads selling grain and division of labour in bagging, transport and marketing of produce[38]

The Manzini Highveld has over 20 per cent homesteads selling grain but in general the Highveld, Middleveld and Lubombo have between 10 and 20 per cent surplus homesteads. On average, those that sell grain have about 10–25 bags for sale, over 30 bags in Manzini Highveld (maize marketing of the surplus occurs in the Ngwempisi and Mahlangatsha RADs). Most of the sales occur locally through the co-operatives or on an individual basis.

Labour for bagging the grain is generally shared by the men and women with some assistance of older children. Labour for transport is more the responsibility of the men, and marketing is done by the men and women. Some assistance from children is also provided.

The survey by Nxumalo[39] indicated that women may sell their crops for cash, those having large amounts selling to the Swaziland Milling Company while smaller amounts may be sold door-to-door or to buyers visiting the homestead. Transport to bigger markets was considered to be a problem.

3. Forest land use

The Fourth National Development Plan states that in 1984 about 121,000ha of the land area in the country were under forests. Of this 103,898 were under commercial forests,[40] with 17,102ha under natural forests.

Natural forests in the country are of greater concern from the standpoint of the environment. Traditionally such forests are used as a source of firewood. It is estimated that firewood contributes about 100 per cent of the energy used in the country.[41]

Other causes of deforestation are over-stocking the Middleveld and Lowveld, excessive burning of the veld during the dry winter, introduction of extensive agriculture under irrigation in the Lowveld, prospecting for mineral and physical infrastructural development. That burning during the dry season will destroy the forests is not debatable. Unfortunately the natural forests in the country are found on grazing land. This further complicates the problem.

4. Livestock

Livestock are important to the economy of the country. However their contribution to GDP, at about 6 per cent in 1977–81,[42] is small relative to the livestock population. Cattle are the most important species of domestic livestock.

In 1985 it was estimated that there were more than 648,000 cattle, over 268,000 goats, about 30,000 sheep, and over 12,000 donkeys.[43] In 1984 there were just over 1,000,000ha of natural veld used for grazing and only

201

about 48,000ha of improved grazing land. This means 952,000ha have to be improved to cater for 858,000 animals. This is considered one of the highest stocking densities in Africa.[44]

The financial performance of livestock in the country reflects the differences between the commercial subsector (TDL) and the traditional subsector (SNL). The commercial off-take was estimated between 14 and 18 per cent as contrasted to 2.8–3.2 per cent on SNL.

The problem of over-stocking is more pronounced in the traditional subsector. The reasons are sociological:[45] cattle are a better investment than banks. According to the Fourth National Development Plan the returns from an SNL herd are around 10 per cent as compared with less than 5 per cent a year from savings accounts.[46] This advantage is over and above the role livestock have in ceremonial, cultural, and social customs. This includes the paying of the bride price, which is a concern for every young man who contemplates marriage. As a result, in 1983 the overall stocking rates on SNL was estimated at 1.9ha per livestock unit. The carrying capacity of land ranges between 3.0 and 4.9ha per livestock unit.

This kind of overstocking has resulted in low calving percentages (30 per cent in 1981) and high mortality rates (up to 7 per cent over the period 1970–81). There is therefore no doubt that the country's economy is losing and, worse still, the natural base is being depleted.[47]

Overstocking is also responsible for the destruction of natural forests[48] and a severe erosion problem.[49] The latter is the perhaps most severe effect of overstocking.

The solution would be to reduce the stocking rate and improve the carrying capacity of the land. Government Fattening Ranches and demonstration grazing areas have been established.

Donkeys have a questionable value in the country and reduction of their numbers is being considered.

5. Energy

Energy is crucial in any development process, whether in the primary, secondary, or tertiary sector. It is required and used by humans in almost all aspects of their endeavours.[50]

All stages of development need energy, but the main difference usually lies in the emphasis placed on types or sources and or in the intensity of use. The implication for its use also depends on the technology attained by the users. Modern methods of energy utilization improve the subsistence level of a society, but the resources have to be properly managed and planned. The use of one resource has direct or indirect effects on other aspects of the environment. The population should be aware of the implications of the use of the different energy sources.

Energy sources include all fuels, water, sunlight, and winds. They can be categorized into primary, renewable, and expendable, but all forms can be traced to the primary.

Primary sources include nuclear fusion, which is the source of radiant energy, providing an inexhaustible supply of energy on earth. Nuclear fission is another primary source even though it produces an insignificant amount of energy compared to nuclear fusion. Nuclear fission releases radioactive energy from some elements, naturally creating geothermal energy from within the earth's crust. However, with the help of modern technology, artificial radioisotopes have increased the amount of energy obtained from nuclear fusion. Wind is another primary energy, created by thermal effects of solar energy.

Renewable energy is created from primary sources. These include solar energy, wind energy, energy from flowing streams, tidal energy, geothermal energy, fuel from trees and other plants. The total amount of potential energy in this category is large in relation to the world's energy needs.

Expendable energy sources include coal, lignite, petroleum products, and natural gas. These resources are being consumed at an appreciable rate.

Swaziland, with a population of 634,000 (1986 census) and an annual rate of increase of about 3.4 per cent, requires energy either locally generated or imported, perhaps in both the traditional and modern sectors. In the traditional sector, fuelwood and farm wastes (stalks, cobs, etc.) and dried dung provide most of the energy requirements.[51] In the modern sector, energy is required to power both domestic and economic development processes. With the growing population, energy requirements will rise.

Income per capita is decreasing, export earnings are rising, and inflation is very high. With agricultural home production dropping the population will in the future be less able to afford the energy needed. Supply is increasing, but not keeping pace with the rate of population increase. In the face of this, the shortfall in energy supply will create a crisis.

Ajakpo[52] states that since the 1970s the country has felt the escalating costs of imported oil and fuelwood shortage. Particularly as the traditional sector is occupied by 85 per cent of the population, 90 per cent of the energy supply source is fuelwood for heating and cooking.

The highlighting of imported oil, which had a contribution to total supply of 13.8 per cent in 1980, has directed attention to the crisis in fuelwood supply.[53]

The industrial sector accounts for 59 per cent of total energy demand, the domestic sector for about 21.7 per cent, while agriculture accounts for only 2.9 per cent. The large demand by industry is attributed to the small size of the country as well as the relatively extensive industrial sector.

This pattern also points out the subsistence level of the agricultural sector, and the basic needs of heating and cooking of the domestic sector, particularly in rural areas where the majority of the population lives.

Table 3 Energy demand by sector (% share)[54]

Category	1980	2000
Urban household	2.9	5.0
Rural household	18.8	14.3
Agriculture	2.9	2.7
Industry	59.0	60.5
Commercial/institutional	2.9	4.6
Transport	13.8	13.0
	100.3*	100.1*

* Figures rounded up

The implications of the above consumption pattern mean there is already some fuel shortage in some parts of Swaziland due to deforestation.

As an alternative, there has been an increase in the use of dung and residue for fuel energy. In other words, with less fuel less food will be cooked. Animal manure is being diverted to cooking and heating instead of to increased food production. This results in the loss of soil nutrients. The soil structure is also destroyed as more organic material is lost to the soil. As food supply falls, clearing of more forest is necessitated.[55]

Woodfuel scarcity has an effect on nutrition. Sometimes food such as beans, which are rich in protein but take long to cook, might be replaced with others that cook easily but have less nutrients. Infant health status is sometimes jeopardized as less sterilization is practised in the bid to save fuel. This means new problems for women who are the main users of fuel.

The proportion of fuelwood consumption and the degree of shortage differs between the rural and urban sectors. Though woodfuel consumption accounts for 35.7 per cent of total energy consumption, rural domestic energy consumption accounts for 18.8 per cent of this total. With fuelwood accounting for 89 per cent of this and dung/residue for 4.4 per cent, kerosene and coal account for 5 per cent. With about 85 per cent of the population deriving 89 per cent of the energy from a source (fuelwood) that is already in short supply, the future looks bleak for the environment.[57]

The sugar industry and wood pulp provide economic benefits as well as fuel sources. They are to a large extent self-sufficient in their energy needs as well as providing fuelwood for some of the rural needs. The greatest shortage is felt in the Middleveld, with the highest concentration of population, where citizens now used barbed wire rather than wood-fences.

5.1 Future prospects
There is need for strong and tangible government commitment and support for re-afforestation. Broad public participation must be rewarded with measures which assure the population of their essential needs.

Table 4 End use fuel consumption for 1980[56]

Category	% share
Woodfuel	35.7
Charcoal	0.0
Dung/residue	23.8
Industrial wood	0.8
Gasolene	5.8
Kerosine	0.8
Diesel	6.3
Aviation fuel	0.4
Residual fuel	5.8
Electricity	6.7
Coal	13.8
Natural gas	0.0
LPG	0.0
Refined oil	0.0

Swaziland's energy consumption according to importance is therefore as follows.

Woodfuel	35.7%
Dung/residure	23.8%
Coal	13.8%
Electricity (hydro)	6.7%

The situation in the commercial wood sector is more encouraging. Usutu Pulp (largest of the firms) diverts its own timber wastes to generate about two-thirds of its electricity requirements. It issues permits for wood collection in the forests.

But there is a rapid disappearance of natural forests in the country. The Ministry of Agriculture and Co-ops has estimated that about 15 per cent of the rural population have to find alternative fuels for cooking and heating, because of lack of wood. Coal consumption for 1980 was 13.8 per cent of total energy. Very little contributes to rural consumption, about 3 per cent, while it accounts for 42.8 per cent of urban domestic use.

Coal reserves are currently estimated at about 200 million tonnes, with only between 20 per cent and 40 per cent of that exported consumed internally. This energy source is not fully exploited. The only mine (Mpaka) had an annual production of 176,000 metric tonnes in 1980 and imports 20,000 tons annually from South Africa.[58]

The existing plant should be modified to burn the country's reserves rather than the imported variety. Improved operations will increase the quality of the reserves. This will be cheaper in the long run. The use of coal could be encouraged to replace woodfuel, to help the treeless landscapes to recover.

Hydro-electric power's contribution to total end-use fuel consumption by electricity is 6.7 per cent. This proportion is low considering the country's potential, estimated to be about 1000 GWH per year. In 1980 SEB had an installed capacity of 50MW. This comprises 40.5MW for the hydro-electric power stations and 09.5MW for its diesel-generating plants.[59] Hydro-electric power generation projects, apart from the relative cheapness of energy generated from water, are a clean source of energy, causing little pollution compared to fossil sources like coal. They lend themselves to a multiple purpose use of water resources, such as irrigation, fishing, settlement, location or relocation, for domestic rural, urban, and industrial uses, and for recreation. The efficiency of hydro-generated power further reinforces the view that this is an energy source for the future.

6. Conclusion

It is clear that government policies on agriculture and the National Development Plans have not addressed the integration of women in agriculture and their contribution as producers who have the capacity to improve the economic growth of their country. As a result the technologies which the women should use are almost non-existent because their contribution is said to be marginal and only for family use, without realizing that women are now cash-crop producers.

It has also become clear that in order for women to contribute meaningfully to the economies of their countries they should be part of the decision-making on what types of technology are necessary for production purposes, their maintenance, as well as their improvement.

Women also have to be trained to maintain productivity so as to be able to sustain food production.

'Land belongs to a vast family of which many are dead, a few are living and countless numbers are still unborn.'[60] It must be borne in mind that this vast family depends on the food that women farmers have to produce; as such, technologies they can use and maintain must be made available so that they can sustain the needs of their nations.

As a sub-region, we have to make an inventory of all the technologies we have in our countries, see how these could be improved to suit the needs of women, and have a sub-regional programme for women's training in their use and maintenance.

Notes

Malawi

Asiedu, J.J.K. (1987). 'The Agricultural Engineer in a Developing Country – Still in Search of his/her Proper Role in the National Development'. Paper presented at the Eleventh Annual Conference of the Association for the Advancement of Science in Malawi (AASOM), 10–11 April, 1987.

Atiemo, M. (1983). 'Smallholder Farmer Maize Shellers. Performances, Limitations and Choice'. Paper presented at the National Conference on Development and Use of Technology appropriate to rural households. Zomba, 18–22 1983.

Bekerson, S. (1983). *Seasonal Labour Association Food Supply and Nutrition in Subsistence and Semi-subsistence Farming Households in Malawi*. Unpublished MS Thesis, University of Geulph, Canada.

Clark, B. (1975). 'The Work done by Rural Women in Malawi'. *Eastern Africa Journal of Rural Development*, 8: 2, 80–91.

Energy Studies Unit, Ministry of Forestry and Natural Resources (1981). Malawi Rural Energy Survey. Lilongwe.

Giles, G.W. (1975). 'The Orientation of Agricultural Mechanization for Developing Countries'. *Journal Agricultural Mechanization in Asia*, 7:2.

Kydd, J., and Christiansen, R. (1982). 'Structural Change in Malawi since Independence. Consequence of a Development Strategy based on Large-scale Agriculture'. *World Development*, 10: 5.

Mkandawire, R.M., Asiedu, J.J., and Mtimuni, B. (1988). 'Women and Food Processing in Malawi'. Unpublished Report prepared for the Ministry of Community Services and UNDP, Lilongwe.

Shellenberg, M., and Nkunika, A. (1988). 'Women's Programmes in Malawi: A Survey on Government and Non Governmental Women's Programmes'. Ministry of Community Services, Lilongwe.

Spring, A., Smith, C., and Kayuni, F. (1983). 'Women Farmers in Malawi. Their contribution to Agriculture and Participation in Development Projects'. Mimeo. April 1983.

Teplitz, W., and Zienth, G. (1988). 'Solid Fuels in Malawi: Options and Constraints for Charcoal and Coal'. Report for the Malawi Charcoal Project, Lilongwe.

Wieneke, F. (1977). 'Die Rolle der Agrartechnik in den Tropen Westafrikas'. *Landtechnik*, 9.

World Survey on the Role of Women in Development (1986). Department of International Economic and Social Affairs. United Nations, New York.

Zambia

Campbell, D., Matiza, T., and Zinyama, L.M. (1987). 'Traditional Household Strategies to Cope with Food Insecurity in the SADCC Region'. Paper presented at the Third Annual Conference on Food Security Research in South Africa, Harare, Zimbabwe.

Keller, B.B., and Phiri, E.C. (1986). 'The Contribution of Women Farmers: Implications for Agricultural Extension Training'.

National Commission for Development Planning (1983). *Third National Development Plan*, Lusaka.

―――― and the University of Lusaka (1984). *Strengthening Women's Participation in Food and Agriculture Marketing: Proceedings of the National Seminar.*

Rothschild, C. (1985). 'The Policy Implications on the Roles of Women in Agriculture in Zambia'.

Sharpe, B. (1987). *Report on the Nutritional Anthropology Investigation of Integrated Rural Development Programme (Northern and Central Provinces of Zambia).*

Sikama, P. (1987). *Household Dynamics in the Cropping Systems of Zambia.*

Small-Scale Producers, Informal Activities and Development in their Social and Economic Context. Case studies on Rural and Urban Zambia. (Report of A Student's Research Project) November 1987.

Third National Development Plan (1983). *National Commission for Development Planning, Lusaka.*

Tanzania

FAO: 'Farm Structures in Tropical Climates' 1986.

Marilyn Carr and Rubby Sandbur: 'Women, Technology and Rural Productivity, Analysis of the Impact of Time and Energy Technologies on Women' 1987.

United Republic of Tanzania/FAO, 'Storage Project' 1986.

African Concord (Bumper Issue), Jan. 1987.

Basic Needs in Danger ILO Report 1982.

'Benki zaombwa kulegeza masharti kwa vijiji' UHURU – Party Daily Newspaper. Monday 13th April 1987.

Drying of food for Preservation/Oil Extraction. Food Cycle Technology source Book No. 1 and 4.

Existing Traditional/Appropriate Technology in Tanzania. – A case Study of Arusha, Iringa, Ruvuma, Kilimanjaro, Morogoro and Shinyanga Regions – Community Development Department – Division of Research and Statistics – July 1987.

Expert Consultation on Women in Food Production – FAO 1983.

Habari za Kukoboa Mtama – Nyenzo kwa Walaji SIDO Hqa.

Household Time Use and Agricultural Productivity in Sub-Sahara in Africa. I.T. Transport Ltd.

Inquest of Agricultural Mechanization Policy and Strategies in Tanzania. Workshop on Farm Tools and Equipment Technology October 1985.

Institutional Efforts in Designing and Developing Appliances for Reducing Women's Workload by A.H. Senyagwa 1987.

'Milling System Eases Plight of Peasant' a report by Ozzie Schemidt and Gerry Toomey for IDRC 1987.

Report on the Evaluation of the New Adult Education Curriculum. Its Relevance and Impact on Women. SIDA/Ministry of Education June 1987.

Reports – The IDRC – After Harvest Vol. 4 No. 4 1 October 1987.

Report on Feasibility of Palm Kernel Oil Extraction in Kigoma Region – Lawrence Limbe 1986.

The Role of Marejea (Crotalia Och.).

Swaziland

1. *The Courier*, No. 55, May–June, 1979, p. 69.
2. *Ibid.*, p. 73.
3. *Ibid.*, p.77.
4. Fourth National Development Plan 1983–8, Swaziland Government.
5. Nkambule, N.M. 1985, *The Soil Erosion Problem in Swaziland* (unpublished).
6. Nxumalo, 1979, *Survey on the Roles, Tasks, Needs and Skills of Rural Women in Swaziland.*
7. *Ibid.*, p. 13.
8. *Ibid.*, p. 11.
9. *Ibid.*, p. 10.
10. *Ibid.*, p. 12.
11. FAO, 1975, *The Role of Women in Rural Development.*
12. Nkambule, N.M. 1988, *The Impact of Agriculture on the Environment. The Case of Swaziland.*
13. FAO, 1982, Environment Import Assessment and Agricultural Development, Rome.
14. Carr, M.K.V. 1987(a) *Irrigation Issues in Swaziland, Large Scale Projects, Outlook on Agriculture* 16.
15. Central Statistical Office, 1984.
16. Carr, 1987(b) *Irrigation Small-Scale Projects*, Outlook on Agriculture 16.
17. FAO, 1982.
18. Kay, M.G. and Carter, R.C. 1984, Health Hazards in Irrigation Development; A Strategy for Improvement, *Outlook on Agriculture*, Vol. 13, No. 3, pp. 125–129.
19. Carr, 1987(b).
20. Nkambule, N.M. 1988.
21. FAO, 1982.
22. Nkambule, N.M. 1988.
23. *Ibid.*
24. Central Statistical Office, 1982.
25. Nkambule N.M. 1988.
26. FAO, 1982.
27. Brader *et al.*, 1985, *Cotton Farming in Swaziland.*
28. Bohlem, 1973, *Crop Pests in Tanzania and their Control.* Verlag Paul Parey, Berlin.
29. Nkambule, N.M.1988.
30. Bermans, 1986.
31. Black-Michard and Simelane, 1982, Study: Small Farms in the Central RDA of Swaziland.
32. FAO, 1982.
33. *Ibid.*
34. FAO, 1980.
35. Walker, 1975, in FAO, 1982.
36. FAO, 1982.
37. Walker, 1975, in FAO, 1982.
38. FAO, 1982.
39. Nxumalo, 1979.
40. Central Statistical Office, 1984.
41. SASREC, 1985.

44. Nkambule, N.M. 1985; Swaziland Government Ministry of Agriculture, 1984.
45. Nkambule, N.M. 1988.
46. Fourth National Development Plan.
47. Nkambule, N.M. 1988.
48. SASREC, 1985.
49. Engoru-Ebinu, 1984, *Population and its effect on the environment*; Nkambule, 1985; Boateng, 1987. Report on Proposal for the Development of an Environment Machinery for Dealing with Environmental Problems in Swaziland, UNEP, MBABANE.
50. Ajakpo, 1988, *Energy Resources and Implications for Use in Swaziland.*
51. *Ibid.*
52. *Ibid.*
53. *Ibid.*
54. *Ibid.*
55. *Ibid.*
56. *Ibid.*
57. *Ibid.*
58. *Ibid.*
59. *Ibid.*
60. Nkambule, N.M. 1988; Upton, 1973, *Farm Management in Africa*, ELBS and Oxford University Press, Oxford.